THE GEOGRAPHY
OF MEANINGS

THE INTERNATIONAL PSYCHOANALYSIS LIBRARY

General Editor: Leticia Glocer Fiorini

Violence or Dialogue? Psychoanalytic Insights on Terror and Terrorism
    edited by Sverre Varvin & Vamik D. Volkan

Pluralism and Unity? Methods of Research in Psychoanalysis
    edited by Marianne Leuzinger-Bohleber, Anna Ursula Dreher, & Jorge Canestri

Truth, Reality, and the Psychoanalyst: Latin American Contributions to Psychoanalysis
    edited by Sergio Lewkowicz & Silvia Flechner

Verdad, realidad y el psicoanalista: Contribuciones Latinoamericanas al Psicoanálisis
    edited by Sergio Lewkowicz & Silvia Flechner

Resonance of Suffering: Countertransference in Non-neurotic Structures
    edited by André Green

Linking, Alliances, and Shared Space: Groups and the Psychoanalyst
    René Kaës

THE GEOGRAPHY
OF MEANINGS

Psychoanalytic Perspectives
on Place, Space, Land, and Dislocation

edited by
Maria Teresa Savio Hooke & Salman Akhtar

Foreword by
Paul Williams

The International Psychoanalysis Library

Routledge
Taylor & Francis Group

LONDON AND NEW YORK

Extracts on pp. 45–48, 53–57 in chapter 2 reproduced from K. Grenville, *The Secret River* (Melbourne: The Text Publishing Co, 2005) by permission of the publisher. © Kate Grenville.

First published 2007 by
The International Psychoanalytical Association

Published 2018 by Routledge
2 Park Square, Milton Park, Abingdon, Oxon OX14 4RN
711 Third Avenue, New York, NY 10017, USA

Routledge is an imprint of the Taylor & Francis Group, an informa business

British Library Cataloguing in Publication Data
A C.I.P. for this book is available from the British Library

ISBN: 9781905888030 (pbk)

Produced for the IPA by Communication Crafts

www.ipa.org.uk

To

Spaces lived in, spaces left behind.
Spaces hardly known, spaces deftly mined.
Spaces beyond classification, spaces well-defined.
Spaces of the body, spaces of the mind.

CONTENTS

I
Space

II
Place, time, and land

III
Dislocation

THE INTERNATIONAL PSYCHOANALYSIS LIBRARY

IPA Publications Committee

The International Psychoanalysis Library, published under the aegis of the International Psychoanalytical Association, is the product of the editorial policy of the IPA Publications Committee: to serve the interests of the membership and increase the awareness of the relevance of the discipline in related professional and academic circles, and to do so through a continuity of publications so that the benefits of psychoanalytic research can be shared across a wide audience.

The focus of the Library is on the scientific developments of today throughout the IPA, with an emphasis within the discipline on clinical, technical, and theoretical advances; empirical, conceptual, and historical research projects; the outcome of investigations conducted by IPA committees and working parties; selected material arising from conferences and meetings; and investigations at the interface with social and cultural expressions.

Special thanks are due to the editors, Maria Teresa Savio Hooke and Salman Akhtar, who have developed this important material, on previously neglected aspects of such an important topic, into a book, and to all the contributors for their dedicated work.

Leticia Glocer Fiorini
Series Editor

ACKNOWLEDGEMENTS

First and foremost, we are grateful to Emma Piccioli, the former Chair of the IPA Publications Committee, who brought the two of us together with the hope of academic collaboration of just the sort this book represents. We also wish to thank the distinguished colleagues who contributed to this volume. We deeply appreciate their efforts, their sacrifice of time, and, above all, their patience with our requirements, reminders, and requests for revisions. With sincerity and affection, we acknowledge the guidance of the members of the current IPA Publications Committee, especially its Chair, Leticia Glocer Fiorini, and the editorial counsel of Cesare Sacerdoti, the Publications Director of the IPA and an ex-officio member of that committee. We are also thankful to Rhosyn Tuta for keeping track of all sorts of matters during the book's actual production, and to Eric King for his very helpful suggestions in the course of editing and producing the book. Finally, we express our thanks to Melissa Nevin, who prepared the manuscript of this book with much effort and dedication.

Maria Teresa Savio Hooke & Salman Akhtar

EDITORS AND CONTRIBUTORS

Salman Akhtar was born in India and completed his medical and psychiatric education there. Upon arriving in the United States in 1973, he repeated his psychiatric training at the University of Virginia School of Medicine and then obtained psychoanalytic training from the Philadelphia Psychoanalytic Institute. Currently, he is Professor of Psychiatry at Jefferson Medical College and a training and supervising analyst at the Psychoanalytic Center of Philadelphia. His more than two-hundred and fifty publications include seven books—*Broken Structures, Quest for Answers, Inner Torment, Immigration and Identity, New Clinical Realms, Objects of Our Desire,* and *Regarding Others*—as well as twenty-one edited or co-edited volumes in psychiatry and psychoanalysis and six collections of poetry. He is also a Scholar-in-Residence at the Inter-Act Theatre Company in Philadelphia.

Bain Attwood was born and raised in New Zealand and has worked and lived in Australia for the last twenty-five years. He trained in history at the University of Waikato, the University of Auckland, and La Trobe University and is currently Associate Professor in the School of Historical Studies, Monash University, and Adjunct Professor in the Centre for Cross-Cultural Research, The Australian National

University. He has published widely on the history of colonialism. His books include *The Making of the Aborigines; In the Age of Mabo: History, Aborigines and Australia; Telling Stories: Indigenous History and Memory in Australia and New Zealand; Frontier Conflict: The Australian Experience; Rights for Aborigines;* and *Telling the Truth about Aboriginal History.* His current research project involves the ways in which Aboriginal sovereignty and rights to land were treated, remembered, and forgotten in Australia by settlers and Aboriginal people.

Kate Grenville was born in Sydney and has degrees in English Literature and Creative Writing. She is the author of seven works of fiction, including *The Idea of Perfection* (awarded the Orange Prize), *Dark Places* (winner of the Vance Palmer Award for Fiction), and, her most recent, *The Secret River* (winner of the Commonwealth Prize and shortlisted for the Booker). She has also taught writing for some twenty years and has written or co-written four books about the writing process, including *Searching for the Secret River.*

Maria Teresa Savio Hooke was born in Italy and graduated in Languages and Literatures at the University of Turin, where she also gained a postgraduate degree in Psychology. She worked for ten years as a child psychotherapist at the Child Psychiatry Department of the University of Turin, where she was also part of the teaching staff. The encounter with British analysts both in Italy and in London was instrumental for further training experiences and contacts with the Tavistock Clinic. She moved to Sydney in 1976, where she trained with the Australian Psychoanalytical Society. As Scientific Secretary of the Society she contributed to raising the public profile of psychoanalysis and to fostering relationships with the allied professions. She is currently President of the Australian Psychoanalytical Society.

Craig San Roque is a Jungian analyst. He trained in London at the Tavistock Clinic and qualified through the Society for Analytical Psychology. As a co-founder of the Squiggle Foundation, he contributed during the 1980s to the integration and application of Winnicott's ideas to child and family care, work with disturbed adolescents, and social psychotherapy. In Sydney, since 1986, he has helped establish the Jungian milieu, psychoanalytic training, and the Masters Program in Analytical and Cultural Psychology. He worked as a community psychologist in indigenous affairs, substance abuse, and mental health in Central Australia from 1992 and has resumed private practice in Sydney.

Eve Steel grew up in the north of England. She trained as a child psychotherapist at the Tavistock Clinic, where she became a senior member of staff in that discipline. She subsequently trained as a psychoanalyst at the Institute of Psychoanalysis in London. Since 1981, she has lived in Melbourne where she is a senior psychoanalyst of the Australian Psychoanalytical Society. She is active in making contributions to clinical and educational work in psychoanalysis and applied psychoanalysis.

James Telfer was born in Sydney. He spent much of his childhood in rural New South Wales. He graduated in medicine at Sydney University in 1970 and qualified as a psychiatrist in 1976. He has been a member of the Sydney Institute for Psychoanalysis, Australian Psychoanalytical Society, and International Psychoanalytical Association since 1992. He is a Clinical Lecturer with the Faculty of Medicine, Sydney University, and a Consultant Psychiatrist at the Royal North Shore Hospital. He also maintains a private practice of psychotherapy and psychoanalysis in Sydney.

Nicholas Twemlow was born in Topeka, Kansas, and received his MFA in Poetry from the Writers' Workshop at the University of Iowa. He was awarded a Fulbright fellowship in 2005 to New Zealand, where he was in residence at the Institute of Modern Letters at Victoria University. There, he received his MA, with distinction, for a collection of poems that explored his Maori heritage, his family's emigration to the United States, and the linguistic fallout of current U.S. foreign policy. He serves as the co-editor of *The Canary*, a magazine of poetry, and is the Feature Editor for *PoetryFoundation.org*. His poems have been published in *Boston Review*, *A Public Space*, *Verse*, and *Landfall*. He is also a screenwriter and has twice been a finalist for the Sundance Filmmakers Lab. His most recent script is a karate drama, which dovetails his lifelong interest in the martial arts.

Stuart Twemlow is Professor of Psychiatry, Director of the Peaceful Schools and Communities Program at the Menninger Department of Psychiatry, Baylor College of Medicine, and the Medical Director of the HOPE unit, Menninger Clinic, Houston, Texas. He is the

Editor-in-Chief of the *International Journal of Applied Psychoanalytic Studies* and has more than two hundred scientific publications to his credit. He is a New Zealand Maori, with forty years' experience in martial and meditative arts. He is a 7th Dan black belt in Okinawa Kobudo (old weapons system) and a 6th Dan in Hawaiian and Okinawa Kenpo Karate. He also has a black belt in Shinko Kaiten Aikido and Eagle Claw Kung Fu. He is considered a master teacher (Renshi), in the Kenpo and Kobudo systems. He is also an exhibited black-ink brush painter and long-time student of Rinzai Zen, part of and developed in his martial arts experience.

Paul Williams is a Training and Supervising Analyst with the British Psychoanalytical Society, a Consultant Psychotherapist in the British National Health Service in Belfast, Northern Ireland, a Professor at Queen's University Belfast and Joint Editor-in-Chief of the *International Journal of Psychoanalysis*. He trained originally as a social anthropologist and earned his doctorate in anthropology through a study of a psychoanalytic inpatient milieu at the Maudsley Hospital, London. He has written widely on the impact and treatment of personality disorders and psychosis.

Thomas Wolman was born and raised in New York City. He attended Johns Hopkins University and Pennsylvania State Medical College. Subsequently he trained at the Psychoanalytic Center of Philadelphia, where he now teaches in both the psychoanalytic and psychotherapy training programmes. Currently he works at the Philadelphia Veterans Administration Medical Center and holds the title of Clinical Assistant Professor of Psychiatry at the University of Pennsylvania School of Medicine. He has written on Winnicott, Mahler, Kohut, and Lacan, as well as on contemporary film and literary themes. He is working on a book about the character Meursualt in *L'étranger,* by Albert Camus.

FOREWORD

Paul Williams

It was with a combination of pleasure, interest, and a certain relief that I read this collection of essays. Pleasure, because the writing is of a standard that will reward the analytically oriented reader; interest, because the subject matter is unusually absorbing and of a type that is increasingly rare in analytic publications; and relief, because we see in these pages psychoanalytic ideas embracing phenomena and concepts that are usually considered to be the prerogative of the anthropological or sociological researcher. As a former social anthropologist who then trained to be a psychoanalyst, I welcome this event. This book helps to move psychoanalysis forward by addressing, in an interdisciplinary manner, the role, function, and meaning of places, displacements, locations, dislocations, migrations, spaces, material contents, and cultural contexts of the lives of specific individuals and groups. The authors of the essays—predominantly but not exclusively analysts—bring analytic thinking to bear on certain powerful, sometimes traumatic environmental influences, and they do so with delicacy, rigour, and, most strikingly, a humane and respectful attitude to their subject. They explore the relationship between analytic concepts and the external worlds of struggling individuals and groups, many but not all of whom are Australian. This is a welcome contribution: the story or stories of what has happened to the indigenous populations of Australia, their relationships with other Australians, and the impact of this cultural history on all Australians, many of whom then bring this history into their psychoanalytic therapy (a history that also affects the analyst), is virtually unknown to those of us outside Australia and, it seems, to many in Australia. The same might be said for New Zealand, also discussed in this book.

Why is a book like this, which deals with the impact of cultural change on personal identity, important for psychoanalysis? First, because analysts and others with a serious, scholarly interest in psychoanalysis do not write enough about the influences and effects of events in the external world. This is understandable, as the respective frames of reference that deal with external and internal reality can differ markedly; yet psychoanalysis and social anthropology have sustained a fertile dialogue since Freud's first interest in anthropological reflections on cultures, social evolution, and their implications for the individual. Psychoanalysis has attracted a small but steady cohort of anthropologists and sociologists who have migrated to the discipline, bringing with them a richness of perspective that has, in my view, deepened our subject. Analysts who have an interdisciplinary capacity or who have systematically studied culture or politics are also well placed to confront the many social, economic, and political prejudices against psychoanalysis. They are equally well placed to challenge the domestication of our theories and techniques. And they may provide insights into the cultural and political conflicts that the discipline is capable of inflicting on itself. By the same token, analysts and analytic thinking have, I believe, a great deal to contribute to the understanding of social and cultural phenomena. If proof were needed of this, we only need to look at the irony in the crisis that confronts clinical psychoanalysis in these "quick-fix" times, in which the numbers of analysands entering treatment are declining. By contrast, there has been a veritable explosion of interest in the insights of psychoanalysis by other disciplines in universities. Media, literature, film, philosophy, sociology, social anthropology, and other departments now regularly engage in dialogue with psychoanalysis. Curiously, it is comparatively rare for this teaching to be done by analysts! The fact that psychoanalysis generates considerable intellectual interest in academia does not solve the problem of its clinical standing in contemporary society. But it does demonstrate a genuine and deep responsiveness in successive generations to the way analytic thought sheds light on hitherto obscure phenomena in a way that no other discipline can.

The editors and authors who have contributed to the original essays in this volume have not set out to produce an anthropological or sociological treatise. They are sufficiently knowledgeable about the pitfalls involved in interdisciplinary writing to have avoided reductionism, over-inclusive thinking, or the inappropriate conflating of paradigms. Instead, they draw out links between psychoanalysis, culture, and history from their well-studied subjects where they feel they are justified: this care and humility of approach only adds to the quality of the finished argument. More than once I found myself thinking "Of course . . ." as the authors tease out implications from cultural facts that seem obvious when they become apparent but, on reflection, are not at all.

The IPA, as well as the creators of the book, are to be congratulated on initiating this publication, and I hope it will be one of many as psychoanalysis claims its rightful place in the analysis of cultural forms. To give a sense of the subject matter of the book and the thoughtful manner in which it is approached, I found myself spontaneously noting, from each chapter, sentences that intrigued or moved me. Here are a few of them:

> "Does the 'average expectable environment' deemed necessary for the unfolding of human psychic life also include a roof over one's head, a solid ground to walk upon, a room, a crib, a bed, a chair, a house, and a street? Are our relationships to our motherlands and their landscapes, vegetation, little and big animals, and architecture mere unconscious displacements of the inner dialogue with our parents or independent of such human relationships?"

> "The line break in poetry and a fumbling pause in free-association constitute [potential] spaces of just this sort. It is at such moments of interpersonal intrigue that silence becomes a closed room."

> "The psychoanalytic consulting room is an exemplary human space."

> "An immigrant becomes a native through a process, not a moment. It has to start with a kind of mourning."

> "Psychoanalysis recognizes the past in the present; historiography places them one *beside* the other . . . in other words, . . . the work of history has rested on some version of the "past/

present opposition".... In relating to the Stolen Generations, historians largely acted out or repeated a past by assuming the position of the victim and/or the resister."

"The contents of this [*Bringing Them Home*] report is not just about crying babies; it is about knowing of violence perpetrated upon innocent children and human beings. To admit the significance of what lies behind this social document is ... to allow other states of mind to be known to us. These states of mind do not belong just to the traumatized victims, but also to the perpetrators. I would see both as Lost Children."

"The issue that has preoccupied my son and me is 'who am I?' Not in the sense of 'I' as an intentional being similar to all other intentional beings, in some particular culture. But 'in the broader sense—that is, where is my home and how am I not white?"

"What are the specific manifestations of the ruptured inanimate background and of the self-righting tendency to redress them? And how do such matters make their appearance in the clinical situation?"

"Displacement is a *double entendre* ... for psychoanalysis, it is the transvaluation of psychic values ... A second meaning of displacement is spatial dislocation. This ... begs a question: what do we mean, in psychological terms, by 'place'?"

"Dislocation, alienation, loss, and the meaning of our geographical environment are becoming more and more relevant in an unsettled world in which migration and movements of refugees and exiles have become an integral part of almost every country. This is a crucial issue both for the ones who leave and for the ones left behind."

There must be few more compelling human difficulties that we as clinicians need to begin to understand. This book brings a sharp analytic perspective to bear on these dilemmas in a way that offers a dimension of meaning previously obscured. Interestingly, the plan for the book grew out of a meeting in 2000 of the Australian Psychoanalytical Society in Uluru, Central Australia, a place of profound significance for Indigenous and Australian cultures. I was reminded of a famous Aboriginal saying: *"Those who lose dreaming are lost."* The wisdom of this understanding of internal and external life is reflected in these pages.

Belfast, 2007

THE GEOGRAPHY
OF MEANINGS

Prologue

Salman Akhtar

Ordinarily in his writings, the pre-eminent psychoanalyst and former IPA President Otto Kernberg shows the precision of a surgeon and parsimony of a banker. His elucidation of erotic desire, however, is strikingly different in tone. It has the music of corporeality and the poetry of longing. Kernberg's (1992) declaration that "a lover's body gradually becomes the geography of personal meanings" is simply breathtaking. Paraphrasing and extrapolating this literary elegance to a different context has led to the title of our book here: *The Geography of Meanings*.

As the book's subtitle—*Psychoanalytic Perspectives on Place, Space, Land, and Dislocation*—readily reveals, our concern here is not erotic desire but the spatial dimension of man's existence, in both its literal and its metaphorical sense. Heinz Hartmann's (1939) early reminder that human psychic proclivities need "environmental releasers" and Harold Searles's 1960 monograph on the impact of non-human environment on the human mind notwithstanding, psychoanalysis has paid less than optimal attention to the space—actual, transitional, symbolic, and imaginary—in which human beings live, create, destroy, and re-create their cognitive and emotional life. Grinberg and Grinberg's (1989) and my own (Akhtar, 1999a) books on immigration do address this issue, but only in one particular context.

1

As a result, questions such as the following have gone unaddressed by psychoanalysis at large. Does the "average expectable environment" deemed necessary for the unfolding of human psychic life also include a roof over one's head, a solid ground to walk upon, a room, a crib, a bed, a chair, a house, and a street? Are our relationships to our motherlands and their landscapes, vegetation, little and big animals, and architecture mere unconscious displacements of the inner dialogue with our parents or independent of such human relationships? Do individuals growing up in rural societies differ in their personality make-up from those who are born and raised in a large metropolis? What is the role of trees, rivers, mountains, and oceans (remember Sir Alec Guinness, who quipped: "I have always found the ocean, no matter what its mood, to be sufficient and good company") in human life? And, what about that of staircases, balconies, auditoriums, and sport stadiums that "contain" us and that of canisters, trunks, envelopes, and mailboxes that "contain" our possessions and messages to others?

However, emphasis upon actual spaces must not lead us to overlook that metaphorical spaces also affect us. Colloquial wisdom becomes our guide here and daily language our textbook. Note the spatially oriented phrases such as "from the bottom of my heart", "deep gratitude", "superficial banter", "the long and short of it", "tall tales", "give him an inch and he takes a yard", and so on. We bury secrets *in* our hearts, come *up* with solutions, wear pride *on* our sleeves, and somehow or the other pull *through* difficult times. Spatial references are abundant in psychoanalytic language as well. While "topographical model", "deep interpretation", "analytic surface", "beneath repression", "incest barrier", readily come to mind, Freud's declaration that "the repressed has a continuous upward pressure in the direction of consciousness" (1915d, p. 151) constitutes an illustration par excellence of spatial moorings of our theory.

Besides these actual and metaphorical spaces lie the imagined and imaginary spaces. The former are ever so slightly out of our sensory grasp and have ontogenetic prototypes in the closed chamber of the primal scene and fantasies about the insides of mother's body. The latter is a psychological "invention" to render the bright expanse of outer space and the dark recesses of intrapsychic life fathomable. Concerns regarding the former underlie agoraphobic and claustrophobic anxieties encountered in clinical practice. Concerns regarding the latter give rise to space travel on the one hand and meditative immersion in quiescent solipsism on the other.

This list of actual, metaphorical, imagined, and imaginary spaces is hardly exhaustive. Michael Balint's (1968) "area of creation" and Donald Winnicott's (1953) "intermediate area of experience" suggest a unique location for the workshop of poetry, sculpture, play, and art; the latter, in turn, creates its own spatial shenanigans as evidenced in the perspectival juxtapositions of Picasso and the geometrical transgressions of M. C. Escher. Balint's (1969) notions of "ocnophilia" and "philobatism", Margaret Mahler's concept of "optimal distance" (Mahler, Pine, & Bergman, 1975), and my elucidation of "psychic tethers" (Akhtar, 1992) all speak to the developmental role of psychophysical space in the mother–child relationship.

And then there are potential spaces. These are gaps that do not exist in or of themselves but are deliberately created for diverse aesthetic or communicative purposes. These are also intervals that are imbued with meanings of their own simply because they represent a missed beat of the heart's communion with the Other. The line break in poetry and a fumbling pause in free association constitute spaces of just this sort. It is at such moments of interpersonal intrigue that silence becomes a closed room, resistance a jammed door, and secret an interpsychic cul-de-sac.

Space, then, is an integral dimension of human mental life. Indeed, the two are in a constant dialectical exchange with each other: space affects the mind, and the mind gives shape and content to space. Time also enters this drama. Division, ownership, naming, use, and population of a given space are altered by passing time. The experience of time, in turn, is affected by the sort of actual and mental space that an individual or a group is in at a given moment. The conflation of "near–far" with "soon–late" is an all too familiar example of such time space conflation.

Elucidation of such issues constitutes the main thrust of this book. It employs a number of contributions from our Australian colleagues, whose voices are generally not heard in Western psychoanalytic circles and who, in some ways, are especially suited to discern the silent language of the disenfranchised and discover the links between new and old traditions of a land. As a result, the book is replete with the poignant history and geography of migration, the triumph and failures of settlement, the halting dialogue with the so-called indigenous people, and the heady intoxication and the tormenting hangover of colonialism. The book also unravels the dialectical exchange between time and space on the one hand and between cultural dislocation and creative pathways back to self-integration on the other. It is a collage of ideas, a symphony of emotions, and a kaleidoscope of theoretical and technical innovation. Following W. H. Auden's statement that "there is no creativity without audacity", the book's mostly solemn tone is occasionally interrupted by blunt, raucous, humorous, and even somewhat spooky passages. It is all very instructive, though, and I submit the book to the readers with the hope that they will find its contents thought-provoking and enjoyable. It is my conviction that the book will—explicitly as well as a bit mysteriously—add to their professional and personal growth.

Introduction

Maria Teresa Savio Hooke

The idea of this book came from the Australian Psychoanalytical Society's 2000 Conference in Uluru, in Central Australia, a place of profound spiritual and cultural significance for both Indigenous and Australian culture. The conference was titled: "This Whispering in Our Hearts: Intuition in the Service of Psychoanalytic Work in the Australian Milieu". The phrase "This whispering in our hearts" (H. Reynolds, 1998) has a double meaning: it refers to the inner distress about the relationships between the indigenous people and the settlers, and it also refers to the intuition needed to read our social and political national milieu (San Roque, chapter 5, this volume). It was the beginning of a new millennium, and—at a time of expansion and reaching-out for psychoanalysis in Australia—we wanted to re-connect with the roots of our culture and identity. Emma Piccioli, who was then Chair of the IPA Publications Committee, and who was interested in cross-cultural issues, suggested a book. As the project evolved, papers presented at other conferences of the Australian Psychoanalytical Society, as well as papers from colleagues in the United States and New Zealand exploring similar or related issues, were added. As such, it is an experiment in multiculturalism.

The Australian indigenous Aboriginal culture is the oldest surviving continuous culture in the world today, going back at least 40,000

5

years. The basis of this culture—which is transmitted orally intergenerationally—is storytelling. The storytelling explains the creation of the land, their deep spiritual connections to it (The Dreamtime), the history and culture of their people, and the social structure of their society and defines life and behaviour in such a social context. Gathered around a campfire in the evening or at a landmark of particular significance, the elders use these stories as the first stage of their children's education. In this way, the Stories of the Dreaming, as they are known, are kept alive and transmitted from one generation to another. Their rituals and ceremonies perform another essential function. They act as a "space" for thinking, as a mental container for thoughts and feelings, as a place where matters can be held in the collective mind and so processed and transformed. The Dreaming has a very powerful psychological function. It is the counterpart of our myths, of our religious narratives, of our literature, a repository of human experiences. Here, the most basic and painful human emotions are given meaning. By being given meaning and historical perspective, they are made bearable (San Roque, chapter 5).

This book is a collection of "stories", and just as the Stories of the Dreaming act as a container of experiences for the indigenous people, it attempts to be a container for experiences that had not had enough exposure in psychoanalytic literature. These include the significance of geographical places and the emotional consequences of the loss of it—dislocation, displacement, dispossession; the meaning of belonging to a place and of losing it. These issues have been overlooked, despite the fact that the history of psychoanalysis has been a history of migration and displacement. As Grinberg and Grinberg (1984) point out, the silence on such matters may be *because* they have been so central in our history.

Between external and internal

Dislocation, alienation, loss, and the meaning of our geographical environment are becoming more and more relevant in an unsettled world in which migration and movements of refugees and exiles have become an integral part of almost every country. This is a crucial issue both for the ones who leave and for the ones left behind. The move away from the countryside towards the cities has also altered our relationship with the land. In a world that moves faster and faster and where local and national communities are breaking down, the finding of roots, continuity, and stability is constantly challenged.

This book explores these issues also in their historical dimension: colonization, forced migration, and dispossession. As the significance of the past is determined in the present, in psychoanalysis when we discuss the past, we are attempting to resolve conflicts in the present. Being aware of our history and of the traumas and atrocities of our past is necessary in order to understand the origins of our prejudice and bias, if we are going to negotiate a way of living in a world where different races, cultures, and religions attempt to cohabit with one another. The Australian writer David Malouf (1998), in speaking about the silence of history, advocates a narrative that would recreate the horror and the deep pain of historical experiences in "an imaginative form that would allow a society to come to terms with itself by taking what it has suffered deep into its consciousness and re-living it in the form of meaning rather than in a muddle or shock" (Lecture 5, p. 1). Here Malouf expresses beautifully what this book is attempting to address. These chapters are not just exercises in history or literature; they also show the relevance of historical facts to the present and that "remembering and working through" is necessary if we want to live in a world of meanings, rather than of raw facts and unprocessed actions. Malouf calls this processing "the deep suffering in our consciousness".

If psychoanalysis is in crisis today, it is also because of our reluctance to engage with the current social and cultural trends and with modern problems. We have lost touch with the early revolutionary spirit of the pioneering times of Freud's Vienna, when our forefathers were at the forefront of all the social issues of the time, from youth issues to child development, from education to sexuality to the women's movement. One of the main contributions that psychoanalysis has made to society since then is the work of John Bowlby (1951) on the effect of lack of maternal care. Bowlby's contribution was born out of the historical and social context of post-war England when, as a consequence of the war, infants and children were separated from their families and were put in homes and orphanages. Today our social context is different. We are still dealing with separation, but for migrants, exiles, refugees, and expatriates it is the separation from their own country and culture, cities and villages, landscapes and architecture—places of familiarity and affection invested with meaning. So it is relevant for us to study the significance of the environment in psychic development: how major environmental changes affect it; how and when these changes become traumatic; and which defensive measures are used to diminish the anxiety and pain related to the loss of it. This is what this book is starting to address.

These diverse contributions have something significant in common. The authors have a particular sensitivity to the trauma of loss and an interest and curiosity in knowing the other's experience emotionally. This counteracts what historically has been a silence, an inhibition of curiosity, "a terror of history" about the issues explored here. Many of the authors share a particular openness, a capacity to put themselves emotionally on the line, to make themselves vulnerable to the experience—a vulnerability to "the other", whether it be a patient, the environment, a location, or a different culture. This makes each chapter not "just another paper", but a testimony of a personal transformation. The authors move away from familiar territory in order to meet the unknown and the unexplored. This has become necessary in order to face, in a real and genuine way, the experience they are describing.

Space

Chapter 1: Thomas Wolman's contribution

The first chapter in this collection is an observation about space. Wolman explores the physical space we live in and the emotional space in which our psychic development occurs, and how the two interrelate with each other. He refers to concepts expressed by psychoanalysts in "spatial terms", since Freud's use of spatial models to illustrate the working of the psychic apparatus. Balint, Klein, Winnicott, Mahler, Bion, all have conceived ideas in spatial terms, like Freud, in attempting to illustrate the working of the mind. Concepts like internal world, transitional space, optimal distance, container/contained are examples of it.

Wolman moves in another direction. Primarily his interest is in exploring how space becomes a "human space" by the fact that we live and conduct our daily activities in it, defined and structured by the way humans use it. By living in it, we humanize space and we domesticate nature. For Wolman each individual and culture creates its own space, which reflects its characters and values. For example, a house or a church is a human space that adapts to the environment but also expresses the cultural values of the individual and the community.

Human space is not just the environment we live in—it is not only the external, it is also the internal space. As well as the need for a good-enough external object that fills the infant's physical environment, the author proposes the need for an internal space. In his view, such space develops through the presence and containing functions of objects, the mother being the primary object. Through adequate containment the infant can develop its own internal space, which enables the development of the mind. Containing "maternal" functions are also described in the space of the consulting room, which will be ordinary enough, quiet enough, comfortable and homelike enough, and in the mental attitude of the analyst needing at times to allow the patient to have an experience of an internal space rather than resorting to a defensive mode. Besides the maternal space, other primary organizing spaces are, for the author, the phallic and the oedipal. In the development of the child, he postulates the child's need for the role of the father in offering boundaries and barriers in the face of delusions of phallic omnipotence and to help in the growth of reality testing.

In this way the child develops its own internal space separate from the parents—for Wolman, a bounded space, a container of thoughts: a mind of its own. The author sees this space—the oedipal space—as equivalent to the analytic space, a space for thinking that is common but separate, where mutual understanding occurs, but also a place of no certainties, of ambiguity and indetermination.

The author then turns from internal space towards external geopolitical realities and looks at the impact that history and politics have on the human space. History, politics, and geopolitics are very closely intertwined: historical events and political shifts change the configuration of nations, affect the life of its inhabitants, and impact in various ways on groups' culture and civilization. For Wolman the idea of unity or stability that we attach to concepts like "nation" or "state" is an illusion: a careful look reveals an inherent degree of fluctuation, instability, and elusiveness not dissimilar to the vicissitudes of the internal space and the evolution of the self.

This chapter is an introduction to the concept of space, both internal and external. With "Experiences Down Under" (chapter 2) and the Twemlows' chapter (chapter 6) there is a shift towards a more personal testimony, where space is conceived as place, as land, as country, and where the vicissitudes of belonging and non-belonging, history, trauma, possession, and dispossession are explored.

Place, time, and land

Chapter 2: Kate Grenville's contribution

Kate Grenville's essay opens the chapters from Australia and New Zealand. Her most recent and highly successful book *The Silent River* deals with the complex issue of the British early settlement in Australia. The chapter is a story within a story; it is, in fact, the account of the journey of writing the book. The main theme is the description of the research into the history of her ancestor, a convict who arrived in Australia as an unwilling migrant; such research becomes an exploration of the author's own family and personal story. Grenville's paper sets the scene for the Australian contributions. The main themes are all represented here: the uneasy feeling of the settler who inhabits a land that he calls home, but that in some ways is still foreign; the guilt for the crimes committed; the secrets and deceits in order to keep the guilt at bay; the sense of identity that does not feel genuine. In order to write the book she had to experience the place the way she thought the settlers had, "as the most foreign place on earth"; and while researching it she realized that behind the silences and the buried information there was a history of crime, violence, and dispossession she had not previously confronted or taken in. She had then to re-examine her sense of belonging to the country and of being Australian, rather than going on trying to prove herself as a true native.

"I had to face the illusory nature of my deep bond . . . an idea of myself as native had to be replaced by the idea of myself as foreign . . . someone that was figuratively an outsider and a destroyer" (Grenville, 2006). The chapter is an insightful account of the novelist's journey into herself during which guilt, loss, and grief had to be faced and worked through. As she puts it in chapter 2: "Inheritors of those settlers—that is, us—have a slightly different journey to go through, but it also begins in loss. The loss is our sense of ourselves as blameless. The mourning has to involve the acknowledgment that we have a home because other people were turned out of it." The account of her experience reminds me of Ellenberger's concept of "creative illness", which he describes apropos of Freud's crisis of

1885. Ellenberger (1970) says that creative illnesses can be found among philosophers, mystics, scientists, and writers and that it occurs in a period of intense preoccupation with an idea and search for a certain truth. The person emerges from it with a permanent transformation in the personality and with a conviction that he or she has discovered a truth. It does seem that, for Grenville, the exploration of the history of her ancestor and the research that followed became her own creative illness, which left her with the sense of having discovered a profound truth about herself and with the internal source for her book *The Silent River*.

Chapter 3: Bain Attwood's contribution

Bain Attwood is a historian. He uses psychoanalytic ideas to understand historical events. In this chapter he is putting on the couch the Australian nation: if Australia is the patient, the disease is the silence about its traumatic past related to the history of colonization. The author uses Freud's paper "Remembering, Repeating and Working Through" as a template for his analysis. He sees the Australian patient as somebody who "resist[s] having a history" and as such, cannot learn from the experience of the past, but is bound to repeat it in the present; a patient who cannot "remember" the crimes and the traumas, inflicted and received and so cannot go through grief and mourning. The author considers the matter of "distance and proximity" in historical work: the crucial issue of how the historian places him/herself in relation to traumatic events that are bound to raise powerful emotional responses. His view is that the modern historian needs to acknowledge and work with these emotional responses from a position of "empathic unsettlement" for victims but also for perpetrators and bystanders. In such work empathy should not be confused with identification with the victims, but should, instead, allow the historian to write history from a position of "historical objectivity". He believes that in recent Australian history—for example, in the narrative of the Stolen Generation (the Aboriginal children separated from their families and put in institutions under a policy of "assimilation")—historians have leaned too much towards identification with the victims and not enough towards historical objectivity. As a result there has been a limited historical understanding and an acting out rather than a working through of the past: "what Freud would have regarded as both too much and too little distance on the part of those relating to this past." This has significant consequences for the present.

The chapter's interplay between history and psychoanalysis is another demonstration—if we needed one—of the usefulness of psychoanalytic thinking in understanding contemporary issues. An important matter raised is the question of emotional distance in relation to traumatic events. Psychoanalysts are faced every day with a similar problem in the consulting room in relation to trauma. How far the analyst is empathic or identified with the patient's suffering is one of the elements that will determine a successful psychoanalysis (Tuckett, 2006). The stance that Attwood advocates of "historical objectivity" is what analysts would call analytic neutrality, a concept that has been misinterpreted because of Freud's unfortunate metaphor of the surgeon, which has been read out of context. Historians—like analysts—if they write history without being sensitive to the underlying affects, end up missing the point; and, if they get too involved in the situation, miss the chance to analyse it. (Tuckett, 2006).

Chapter 4: Eve Steel's contribution

Eve Steel's chapter was written in response to a request that I made, as Scientific Secretary of the Australian Society at the time, to present a paper on the *Bringing Them Home* report to an Open Day of our conferences. The lost children of this paper, or, as they came to be called, The Stolen Children or the Stolen Generation, are the 30,000 Aboriginal children who were taken from their families between 1910 and 1970 and put in religious institutions, out of a government policy of assimilation. This was an attempt on the part of the government to "dilute" aboriginality by removing them from their families of origin and encouraging future mixed marriages. The publication of this report had a profound impact on Australian public life and on Australia's collective conscience and was a fundamental step in breaking the "great Australian silence" on its history and on the crimes perpetrated against the indigenous population.

Steel's title, "Lost Children", denotes both the children who were called the stolen and those who were behind the action of stealing them. This is a distressing, disturbing, and confronting paper in which the plight of the "lost children" is explored in both sociocultural and psychoanalytic aspects. In fact the author considers the lost child in the outside world and the lost child in the internal world, against the background of the children's rhyme "I'm the king of the castle, you're the dirty rascal", which becomes a metaphor for the see-saw position of superiority/inferiority sociologically, politically, and internally. Such an exploration does not relate only to Australia and does not concern only the past: in fact, the stealing of children occurs today under different forms and denominations, and the trade of children from poor countries to rich countries is alive and well. The historical background of this chapter is the Australia of the 1950s, dominated by a belief in racial superiority and protectionism that went under the name of "White Australian Policy" and by the stronghold that the Church, both Catholic and Protestant, had on public life. The author paints a fresco of early life in the colonies where the two main powers—Church and colonial—were allied in an ideology of superiority and dominance over the land and its indigenous inhabitants. For Steel the historical dimension is also a contemporary dimension: history is always contemporary history; each time that internally and externally a position of superiority and "divine right" dominates, awful things continue to be done to the powerless and to the ones without a voice.

The question is posed: How could these horrors have happened? Which state of mind makes the perpetration of such horrors possible? She focuses on intergenerational transmission and examines how, if not metabolized, the traumas and experience suffered are unconsciously passed over through generations. In this case, the traumatic experiences of the first migrants—the unwanted English, Welsh, Irish, Scottish, kicked out as "dirty rascals" from their own countries—were passed on to the Australian indigenous people, who became the unwanted ones, kicked out of their own land and massacred. Additionally, the punitive and abusive experiences suffered by the members of religious orders in their churches and convents at the time were also passed on to the aboriginal children, who ended up suffering the same cold, abusive, punitive treatment their guardians had suffered.

The author reminds us of the dangers inherent in working with traumatized people: of the risk in believing that telling one's story is healing in itself and of the need instead of skilful work in order for processing and working through to occur. Quoting Freud's

"Remembering, Repeating and Working Through", she emphasizes the need of working through in order to develop a third position in the mind: the position of the observer or the bystander. For the traumatized person, the development of such a position is a fundamental step in being able to let go and mourn; the alternative is to remain stuck in the see-saw position of victim/perpetrator.

As I mentioned, the chapter has a broader psychoanalytic dimension. In fact, the author sees the brutalization of the Aboriginal children not only in the historical past but as the brutalization of the child in the adult that goes on in the present, each time that we are in the "king of the castle" position and we project our own "dirty rascal" onto someone else. For the author (personal communication), there is a lost child in all of us when "our out-of-touchness with our own centre, our blindness, our not wanting to know what cannot be tolerated" have the upper hand.

The authenticity of this chapter makes it powerfully relevant in the present and raises an important issue regarding trauma. In addressing how we listen to the account of the traumatic experience, Steel says that it is necessary to hear the story of the victim and of the perpetrator from a position of internal conviction that we all carry both sides in ourselves. Only out of a profound awareness of this truth will we be able to develop empathy, rather than judgement and blame, and will we avoid getting rid of what is unpalatable in ourselves onto the other.

Chapter 5: Craig San Roque's contribution

San Roque's chapter is a reflection on the experience of a Jungian psychoanalyst working within the Aboriginal community in Central Australia. The author's interest for the "other", his wish to know the other emotionally, the curiosity that propelled him to make the geographical journey to central Australia, give this chapter a moving and very personal quality. In the words of San Roque, it is an emotional journey of discovery of the "half of my substance [that] was missing". If one thinks of Bion's three different ways of relating—through knowledge, through love, and through hate—this chapter conveys a relationship with Central Australia and with the Aboriginal people through knowledge and love. The interest, curiosity, and openness to the experience become, for the author, transformational.

The chapter tells three intertwined narratives. The first is the narrative of the author, his leaving the oppressive cultural somnolence of Australia of the late 1960s and going to London for his psychoanalytic training, his return in the late 1980s, his travelling to work with the Aboriginal communities in Central Australia where he would live for 10 years immersed in indigenous mental health, law, alcohol use and abuse, petrol sniffing, and community action.

The second intertwined narrative is the author's preoccupation with the issue of psychic pain—the psychic pain in the Australian milieu—and his belief that the nature of the Antipodean pain cannot be understood unless one goes back to its roots in the events of the eighteenth, nineteenth, and twentieth centuries, a period of displacement and massacre of the indigenous population.

The third narrative is the author's belief that psychotherapy becomes a false self-exercise if it is transported unchallenged from Western societies and applied in Australia, without taking into account the specific qualities of psychic pain as it is experienced in that country.

The chapter then moves into indigenous contemporary reality and explores intuition as the mode of communication between the two cultures. This transports the reader into a different space and dimension: under the influence of *Tjukurrpa*, the *"Dreaming of the country"*, which San Roque understands as a mental container of emotional experiences, a space that functions as a mind to be used for reflection, thinking, and metabolizing. For the author, Tjukurrpa is not only the container of oral tradition of Aboriginal history, but an active psychic force with a powerful contemporary function. San Roque's understanding is that when Tjukurrpa is not present, there is no possibility of doing the emotional work that allows the holding and processing of a problem in the collective mind. This understanding is applied with very interesting results to the problem of alcoholism and intoxication, endemic and insoluble among the Aboriginal people. Alcohol was imported to Australia by the Europeans; it was as such unknown to Aboriginal people. It is something for which the Aboriginal culture does not have a song, a myth, or a dreaming, nor an oral tradition, so these issues cannot be talked about or shared. San Roque, who worked on many community projects on petrol sniffing and alcohol abuse, over the years developed a project based on the Dionysian legend—the Sugarmen/Dionysius Intoxication project—with the idea of providing indigenous people

with an equivalent to Tjukurrpa. This was then used to start giving
words and a cultural context to intoxication and drunkenness. San
Roque's experiment of working with and within another culture is
one of the few examples where the two cultures—psychoanalytic
and Aboriginal—have been working together, with fruitful results
on both side. Similarly to the Twemlows' concept of multicultural
identity, San Roque's approach opens up new perspectives on bridging cultural and social divides.

Chapter 6: Stuart and Nicholas Twemlow's contribution

The issue of cultural identity is at the centre of the Twemlows' chapter. Erikson (1950) already attempted to include cultural identity as
part of the process of emotional development and made the point
that a complete personal growth implies the integration of our own
cultural identity. The Twemlows develop this concept further and
contend that a rich and mature sense of self (a true self in Winnicott's sense) comes from the integration of our different cultural
selves, of one's various cultural self-representations. The narrative—
one would say, the clinical material that provides the evidence for
this hypothesis—is the personal experiences of the two authors, a
well-known psychoanalyst and his son, a poet and art graduate. In
this chapter they explore their Maori roots and heritage during a
momentous trip to New Zealand.

The impetus for the trip is similar for both father and son: a
search for their own roots. For the father, the precipitating factor is
the announcement he receives during a psychoanalytic conference
that his natural mother is dying and the emotional collapse that follows: a cluster of experiences of loss brought to the surface by the
news, which burst open in a sort of temporary breakdown.

In their chapter the authors attempt to make sense of their experience and to articulate its psychological meaning. They use Winnicott's concept of potential space and Ogden's concept of dialectical
process. The exploration of the Maori culture, and the discovery of
aspects of their own lives influenced by such culture, leads them to
conceptualize the total self as a composite of many parts, of different
cultural identities in dialogue and in a fluid relationship with each
another, and to propose the concept of multicultural identity. This
concept leads to what is the most interesting and far-reaching reflec-

tion of the chapter—knowing who we are and being aware of the various mixes of our cultures may allow us to transcend prejudice and bias, especially racist bias. The Twemlows, in fact, believe that as we are more mixed-breeds than we think we are, as our bloodlines are more mixed than we think they are (as some DNA studies seem to imply), it follows that the black and white division on which most racism is based is a false dichotomy and that racial purity is an illusion. "The realization that we are all 'half-breeds'—that is, all of mixed racial descent—can help us feel a closer connection with others who appear to be culturally and physically different." The authors' suggestion is that the multicultural identity of an individual—exemplified by the description: "I am not just a Jew, I am not just a New Yorker, I am not just an African American, nor only my parents' child. I am more than the pieces patched together"—is critical to the full development of mental health. This concept could prove of great social benefit—especially at a time such as ours of mass migration, globalization, and acute racial, religious, and cultural tensions—as it speaks for tolerance of differences rather than prejudice, and it speaks for reason and moderation rather than extremism and absolutism. It is also a concept that anyone with mixed cultural heritages can relate to, as it helps to make sense of living with the coexistence in oneself of mixed heritages and different cultures.

Dislocation

Chapter 7: Salman Akhtar's contribution

While much has been written in psychoanalytic literature about loss of a person, much less explored has been the theme of loss of places, of familiar surroundings, of objects that are part of the "ordinariness" of everyday life. Salman Akhtar, in his multilayered and rich chapter, looks at the role of places in our life and the effect of dislocation on the mind and on the internal structure of the personality. The author uses and extends the concepts of "environmental releasers" (Hartmann) and of the "waking screen" (Pacella) to include also the relationship with the environment as formative in our psychic development. He believes that inner stability is never acquired once and for all and that our internal structure requires constant input from the outside. Major changes and disruption in the environment affect and threaten the sense of safety of the individual and, as such,

become traumatic. In this chapter he considers what makes environmental changes traumatic, the impact they have on the human
mind, and the defensive measures used to deal with the anxiety and
pain related to the trauma.

The chapter heightens the reader's awareness of physical surroundings, of the "spirit of the place". It focuses the mind on the
relevance of the ordinary, of the familiar, what David Malouf infers
as the culture of small things: "the fact is that the whole of a culture
is present in all its complexity in small things as well as large" (1998,
Lecture 1, p. 4) and in his understanding that a culture is represented in objects and sites that contain layers of history, memories, and
traces of personal events which make it significant and meaningful
(2000, p. 4).

Of particular interest is the part that deals with the defences put
in place to cope with trauma and loss. Such a description will be very
familiar to those who have been migrants, exiles, or refugees, and
it ranges from the denial of the loss to the manic adoption of the
new country's way of life, from the return-fantasy to the re-creation
of the idealized home, to the wish to make reparation out of the unconscious awareness that leaving home also means having attacked
home-motherland.

The technical implications of working with patients who have suffered the trauma of dislocation and displacement are addressed in
the two clinical chapters of this collection: those of Salman Akhtar
and Jim Telfer. Akhtar offers very clear guidelines for the work with
these patients and suggests technical adjustments that are based on
his experience with exiles, refugees, and settlers. The emphasis is
on developmental work, on validating feelings of dislocation, and
on being receptive to non-human aspects of transference and countertransference—what Akhtar calls the environmental transference.
The author believes that: " Only [after this type of work] can analysis—in its traditional sense—begin, proceed, and be meaningful."

Chapter 8: James Telfer's contribution

Telfer's chapter looks at dislocation as it is represented in the mind
and investigates the issue through clinical work. The author gives
a moving and vivid account of the work with a displaced person, a
young librarian who experiences feeling of unreality and disconnec-

tion from people and places. The patient is also displaced and alien from herself, as she exists only in the way others see her, fitting into the perceived image constructed for her by the mother. She comes from generations of displaced people, where emotions related to migration, dislocation, and loss had been always denied.

We follow the analyst's mind struggling to reach a patient who creates in the session a comforting and alluring sense of "always having been here" and "always having known him", not able to bear any feeling of separation from the analyst. There is a striking description of how any "new" comments and interpretations are archived by the patient, as a good librarian would do, in old familiar files—nothing is allowed to be new. In his attempts to make sense of his experience, the analyst reaches both inside and outside himself, searching for inspiration. He uses a concept from group work, "genius loci" (or spirit of the place), which helps him to focus on the physical aspects of the consulting room, where images evoked by the room—lights, shadows, noises—provide food for metaphors for the analyst. These turn out to be helpful in slowly re-connecting the patient with a sense of place and time, talking in metaphors being less threatening to the patient than transference talk. Telfer uses this talking in metaphors to connect the patient with the consulting room as "a place" of emotional meaning, and he sees it as the first step in a delicate work of re-connection of the patient with the person of the analyst.

This use of the physical environment as a source of meaning, and as a way of linking the displaced person to a place, has many points in common with Salman Akhtar's comments on technique.

Akhtar and Telfer both address two intertwined issues: one familiar enough, the ongoing discussion in psychoanalysis today about working with traumatized patients; the other much less familiar, which is the analytic work with displaced patients, who are also traumatized but in a different way. Telfer's patient is both heavily traumatized and displaced. Both analysts intuitively sense their patients' need for a delicate work of gluing, mending and sewing the fractured, lacerated bits of their experience and how this can also occur through a work of re-connection to the immediate physical environment of the consulting room. Both analysts also believe that this has to come first, before venturing on to more in-depth work. This may be a less threatening and more meaningful way to help the patients feel understood.

I

Space

1

Human space, psychic space, analytic space, geopolitical space

Thomas Wolman

Space has played a part in psychoanalytic thinking since Freud used a series of spatial models to portray the workings of the psychic apparatus (Letter to Fliess, 6 December 1896, in Masson, 1985; Freud, 1900a). One model showed a series of systems or plates in a three-dimensional array. Another depicted a kind of optical apparatus. These diagrams, and indeed the very notion of an "apparatus", are inherently spatial. Certain ideas such as the body image and the ego-boundary were also conceived in spatial terms (Schilder, 1935). From the latter we get the basic analytic distinction between "interior" and "exterior". Psychic locality is an axiom of psychoanalysis that underlies both the first and second topography. In two representations of the second topography, Freud (1923b, 1933a) shows the different parts of the mind occupying adjoining and overlapping "neighbourhoods", with complex interrelationships. And it was natural for analysts to think of the unconscious as occupying an *area* of the mind. In the same vein, spatial thinking was recognized in dreams, where the unconscious may be represented by a cellar or basement, or perhaps by its opposite—a mouldy old attic, filled with discarded papers and objects.

However, the role of space as both metaphor and object of investigation remained marginal in the history of psychoanalysis until recently. One might say it faded into the "background". Its return as a subject of interest began in 1961 with the publication of Stone's monograph, *The Psychoanalytic Situation.* At this juncture, a clear distinction was made—one that was always implicit—between the psychoanalytic situation and setting, and the psychoanalytic process. The former was defined as spatial, the latter temporal. In 1967, Bleger made a similar distinction between the psychoanalytic "frame" (spatial) and process (temporal).

Meanwhile, in Britain, a very original concept of space—so-called intermediate or "potential space"—had been conceived by D. W. Winnicott (1951). In part because of the challenges of visualizing "potential space", this sophisticated concept took time before being assimilated into the analytic mainstream. But once accepted, it opened up everyone's thinking to the more general problem of space. Winnicott himself had formulated his concept, in part, as an alternative to Melanie Klein's internal world (Segal, 1964). It was already becoming fashionable to speak of the child's internal or representational world as constituting the area of the psyche—the stage, if you will, where conflicts and antagonisms played themselves out. In this mostly British context, Balint (1968) proposed an entirely new topology of the mind, consisting of three "areas": the Oedipus conflict, the basic fault, and the area of creation. With the confluence of all these new ideas, the psychoanalytic setting could be rechristened: "The Psychoanalytic Space". Thus in the 1980s and 1990s a spate of articles appeared in the psychoanalytic literature with the word "space" in the title (Modell, 1992; Weiss, 1997).

These ideas were all circulating when Margaret Mahler (Mahler, Pine, & Bergman, 1975) conducted her research on mothers and their infants and toddlers. Strongly influenced by Winnicott, Mahler introduced concepts with a spatial quality: "emotional refuelling", "darting away", the upright perspective, and, of course, the famous "optimal distance". She demonstrated how the mother acts as a beacon in her child's construction of a personal space. In this tradition, Akhtar (1992) wrote about the child's planetary movement around the mother, involving tethers and other objects, and later extended these views to the psychosocial dilemmas associated with immigration (Akhtar, 1999a).

The contemporary work of Bion (1977b) and Lacan (Fink, 1997) was less well known outside the United States. Working in parallel, these two theorists embarked on an ambitious reworking of Freudian theory. Each made extensive use of spatial models. Bion (1977b) constructed the "Grid"; Lacan, the "schema L" (Evans, 1996). These complex diagrams were designed to reveal the logic behind diverse clinical phenomena. Bion applied a Euclidian model of multidimensional space to the problems of psychopathology. Lacan followed a non-Euclidian approach, initially experimenting with topological objects, such as Möbius strips, Klein bottles, and the "cross-cap". Later in his work, topological models gave way to a study of Borromean knots.

Human space

Psychoanalysis does not deal with the space found in nature, and certainly not the vast expanse of "outer space". For analysis, space does not exist outside a context of human objects. Human space is produced by the objects that dwell within it, in their character, and in their various arrangements. Human space is structured by definition, whether we speak of "interior space" (the space of the mind) or ordinary, external space. A human being requires a place to "dwell". We call this place by a number of names: one's own little corner of the world, home-base, or the place where one lives with oneself.

A beautiful short poem by Wallace Stevens (2005) shows the humanization of space. In the poem's inaugural act, a person who says "I" places a jar atop a hill in Tennessee. In so doing, he or she adds a human, subjective element to the landscape. The placement of the jar immediately redefines the area as a human space. The jar works as a single point of orientation. Everything in the surrounding landscape can now be seen in relationship to the jar. Nearness and remoteness may be assessed and experienced. Pre-jar, the wilderness was uncharted; post-jar a human space is established.

The issues of human space must be addressed by all human cultures. Each culture creates a human space that adapts to its environment and embodies its values. Because of the isolation of rural societies, a premium is placed on gathering places like churches and meeting-halls. And the home must compensate for a lack of near neighbours. In any society today, you can walk into a home and see immediately that you are in a human space even if you don't recognize the significance of the objects that constitute it.

Rural societies thus are able to "domesticate" a portion of the natural world. Domestic plants and animals are drawn into the human realm. But such societies must also confront the larger, wilder space of Nature—the Nature beyond the hill in the Wallace Stevens poem. Since ancient times, humans have divided Nature into sea, sky, and land. Of these three expanses, the sea is the true *terra incognita* because it extends in all directions without any landmarks, unless we count the sharp natural boundary between sea and land. On the rolling sea the horizon operates as a kind of false landmark, ever receding as we approach it, and giving the impression of a space without limit. As a corrective to the amorphous oceans, the sky stands as a fixed dome that is entirely structured by the position of the stars, especially the fixed polar star. Humans have known celestial geography since the Stone Age. Indeed, places like Stonehenge seem to have served as astronomical orientation devices. And through their verticality these structures connect the sky and the land, as mountainous terrain does naturally. It is therefore no accident that advances in navigation all depend on knowledge of the sky. The structure of the heavens allows sailors to get their bearings on the oceans.

Land falls half-way between sea and sky. Portions of land such as desert and ice cap resemble the sea in its amorphousness. The emptiness of deserts finds its counterpart in the extreme density of jungles, where human orientation also veers towards the impossible. But much land is either cultivated or possessed of a familiar, comprehensible topography. Societies differ in their approach to this two-sidedness. Hunter gatherers tend to view natural space as indivisible and placed outside the human realm. They may see themselves dwarfed by the huge scale of nature. Modern humans tend to look upon land as divisible and available for human appropriation. Land can be owned, sold, traded, and subdivided. This is part of the global tendency towards domestication that is affecting wetlands and rain forests around the world.

In our era, modernism has made it harder to preserve the "liveability" of human space. A landmark book, in this respect, is Jane Jacobs's *The Death and Life of Great American Cities* (1993). She argues cogently against the destruction of human neighbourhoods by superhighways and high-rise buildings. For Jacobs, the local neighbourhood is the urban human space par excellence.

The psychoanalytic consulting room is an exemplary human space. It is usually a well-appointed room filled with human objects: a couch, chairs, doors, windows, toilets, objets d'art, carpets, pictures, knick-knacks, lamps, a desk, bookcases, assorted papers, plants, screens, vases, and so on. The element of design (i.e., structure) is obvious, as is the human "lived-in" quality.

Winnicott perfectly captured the "ordinariness" of the consulting room in the following quotation:

> This work was to be done in a room, not a passage, a room that was quiet and not liable to sudden unpredictable sounds, yet not dead quiet and not free from ordinary house noises. This room would be lit properly, but not by a light staring in the face, and not by a variable light. The room would certainly not be dark and it would be comfortably warm . . . and probably a rug and some water would be available. [1954, p. 285]

The quote emphasizes the home-like aspects of the room, its lack of pretentiousness, its relative comfort, and its protection from extreme changes. Interestingly, the only object mentioned is the rug, which, besides adding to the room's warmth, might also remind us of the original transitional object (a blanket, say), along with the likelihood of pillows on the couch and chairs.

The analyst's conduct is structured and limited by the human space shared with the patient. He or she speaks in a conversational tone and does not allow a silence to go on past the point of no return. Nor will the analyst interrupt a silence (as we shall see) that circumscribes, perhaps for the first time, a real personal space for the patient. And as in the old joke, if the patient walks towards the window intending to jump, the analyst does not continue interpreting, but gets up and stops the patient. If the patient needs to sit up for a while, she sits up, or if she needs to use the toilet in mid-session, so be it. As Greenson (1967) emphasized in the 1960s, if the patient has suffered a loss, or has celebrated a significant anniversary, the analyst acknowledges it.

The human space dictates that there are no absolutes in psychoanalysis. Any "rule" may be broken whenever the human context demands it. Even the fundamental rule is no exception. It primarily applies to the patient's openness to future revelation. If a patient begs not to have to tell something today, the analyst will accept it. This instance may bring to mind Freud's technique in the Rat Man case. Although Freud (1909d) did not give his patient this leeway, he was more than willing to help him tell his horrifying tale. It was as if he was saying: Yes, we cannot ignore the rule, but we can still engage with it as a common task, in a human fashion.

The mention of the fundamental rule reminds us that psycho-analytic space is made for talking and keeping silent—both quintes-sential human activities. For this reason it is useful to visualize the analytic space as a "frame", like one for a picture or a photograph. In film theory (Casabier, 1976), the frame has a very specific meaning: whatever happens inside the frame is meaningful. For example, if one sees two men moving towards each other inside the film frame, it means there is going to be an encounter. But if the same thing occurs on the street, one may not make that assumption—perhaps the men are just "passing by". If we say that the human space of the consulting room "frames" the unfamiliar aspects of analysis—the use of the couch, the analyst's silence, the lack of inhibition in speak-ing—then these features become potentially meaningful. That is to say, the "frame" prevents analytic work from feeling "weird" or "sur-realistic" or "unsociable"—as it not infrequently does to patients at the beginning.

Maternal space

Human space begins to take shape in the early relationship with the mother. There are three maternal objects that play an essential role in the first structuring of space. The object most closely associ-ated with the mother is the "vessel". Its psychoanalytic counterpart is the "container", which forms an important theoretical term in Bion's thinking. Bion (1977b) thinks of the container as the moth-er's reverie, processing and containing the infant's chaotic feelings, especially hatred.

There are various ways to conceive the vessel's function. We can view it positively as "containing" something—in this case, the infant's fragmentary experience. The word "contain" also suggests a barrier against the centripetal force of overflow and bits flying apart. It thus allows an unstable mass to somehow hold together. But we can also view the vessel negatively as preserving the emptiness within it. In other words, it is precisely the empty space inside that is preserved from impingements from without. Indeed, we could take the step of saying that the vessel *is* this emptiness—the essence of its container function.

This later feature can be seen in adult analyses when long periods of silence are required. These silences may occur after the patient has succeeded in overcoming a manic defence of constant activity or of obsessive thinking that made it impossible for his mind to be at rest. Once a state of silence is achieved, intervening would only rekindle the manic defence. The patient must have the opportunity of experiencing the silence uninterrupted. The presence of the analyst helps to hold the empty space together, making possible a true interior space.

Here is an example of the positive aspect of the container, from a paper by Khan:

> not only was each session an isolated happening, with no before and after, but it was also a clutter of bizarre bits and pieces of her random perceptions and volatile affects. Yet I had this sure feeling that Caroline was making a very private use of the analytic space and, gradually, even of me as a person. But she kept it all strictly to herself. [1983, p. 103]

The second maternal object is the beacon or lighthouse. I take the lighthouse reference from the novel *To the Lighthouse* by Virginia Woolf (1927). In Part One of the novel, Mrs Ramsay *is* the lighthouse. She is the hub around which her large extended family revolves. We know, of course, that the infant begins to recognize the human configuration of nose, mouth, and eyes very soon after birth (Mahler, Pine, & Bergman, 1975). Soon the mother's face and look become the guide or compass to the surrounding space. At this stage, it is the mother's constant presence that humanizes the space and makes it safe and liveable for the child's explorations. Once the infant learns to crawl, his exploration of the space around the mother becomes a form of *reconnaissance*. To reconnoitre means both to explore and to recognize the space, in its intimate relationship with the mother. At some point, the mother introduces objects to her child—often ones associated with her person, like jewellery—which continues the structuring of space around her.

In the earliest years, the absence of the mother even for a short interval leaves the child without any orientation in space. Winnicott (1963b) called this experience a primitive agony analogous to falling for ever. The phenomenon of stranger anxiety also demonstrates the 8-month- to 1-year-old child's sensitivity to disruptions in the "beacon" function. In severe cases of stranger anxiety, the child tries to look away from the stranger. Fixing upon the stranger's face causes a "defamiliarization" of space, with the resulting panic. In all subsequent stages, object loss causes a perturbation in the child's and adult's sense of personal space. The idea of being "lost" always includes the meaning of not knowing where you are in relationship to the mother-as-beacon. Adults who have lost a spouse, for example, often complain of not knowing who they are any more, or where they are headed.

A powerful aid in this regard is the transitional object, which can serve as a mother surrogate. Any object associated with the mother can provide a focal point for personal space in the mother's absence. Another sign of the spatial nature of the transitional object can be found in its materiality, a quality that counterbalances its role as mother surrogate. Winnicott (1951) noted that the child's first possession was usually a piece of soft cloth, like a handkerchief or blanket. It had not only to be soft, but also pliable, malleable—in short: an object of great plasticity. It can be folded, twisted, crumpled, or gathered. It can flap in the wind or seem to float on air as it descends. It is quite protean in its manifestations.

In truth, the transitional object embodies an omnipotential space. It is not so much formless as the series of all potential forms. Its quality of seeming alive, noted by Winnicott, may derive from this dynamic property. We can observe it in Winnicott's own "squiggle" drawings (1971b). We can think of the transitional object as a kind of "squiggle" drawing in three dimensions. Such a moving form can never become fixed or finished like a fully formed external object. It can be a knotted cloth, which suggests a doll, for example, but it can never be a doll. A doll—or any other fabricated object—loses its omnipotentiality.

The three objects—vessel, beacon, and blanket—all have important effects upon the consulting-room space. In order to maintain the container function, the analytic space should be non-intrusive. It should be warm, comfortable, and lived-in, but not a "designer space". Nor should it be an example of modernist minimalism, at least in my opinion. The paintings on the wall, for example, should be decorative but not so dramatic or compelling (or seductive) in themselves that they divert attention to the surrounding space (and, by implication, away from the process). For the same reason, analysts avoid the use of bizarre objects or anything that smacks of surrealism. There is plenty of the latter in all our dreams and unconscious productions. In short, the consulting-room space, with its familiar placement of desk, chair, and couch, constitutes a background and support for the psychoanalytic process.

The analyst must be aware of his or her potential role as beacon for the patient—a role that is substantially eclipsed by his or her position out of the patient's line of sight. Some patients cannot tolerate the loss of face-to-face contact and cannot use the couch at all. Others will turn around to see the analyst's face or will request to sit up for a period of time. These difficulties may indicate that the analytic space has become frighteningly unfamiliar or amorphous for the patient. The patient's demands for guidance—almost ubiquitous in many analyses—stem in part from a need to situate the analyst within the treatment space. In the early stages of any analysis, mutual "situating" helps establish the analytic "situation".

Pillows are a common surrogate for the maternal aspects of the analyst. They are soft, pliable, and reminiscent of the mother's breast. These and other soft objects like throw-rugs or bean-bags can be moved and rearranged by the patient. Such objects provide a sense of familiarity and, therefore, orientation within the consulting room. They also ensure that a portion of the analytic space remains under the patient's control. The patient can hold the pillow or put several under his or her head, lay a blanket over him/herself, or even line up a series of objects near him or her on the couch. The analyst can freely opt to analyse this behaviour at any point, or to let it alone.

Phallic space

Picture a cityscape like Paris, with the Eiffel tower looming over a wide expanse of scaled-down nineteenth-century buildings. In this picture the tower dominates all the space around it. It does so in three ways: (1) Its verticality leads the eye to the heavens and emphasizes the smaller scale of the houses. (2) Everything in the cityscape is visualized in relationship to the tower. (3) If we picture the cityscape as lines of force like those made by iron filings laid out on paper over a magnet, then all the lines of force go towards the tower, then up its length, and finally out into the sky. The tower channels the multidirectional energy of the cityscape into one unified flow.

The myth of the Tower of Babel explains the monolithic character of this kind of space. In the biblical story (a variant of the oedipal myth, according to Bion, 1977b), the people undertake the building of a tall tower. Their aim is to literally touch the sky. In other words, they see no inherent limit to the height of the tower. The tower represents the unified energies of the people—their almost unlimited capability when everyone pulls together and all the collective energy moves in the same direction. We can compare the tower to a laser which aligns all light photons in the same direction. The result is energy concentrated to a prodigious intensity.

In the story, God destroys the tower in order to punish the hubris of the people. And he punishes them further by dividing them into an ever-expanding number of language groups, each unable to understand the other. Surprisingly, the punishment is not as severe as it could have been. The destruction of the tower and the consequent loss of any principle of unity or organization could have left the people impotent and blind. In spatial terms they would have been consigned to the wilderness. Their lesser penance was to be separated into a multiplicity of neighbourhoods, each with its own particular structure. Each neighbourhood (language) is a valid human space. Neighbourhoods can exist side-by-side—that is, they can coexist—but they are never on exactly the same page (inhabiting the same space). The same language barrier keeps any two individuals from fully understanding each other.

The myth makes it seem as if phallic space—the building of the tower—is possible but for the wrath of God. However, the myth may simply point to an inherent impossibility. The multiplicity of languages that defines human beings can never be unified. Each language maps the social and psychic space in a slightly different way. In transposing one space upon another, something is always lost. However, the idea of phallic space, which would include perfect communication among humans, persists as a fantasy.

We could also say that phallic space is a universal idea (building the tower) that reappears in every generation of children. According to Freud (1909b), the idea occurs as the theory of phallic monism—the idea that everyone, male or female, possesses a penis. Less familiar is the overarching manner in which the theory structures the human space of the child. This can be seen clearly in Freud's case of Little Hans. When Hans discovers the self-importance of his own penis as a source of pleasure, it quickly becomes the primary organizing principle of his life. With the phallus, he is able to distinguish inanimate from animate (largely human) space. And within the space of living creatures that surround him, the phallus is the master signifier—the primary landmark that unifies what he sees. Whenever he is out and about, the reassuring sight of the phallus in animals serves as a linchpin holding the entire living space together.

He is very anxious to confirm its existence in all humans, as this would be a powerful proof of the unity of the world. When he sees his little sister Hannah being given a bath, he discounts the importance of what he sees. There are two aspects to this well-known "misperception". One, the principle of unity itself, is so powerful that it can unite seemingly contradictory elements. Two, accepting that Hannah lacks a penis would cause his phallic space—that is to say, his whole world—to unravel. At this stage, we could say that castration is unthinkable. For the moment, the theory, the world view, and the phallic organization of space still hold.

There are remnants of phallic space in the idea of complete or perfect analysis. The space of the consulting room can approach phallic space when it is too neat or too well organized or designed (e.g., by a professional designer) so that everything fits down to the last "accent" piece. For analysis, the hallmark of human space is the piece that doesn't fit, the little enclave of messiness in a haphazard pile of papers, the non-perfect alignment of chair and couch, and so on.

Similarly, in her or his technique, the analyst usually avoids all-encompassing constructions of the patient's entire past history or the "key" to a patient's personality. The patient's fantasy that the analyst holds the "key" is a normal part of the transference, but the analyst must avoid the illusion that he or she does indeed possess "it". The closest the analyst may come in interventions is a construction of a key piece of the patient's early history. In the same vein, the analyst steers clear of interpretations that say too much, or that give too comprehensive explanations of dreams. There must always be something that doesn't "fit". There must always be something lacking that only the patient can try to fill. When the patient says "that's not quite it" and then proceeds to bring up some new piece of material, the process moves forward.

Oedipal space

Phallic space is potentially unlimited, at least in the vertical direction. But after the tower falls (castration), the resulting oedipal space is bounded. The tower is replaced by a barrier, boundary, or limit. As a spatial concept, the barrier has a venerable lineage within psychoanalysis: Freud talked of the "incest barrier" (1909b), the "repression barrier" (1909b), and the "stimulus barrier" (1920g). Bion introduced the "contact barrier" (1977b). In a spatial context, a barrier limits the extent or expansion of space. Instead of a single, monolithic space, there are multiple bounded spaces. There are, thus, multiple language groups, neighbourhoods, individuals, and areas of the psyche.

We can see how a first barrier is constructed by reviewing Little Hans's navigation from phallic space towards oedipal or paternal space. Hans's theory of phallic monism—the viewpoint that all living entities possess a penis—is put to the test in several terse dialogues with his mother. In these short conversations the mother neither confirms nor denies Hans's theory. But one thing is clear: the questions Hans asks her seem to violate some invisible boundary. His first question, "Mummy, have you got a widdler too?" (p. 7) does not receive an answer, but instead yields another question: "why?" Shortly thereafter, the mother issues her famous castration threat after she finds Hans with his hand on his penis. Sometime later, as Hans stares at his mother's "widdler", she says: "what are you staring like that for?" (p. 9).

These boundary violations begin to undermine Hans's sense of security linked with his theory of phallic monism. According to the theory, there should be a phallus in the place where he expects it. The assumed phallus holds the space together and allows Hans to know where he is. But the theory is not working. Not only is he unsure whether the mother does indeed possess the phallus, but he is doubly unsure where *he* is situated within the space. When talking with his father about the well-known giraffe fantasy, he crumples up a piece of paper to demonstrate the "crumpled giraffe". The crumpled giraffe is himself—or, rather, what has happened to his personal space. The undermining of the theory of phallic monism leads to a temporary "crumpling" or disintegration of Hans's psychic space. This is one meaning of castration for Hans.

In other language, we could say that Hans occupies the place of the mother's phallic object. In a spatial context, there are two possible reasons why being in this place leads to disorientation. If we first assume that, as phallic object, he "completes" the mother—then he is simply part of a monolithic space that is unbounded. All places in such a space would be the same. Second, occupying the phallic place, Hans cannot orient or locate himself *in relationship* to the phallus. It is sort of like standing on the North Pole, where all directions face south.

We can also describe Hans's predicament in spatial terms as falling into a hole. The "hole" is first and foremost a hole in his precious theory. The mother has already tried to poke holes in the theory and was partly successful. Even one hole in the theory is too many. The theory of phallic monism is by definition complete, comprehensive, and systemic. The foundation of the theory is that everything in the sphere of sexuality can be tied together into one neat package. One flaw, and the whole "edifice" unravels. Thus a small hole becomes a gaping hole that swallows up the whole (including Hans).

By our terms, the "hole" occurred in the space between Hans and his mother. We have seen that the mother's little jibes have created "pitfalls". Hans keeps falling into these pitfalls without knowing how or why. In essence, they amount to one gaping hole that now takes up the entire space. The hole is not the empty space inside the walls of a vessel. It is more in the nature of a "void". A void is by nature unstructured and uncharted. Moreover, it is dynamic and annihilating. It voids. It threatens to void Hans's very being. In his fantasy, he is being devoured by the mother. He has lost the ability to locate himself in a space that has become a treacherous sexual "no-man's land".

It is at this point that the father's role proves critical. In several conversations with this son, he helps explore the idea of a boundary or barrier. (Freud, 1909b, immediately links it to the incest barrier.) Father and son see a flock of sheep confined to an area by a low enclosure made of rope. The rope effectively keeps the sheep in bounds. Hans questions his father about the security of such a measure since it would be easy to step right over the rope. The father introduces the idea of "authority" in the form of guards, policemen, and ultimately God. Implicit is the notion of prohibition. He neglects to emphasize that he himself has something to do with this "authority", but, nevertheless, the idea of a rudimentary barrier is formed.

Hans quickly uses the newly discovered boundary to separate himself from the uncharted regions of "maternal space". The other side of the line is literally "out-of-bounds". This side of the line is structured human space, which can be shared with his father. For Hans, the main function of the boundary is orientation. The boundary allows Hans to know the barred direction. He follows the directive, "Don't go there". Knowing one compass direction, he can deduce the other three. Thus he can figure his location—in a rough manner—on this side of the line.

Naturally, we can draw this boundary across several possible spaces. We have been talking about the one between maternal space and Hans's own space. The maternal space includes the space of maternal sexuality—the so-called dark continent. The same boundary also produces the area of the forbidden, an area that had not previously existed for Hans. In the case history, he begins to express shame about exhibiting oneself, for example. With the onset—or at least the reinforcement—of repression, the boundary then becomes the repression barrier.

Oedipal space and psychoanalytic space

One of the oedipal achievements is the realization that parents cannot read their children's thoughts. Thoughts must be spoken in order to be heard. With the bounding of his own space, a child realizes he has the freedom to keep his thoughts to himself. This bounded private space, also known as "interior" space, is present in all social interactions, including analysis. In analysis the autonomy and privacy of the individual is respected. Even guided by the fundamental rule, the patient will always be withholding something. This is respected because the patient is granted the freedom to not say something. Over the course of an analysis a patient will reveal "secrets"—that is, has consciously withheld information—at various times. And, of course, the analyst almost always keeps his or her thoughts to him/herself, unless he or she decides to say something to the patient.

Personal private space is one of at least three spaces that make up psychoanalytic space. We can highlight the distinguishing feature of each space by comparing the space of the waiting room with that of the consulting room proper. The waiting room is, on the one hand, a space of private, introspective reverie. The quiet atmosphere, with classical music playing at low volume, promotes this atmosphere. You can be alone with your thoughts even if there are other patients present. On the other hand, the other patients transform the waiting room into a sort of "common room". It is a shared space, even if the shared element is precisely the sense of privacy. The commonality of the space is both literal and figurative. Metaphorically, the analysands are in the same boat. They are all going through analysis with the same analyst. If they do talk among themselves, a tone of complicity prevails, even if they manage to avoid talking about the analyst. In the oedipal context, they are siblings.

In the consulting room, the common space can be defined as anything that brings about a meeting of the minds. In ordinary space, this might be the area near the door where greetings and goodbyes are said. Common space is also present whenever analyst and patient are in tune with the same emotion via empathy. If this feeling is expressed in a felicitous phrase, the meeting of the minds is confirmed. A third area lies in the related issue of mutual understanding. Especially at the beginning, the patient is at pains to present a consistent picture of herself to her analyst. She seeks confirmation in this depiction. She wants the analyst to see her as he sees herself. And in all her communications with the analyst, she wants to ensure that he understands what she is saying and what she is experiencing. In the current vernacular, she wants to know if the analyst "gets her". Thus, if the analyst hears what she says in a different way from how she intended it, she will want to correct the discrepancy immediately. If the analyst says something that sounds obscure she will ask him to repeat it or paraphrase it or clarify what he means. The entire intent is to get each other on the "same page" and have a meeting of the minds.

In oedipal space, the father's word substitutes for the lost and renounced phallus. The father's word is like a promise that the child will become the person he can be. A promise is not a guarantee this must be so; the child must take his father's "word" for it. Nor is the "word" a recipe, formula, or algorithm for how to get there. The "word" can structure analytic space first as a maxim or motto—words to live by. Such words express a value associated with the father or the parental couple. A value is neither guarantee nor formula; it is not always reached and the paths to it are not always marked. But it is a defined locus in human space. In the psyche, it forms the seed of the ego-ideal.

To examine the effect of such an ideal on analytic space, let us consider a written maxim hung on the wall of the waiting room. These words may express how the analyst views the analytic process. One such maxim invoked the image of two combatants in an arena. Taken literally, these words would define analysis as an oedipal competition. But if taken in the sense of "do not be afraid to be who you are", they might not seem so anti-analytic. And even without a maxim on the wall, the objects in the analyst's consulting room, as well as words overheard, offer clues to the analyst's ethical and aesthetic ideals.

Some ambiguity is necessary concerning the analyst's ideals, because otherwise his or her position will become fixed in analytic space. That is to say, the patient will know exactly where the analyst stands. In such cases the analyst's ideal is like a global-positioning device for analytic space. Knowing the exact location of the analyst, the patient can then position him/herself accordingly. The patient can completely identify with the analyst's values or, alternatively, can reject them out of hand. The patient can take whatever distance she or her wants from them. The patient can even update them for the new millennium if they appear archaic.

Such a fixed position fails to take into account the patient's unconscious desires, which never remain fixed or unified. The second model of oedipal space builds in the necessary indeterminacy. In accord with the "word", this space is fully structured but not unified. Neither the analyst nor the patient can find a single location within it that says: This is my spot—this is exactly where I am. The analyst positions him/herself in an area of indeterminacy. He or she certainly occupies a finite area (behind the patient!) but his or her exact location within it can never be specified. For the patient, indeterminacy is defined as a bi-focal location. In effect, the patient is present in two locations at the same time. This division separates the conscious from the unconscious, one individual from another, and one group or agency from another.

An example drawn from the psychopathology of everyday life will illustrate this split. I had applied for a job, and my contact person raved about my qualifications. I was the perfect fit for the position. It was a foregone conclusion. Of course I was pleased, and I accepted this view of myself. But then weeks went by without a call. Finally, I telephoned and asked my contact person whether I was still being considered for the job. He replied: "Oh, yes absolutely!" At this very moment the phone went dead, because he had spilled a cup of hot coffee on his lap. This action coupled with his words struck home to me that I was not going to get the job. Later, my contact person reluctantly confirmed that this was indeed the case.

At the moment when I achieved this "insight", I was suspended between two positions. I knew I was facing an unpleasant truth, but part of me wished it were not so and hoped that I would turn out to be wrong. Later when I had assimilated the new truth, I explained to myself that I was probably better off and that it would have been a mistake to have taken the job. Thus the unity of the ego prevails before and after. But at the moment of "insight", one could say that I occupied the split between my position as "accepted" and my new position as "rejected".

The area of indeterminacy is produced by the parental word, which is incapable of completely mapping human or psychic space. If we view the "word" as a complex web of associations, then in any act of speech, something—perhaps something precious—always falls through the cracks. It is important to keep in mind that this indeterminate "something" only exists as a by-product of the network or "map" itself. Lacan called this "something" the object (a) (Evans, 1996), even though it is imperceptible. Although it seems hypothetical, to say the least, this object does have the merit of explaining a paradox—that something in analytic space can guide your path, even lead you on, so to speak, without ever being strictly locatable. Thus the analyst can direct the treatment without having any special "end" in mind.

These divisions in space always involve the spoken word—the sine qua non of psychoanalysis. It occurs first with the effort to verbalize or "spell out" the previously half-formed thoughts floating in the mind. This turns out to be harder than it looks. Sometimes patients remark that what they feel or think is indescribable. The verbal description pales in comparison to the interior experience. The words may seem trite or clichéd. No matter what words are used, something is always lost in translation. So already there is a split between the introspective patient sitting alone and the analysing patient lying down.

The space inside the consulting room is, of course, dominated by the presence of the analyst. The analyst's "word" takes on weight in the transference. The implicit promise behind the analyst's "word" structures the whole analysis. The patient is usually willing to give the analyst the benefit of the doubt and to take his or her "word" that the analytic work will lead somewhere. As the work deepens, the analyst and his or her "word" become the focal point in the treatment (the transference neurosis). In many respects, the analyst's words create structure. His patient uses the constant and predictable elements in his speech to get his bearings in analytic space. Yet the patient can never pin the analyst down to one point of view, one meaning, or one comprehensive explanation. The patient is thus in the strange position of using the analyst's words to get her or his own bearings, while never being able to get a *fix* on the analyst's position with respect to her/himself.

This phenomenon can be seen clearly in those moments when the analyst says something unexpected. The analyst may have given many interpretations of the same type, and some may have been repeated over and over again. But there may come a point when the analyst says something quite out of character or at variance with the rest. The patient will often be surprised or shocked and may feel that these words have "come out of the blue". Sometimes the meaning of the words is not immediately clear. Yet they have an effect on the patient, often leading to the production of new material.

In the same regard, the patient may surprise her/himself by saying something unexpected, perhaps blurting out a long stream of invective against someone she or he thinks of as a friend, or making a slip of the tongue, as in the example I gave. In these cases the analyst has only to repeat or highlight what was inadvertently said. In either case, the surprising words jar the patient out of her or his former position, making her or his exact location in analytic space problematic.

Geopolitical space

At this juncture, allow me for a moment to veer away from depth psychology to the hard realities of the impact that history and politics have upon human space. This is an area fraught with logical, conceptual, and metaphorical conundrums. Take, for example, the concept of a "nation", which in common parlance seems self-evident but upon closer scrutiny turns out to be elusive. The concept raises all sorts of questions. Does a "nation" have to have territorial boundaries? What sort of symbolic significance do the borders of such a territory (Falk, 1974) come to acquire in the human mind? How does a redrawing of borders between countries affect the sense of nationhood of those affected by such seemingly arbitrary geopolitical acts? What is the relationship between "nation" and "state"? Is "nation" itself a conceptual monolith, or might it contain micro-nations within it? Can there be emerging "proto-nations" that are invalidated as misguided uprisings by a majority invested in cohesion? Clearly, one can go on and on with such queries, but the point is incontestable: "nation" is a slippery concept. And, once established, the instability of the concept produces daunting consequences, ranging from the extremes of maudlin sentimentality to vicious and divisive politics. Illustrations range from the grand scenarios of changing German configurations, the collapse of the Soviet Union, and the bloody splintering of the erstwhile Yugoslavia, to the seemingly trivial but nonetheless painful division of Cyprus into Greek and Turkish sections, the unblinking swallowing up of Tibet by China, and the tragic warfare in the East Timor region of Indonesia.

Such upheaval, even when locally contained, is often the result of policy shifts taking place in distant, economically powerful entities. Alongside this "wave effect", there is also the issue of colonization and, in our time, neocolonization. The former lands upon the local—or, as the terms of the discourse dictate, "native"—peoples and their ways of life rather like a hammer upon an anvil. That colonialism—especially in its "enlightened" incarnations—can bring some "reforms" is hardly questionable, but who gets to define these changes as "reforms" in the first place?

Economic improvement, under these circumstances, can, in the end, exploit and smother the local pride. In this regard, we know that such broad geopolitical changes can lead to a collapse or deflation of the local cultural spaces. Hence, myths begin to undergo disuse atrophy, heroes change, and, bit by bit, history is rewritten. Content with a hybrid society for a while, the masses sooner or later stand up. The struggle that then ensues is labelled as "insurgency" and "terrorism" by the occupiers and as "liberation movement" by the politico-economic underdogs. Sometimes the latter are victorious and enter the negotiating space in international dialogues. At other times they are vanquished. Their slogans fade, and their poems are scattered as literary debris. An even more tragic outcome may occur when the colonizer leaves and the newly quenched "villain hunger" (Akhtar, 2007) turns upon itself. Ethnic minorities are then raped and massacred. Examples of the three outcomes are widespread and can easily be detected in the history of India, the Middle East, and the colonized portions of Africa. Partitions of countries left behind, assimilation of one nation into another, genocides, and territorial continuing conflicts hardly compensate for the pride regained by returning the names of cities and countries to their pre-colonial (and ironically, at times, truly ancient) forms.

Three other intersections between history, politics, and human space are to be noted: the flight of the persecuted; migrations of the colonized; and the grave—though not fully recognized—impact of what is euphemistically called "globalization". The most prominent illustration of the first is the post-Holocaust diaspora of European Jews. The heinous crimes of Hitler and his diabolical lieutenants not only left millions dead, but also produced a staggering number of refugees. The psychological toll on this population and its transmission to subsequent generations (Brenner, 2005; Kestenberg, 1980, 1989; Kestenberg & Brenner, 1996; Kogan, 1995) is a matter of worldwide record that only the deluded attempt to deny.

There are other populations that have fled the tyranny of regional despots, pillage of their abodes by foreign powers, or occupation of their lands by forceful outsiders. Exiled groups of this sort include Haitians, Palestinians, Cambodians, Vietnamese, Laotians, and now Sudanese, Afghanis, and Iraqis. Each group carries with it a sleeve of "old culture", though the nostalgia for it may emerge years or even decades later. Meanwhile, the wounds of dislocation fester underneath the necessities of adaptation to the values of their adopted land.

In contrast are the voluntary immigrants who leave their lands in search of economic prosperity. Their emigration is apparently unforced. However, a deeper look causes one to question the "voluntary" nature of even these journeys. Driven by colonial brainwashing—the postcolonial hangover of idealizing the master—they resemble Salman Rushdie's (1980) *Midnight's Children* after all. It is as if a powerful magnet has pulled away from the field and fine steel shavings are following in the wake of its hypnotizing pull. In other words, refugees are "pushed" to dislocate and immigrants are "pulled" to fracture their historical identities. Although different, either fate is tragic in its own way. And yet, the broadening of the ego sphere and the relaxation of the superego that often results from such migrations can mitigate the negative effects.

What does remain constant in this saga is the condensation and telescoping of lands, loyalties, and legacies. All these spatial dislocations—especially those on a broad scale—must inevitably pose the question of globalism, which seems to treat the entire planet as a single economic entity. The concept is as slippery as that of "nation". Does it foster exploitation on a massive scale or, rather, universal opportunity? As a process, is it unifying or fragmenting? And is it dominated by the United States of America, or will the latter prove to be dominated or even "balkanized" by it? Globalism—and, indeed, all the geopolitical processes mentioned in this section—imply the importance of geography, or, to coin a phrase, "earthspace". Both globalism and the environmental movement seek to view "earthspace" as a unified entity, just as peoples view their "nation" as a unity. This development can be seen as salutary if it leads various nation-states to collaborate vis-à-vis environmental protection, share knowledge, and meaningfully barter resources. At the same time, globalization has the downside of crushing regional cultures, resulting in considerable "civilizational anxiety" (Lear, 2007). A regressive clinging to an idealized past and fundamentalism form the next steps in this diabolical chain of events.

Concluding remarks

In this chapter I have endeavoured to explore the concept of human space as a model for psychic space. I have examined several types of space and assigned to each a characteristic object. I assumed from the start that human space arises from the configuration of objects and thus can orient itself around one particular or exemplary object. In writing about space I found the subject expanding in all directions. I have only been able to touch upon a few aspects. In my three conclusions, below, I indicate additional aspects of space or uses of spatial metaphors that could be pursued further.

My first conclusion is that the time-honoured split in analytic thinking between interior and exterior space is not as critical in this model of human space. In human space, exterior space and interior space resemble each other somewhat. In one we have "décor" and in the other the staging of fantasy—which is usually structured as a "scene" or "scenario". The radical division between "internal" and "external" belongs to the area of the pathological, One example would be the split between Winnicott's true and false self (1960a). In my view, the major division is between human space—internal or external—and what I call uncharted space or the void. In Lacan's terminology (Evans, 1996), this corresponds with the barrier of the Real.

I also conclude that human/psychic space is not static, as is usually supposed. Even a "still life" has an inherent sense of movement and energy. We can see or sense this quality in all good paintings. In my view, the human object produces a flow of movement in the surrounding space much like in Stevens's poem "Anecdote of the Jar". In this chapter, I have used phallic space as an example of the movement of energy. However, one could also envision a flow of energy in the vessel—the circulation around the sides, for example, or in the varying tensions within oedipal verbal networks.

This dynamic quality suggests the element of time. In my opinion, time is the repressed dimension of space. There is always a hidden reference to time in human/psychic space (the clock on the wall?). The initial division of the analytic situation into process and setting artificially splits time and space. As in physics, it may be more fruitful to think of chunks of "space–time". In any case, there is a large area of inquiry in the relation of space to time. I propose, for example, that much of psychic space is the *fixation* or freeze-framing of time.

And I found certain anomalies in human space that may be jumping-off points for a topology of psychopathological states. The point is often made, for example, that severe depression causes the collapse of interior space and a corresponding sterility in exterior space. Bion (1977b) has used spatial metaphors for traumatic experiences in the life of psychotics. The idea of a "screen" is useful for exploring conditions such as the "as-if" personality. Expansions, contractions, twists, holes and knots, being themselves anomalous and "irregular", lend themselves to the visualization of a variety of extreme mental states.

Finally, I have sought to portray the unity of space—and therefore of geopolitical entities—as a powerful myth or illusion dismantled by the destruction of Babel. The closer one looks at "nations", "empires", or "states", the more one sees evidence of internal disunity, which is not to deny those historical moments in which unity is achieved. In this sense, geopolitical space shares something in common with the space of the individual ego—that seemingly impregnable fortress that yet reveals hidden cracks, fissures, and "faults" (Balint, 1968).

II

Place, time, and land

2

Unsettling the settler:
history, culture, race, and the Australian self

Kate Grenville

I've spent the last five years writing a book about "settler" Australians. It's a novel about a representative settler, William Thornhill, who comes to Australia as a convict—and at the end of his life recognizes that this foreign place has become his home. It's a complicated sort of home, though, because in some ways it is still foreign.

What I'd like to talk about is not so much the content of the book as the journey of writing it. As I wrote I found myself caught up in questions I'd never asked before—questions about what it means to call Australia home. Can your own place still also be a foreign one? What does it mean to be descended from that first generation of settlers, and what happens when you immerse yourself in the documented history of this place?

> The *Alexander*, with its cargo of convicts, had bucked over the face of the ocean for the better part of a year. Now it had fetched up at the end of the earth. There was no lock on the door of the hut where William Thornhill, transported for the term of his natural life in the Year of Our Lord eighteen hundred and six, was passing his first night in His Majesty's penal colony of New South Wales. There was hardly a door, barely a wall; only a flap of bark, a screen of sticks and mud. There was no need of lock, of door, of wall; this was a prison whose bars were ten thousand miles of water.

Thornhill's wife was sleeping sweet and peaceful against him, her hand still entwined in his. The child and the baby were asleep too, curled up together. Only Thornhill could not bring himself to close his eyes on this foreign darkness. Through the doorway of the hut he could feel the night, huge and damp, flowing in and bringing with it the sounds of its own life: tickings and creakings, small private rustlings, and beyond that the soughing of the forest, mile after mile.

When he got up and stepped out through the doorway there was no cry, no guard: only the living night. The air moved around him, full of rich dank smells. Trees stood tall over him. A breeze shivered through the leaves, then died, and left only the vast fact of the forest.

He was nothing more than a flea on the side of some enormous quiet creature.

Down the hill the settlement was hidden by the darkness. A dog barked in a tired way and stopped. From the bay where the *Alexander* was anchored there was a sense of restless water shifting in its bed of land and swelling up against the shore.

Above him in the sky was a thin moon and a scatter of stars as meaningless as spilt rice. There was no Pole Star, a friend to guide him on the Thames, no Bear that he had known all his life: only this blaze, unreadable, indifferent.

All the many months in the *Alexander*, lying in the hammock which was all the territory he could claim in the world, listening to the sea slap against the side of the ship and trying to hear the voices of his own wife, his own children, in the noise from the women's quarters, he had been comforted by telling over the bends of his own Thames. The Isle of Dogs, the deep eddying pool of Rotherhithe, the sudden twist of the sky as the river swung around the corner to Lambeth: they were all as intimate to him as breathing. Daniel Ellison grunted in his hammock beside him, fighting even in his sleep, the women were silent beyond their bulkhead, and still in the eye of his mind he rounded bend after bend of that river.

Now, standing in the great sighing lung of this other place and feeling the dirt chill under his feet, he knew what life was gone. He might as well have swung at the end of the rope they had measured for him. This was a place, like death, from which men did not return. It was a sharp stab like a splinter under a nail: the pain of loss. We would die here under these alien stars, his bones rot in this cold earth.

He had not cried, not for thirty years, not since he was a hungry child too young to know that crying did not fill your belly. But now his throat was thickening, a press of despair behind his eyes forcing warm tears down his cheeks.

There were things worse than dying: life had taught him that. Being here in New South Wales might be one of them.

It seemed at first to be the tears welling, the way the darkness moved in front of him. It took a moment to understand that the stirring was a human, as black as the air itself. His skin swallowed the light and made him not quite real, something only imagined. His eyes were set so deeply into the skull that they were invisible, each in its cave of bone. The rock of his face shaped itself around the big mouth, the imposing nose, the folds of his cheeks. Without surprise, as though he were dreaming, Thornhill saw the scars drawn on the man's chest, each a neat line raised and twisted, living against the skin.

He took a step towards Thornhill so that the parched starlight from the sky fell on his shoulders. He wore his nakedness like a cloak. Upright in his hand, the spear was part of him, an extension of his arm.

Clothed as he was, Thornhill felt skinless as a maggot. The spear was tall and serious. To have evaded death at the end of the rope, only to go like this, his skin punctured and blood spilled beneath these chilly stars! And behind him, hardly hidden by that flap of bark, were those soft parcels of flesh: his wife and children.

Anger, that old familiar friend, came to his side. Damn your eyes be off, he shouted. Go to the devil! After so long as a felon, hunched under the threat of the lash, he felt himself expanding back into his full size. His voice was rough, full of power, his anger a solid warmth inside him. He took a threatening step forward. Could make out chips of sharp stone in the end of the spear. It would not go through a man neat as a needle. It would rip its way in. Pulling it out would rip all over again. The thought fanned his rage. Be off! Empty though it was, he raised his hand against the man.

The mouth of the black man began to move itself around sounds. As he spoke he gestured with the spear so it came and went in the darkness. They were close enough to touch.

In the fluid rush of speech Thornhill suddenly heard words. Be off, the man was shouting. Be off! It was his own tone exactly.

This was a kind of madness, as if a dog were to bark in English.

Be off, be off! He was close enough now that he could see the man's eyes catching the light under their heavy brows, and the straight angry line of his mouth. His own words had all dried up, but he stood his ground.

He had died once, in a manner of speaking. He could die again. He had been stripped of everything already: he had only the dirt under his bare feet, his small grip on this unknown place. He had nothing but that, and those helpless sleeping humans in the hut behind him. He was not about to surrender them to any naked black man.

In the silence between them the breeze rattled through the leaves. He glanced back at where his wife and infants lay, and when he looked again the man was gone. The darkness in front of him whispered and shifted, but there was only the forest. It could hide a hundred black men with spears, a thousand, a whole continent full of men with spears and that grim line to their mouths.

He went quickly into the hut, stumbling against the doorway so that clods of daubed mud fell away from the wall. The hut offered no safety, just the idea of it, but he dragged the flap of bark into place. He stretched himself out on the dirt alongside his family, forcing himself to lie still. But every muscle was tensed, anticipating the shock in his neck or his belly, his hand going to the place, the cold moment of finding that unforgiving thing in his flesh. [*The Secret River.* Grenville, 2005, pp. 3–8]

What draws a writer to one subject rather than another? This book started as an exploration of family history. My mother had told me about our convict ancestor, Solomon Wiseman. He'd worked on the docks in London, committed some offence, and was transported in 1806. By 1812 he was a free man and by 1817 he had "taken up land" on the Hawkesbury River. He made a bucketload of money and died rich and respectable.

For years this was just a family story—a kind of sealed capsule, its telling a ritual always in the same words. You either swallowed it whole or you refused it, but you didn't take it apart and examine it.

The Reconciliation Walk in 2000 was the thing that burst the capsule open for me. During that walk I met the eye of an Aboriginal woman and we smiled at each other. But even as we were acknowledging each other, I had a shocking thought—shocking because it had never occurred to me before. My great-great-great grandfather had been right here, underneath the bridge, when he was landed off the boat in 1806. Her great-great-great grandfather might have been there too. They might have glanced at each other, the way she and I just had. Would they have smiled at each other in mutual acknowledgement, as we had?

I didn't know a lot about early Australian history, but I didn't think so. There'd have been distrust, perhaps open hostility. And what about when Wiseman went up to the Hawkesbury and "took up" land? What about the Aboriginal people whose land it was—how had Wiseman persuaded them to give it up?

It was the time of the history wars—historians at each other's throats over what kind of violence might have taken place on the frontier—how much there'd been, or even whether there'd been any at all. In the moment of smiling at that woman, the history wars became something more than academics bad-mouthing each other. Suddenly, history had a very personal face, the face of my own ancestor. I needed to know more.

I started with research in the archives and began with that "unknown offence" that Wiseman had committed.

Four generations of my family had repeated the statement that we didn't know what that offence was. And yet, when I went looking, I found it in a quarter of an hour. The family story had denied knowledge of the crime but had kept alive the two facts that made it easy to find out: the date of Wiseman's arrival here, and the name of the ship he came on. If you know those two things, you can just go straight to the transcripts of the Old Bailey trials, on the open shelves of the Mitchell Library.

He was just the most ordinary sort of crook—nothing very exciting or glamorous about stealing a load of timber. But that search for his crime told me something much more interesting than the nature of his crime—something about stories and the people who tell them. The family story pretended it didn't know. But at a deeper level it knew that it knew—and made sure that the key to that knowing was there for anyone who went looking. It was revealing, even in the act of concealing.

The idea of concealing and simultaneously revealing became something of a motif in the journey I had begun.

For a start, I realized that I knew much more about the frontier and its violence than I'd ever let myself know that I knew. I may not have known the details, but I'd always known the broad outline of the story. A simple one, really. We—Europeans—had arrived and displaced the people who were already living here. Some of the dirty work had been done by smallpox and measles, but we all knew there'd been violence as well. In my own family it took the form of a vignette of my great-grandmother: the story about her was that "she always had a gun loaded in the corner of the hut—not to use, just to show them she had it".

It also dawned on me how the language itself was an accomplice in this knowing and not-knowing. There was a of linguistic sleight of hand going on—the land wasn't really "taken up", it was just "taken". The word "dispersed" that I came across so often in the sources—as in "we dispersed them in the usual manner"—this bland little word often meant shoot.

This sleight of hand wasn't a conspiracy, there was no conscious intent to deceive. "Taken up land" or "disperse" weren't words that lied, exactly. They were sort-of true, so that the people using them didn't have to acknowledge to themselves that they were fudging.

I started to wonder where my own sense of "being Australian" came from. To do that I found myself going back to childhood.

I grew up in the city but with a sense of the bush as the real Australia. I loved the bush—my family did a lot of camping. I'd go off for the whole day with a knapsack of food and a penknife (and Condy's crystals in case of snake bite). Later as a university student I went on week-long canoeing trips with friends, out of touch with anyone, no mobiles, just us and a map. We took pride in foraging for what these days we'd call bush tucker. We'd try to go barefoot (though not for long). On one memorable occasion I killed, cooked, and ate a snake.

This was all in the context of assuming that the Aboriginal people were "all gone", as the family story had it. On our family picnics Mum would always look around at some creekside or beachside spot and say, "The blacks must have done well for themselves here." So there was a sense of them having been there, underneath our own lives, but somehow—blamelessly—now vanished. The bush was ours to inhabit.

What I now see as revealing is the way I chose to inhabit it. All that barefoot stuff, all that going feral and eating snakes—I was mimicking what I thought of as Aboriginal ways.

What I was declaring, I think, was that I had a right to be there because I had taken over the bond with the land that they had had. They had disappeared and had passed the baton to me. It was as if

I was saying, "I am the 'native' now—look how fearlessly I kill and cook and eat that snake! So this is truly my place."

I'll talk in a moment about where the "going native" illusion has gone for me, and what I think it's about, but it's still alive and well. When I was writing *The Secret River* and I'd tell people what it was about—a questioning of what happened on the frontier—a frequent response was to fire up with instant indignation and say something to the effect that "I love this place as much as the Aboriginal people do." Now that the book has been published, one of the most common questions is about the Aboriginal connection to the land—I'm often asked what that is and how it's different from the love of the place felt by non-indigenous Australians.

The implication behind these questions is that Aboriginal people may claim a special bond to the land, but in fact non-indigenous Australians can have just as strong, even spiritual a bond. We can be white blackfellers.

Of course, it's true that we settlers can have a powerful and genuine love for this place of ours. But I'm interested, for the sake of exploring, to question that feeling of belonging.

It intrigues me, for instance, what happened to the word "native". The first settlers called the Aboriginal people "Indians" or "the black natives". But within a very few years, the word "native" had shifted its meaning 180 degrees—it came commonly to mean not an Aboriginal person, but a white person born in Australia. A kind of linguistic appropriation, if you like, echoing the appropriation of the land itself that was going on.

In metaphorically leaping off the boat and calling ourselves natives, we short-circuited something important in the settler experience. An immigrant becomes a native through a process, not a moment. It has to start with a kind of mourning. Whatever they might later gain, immigrants first of all suffer a loss—of homeland, of the identity with living in the place that's home. Once that mourning has been lived through, the next part of process can take place—a series of adaptations, a gradual process of putting down roots. The end of that process is a real belonging in the new place.

Inheritors of those settlers—that is, us—have a slightly different journey to go through, but it also begins in loss. The loss is our sense of ourselves as blameless. The mourning has to involve the acknowledgment that we have a home because other people were turned out of it.

What our ancestors did, and from which we benefit, was a bad and sad thing, but also a fairly normal human act. The history of the human race is, by and large, the history of one set of people displacing another set. What's useful is not either to criticize or to defend what those settlers did, but to think about the traces of their actions on our present psyche.

If we can't acknowledge that we are, in some sense, interlopers, we live with the anxiety that the reality of that fact will break through the crust of belonging. We might have to work a bit too strenuously to be a true blue Aussie fair dinkum mate out in the bush going barefoot and eating snakes.

So no wonder the moment with that Aboriginal woman on the bridge was so disorienting to me. A complicated grief happened, a grief with a kind of outrage tangled up in it. It felt as if something had been taken from me, and it had been. What was gone was my thoughtless taking for granted that this was my place.

I did a huge amount of research for the book—more than any sane person would really have to do to write a novel. It was as if I wanted to go back to that founding moment and live through it for myself, detail by detail.

I was writing about a family of settlers—their story was the literalization of my own new sense of "outsiderdom". To them, this was the most foreign place on earth. In order to write about them, I had to share that feeling.

I spent many days and a few nights in the bush on my own. The place itself—the landscape of the lower Hawkesbury—is frightening. The bush is as crumpled and intricately folded as a piece of scrunched-up cloth. When I took a few steps off the track one day—just to get the feel of not being on a track—it was terrifying how quickly I felt lost. The place swallowed me, disoriented me, got to me in some way so that it was a huge intellectual effort to remind myself that the track was behind me, and I had only to turn, take six steps, and I'd be back on it.

Trees gestured at me from the corner of my eye, and I whirled around, sure it was a person. These days there was no one there with a spear poised to throw, but 200 years ago there might have been. Thornhill would have seen—or thought he saw—fleeting black figures everywhere, flickering among the light and shade. He'd always have felt watched.

I began to understand that fear, and I could see how it could make you do things you might not otherwise do.

The bush at night makes you feel very small, very alone, very vulnerable. The wind in the trees is speaking a language you don't understand. The weird little night-noises—the cracklings and snappings, the hums and ticks—all tell you that there's a life going on here that you have absolutely nothing to do with.

Lying there in my sleeping bag trying not to think about snakes and funnelwebs was uncomfortable, but it was also rewarding. Once I could drop all that barefoot-in-the-bush stuff, it was amazing how easy it was to accept that the bush had always felt eerie. You can live with eeriness. You don't have to pretend it isn't there.

I'd expected resistance to this book, *The Secret River*, even anger. What I've found is a huge hunger to know—the same hunger that drove the writing. For many people the book is really just a lever with which to open the can of worms about their own feelings. There are a lot of questions, a lot of anxiety. What should we feel about the stolen gift that our forebears have made to us? But there's also a willingness to voice the anxiety.

Fiction is a good medium for entering anxiety-producing situations and being able to stay with them for long enough to learn from them. It's a vicarious experience, and one that's under your own control—you can identify only as closely as you want to with the characters. You can close the book any time it gets too much. And fiction offers a compensatory pleasure that offsets the discomfort—the satisfactions of narrative and the sensual pleasures of language.

At the end of *The Secret River*, Thornhill has made good, made lots of money, has driven the Aboriginal people away. He's won. But he's infused with a kind of melancholy, some gnawing feeling of something not being finished, not right. His trouble is that things have happened that can't be talked about. Violence has created a no-go area around itself. There's a silence, a gap, where there should be acknowledgement. Thornhill knows the gap is there, but can't let himself feel it. Knowing, but not-knowing, he's suspended in an emptiness that he seeks to fill without knowing how.

> As each day ended he sat in his favourite spot on the verandah, spy-glass in his hand, watching the sunset glow red and gold on the cliffs. He had had a bench made, not too comfortable, a plain wooden bench, that was what suited him. He would have Devlin

bring him a madeira on a silver tray, and a cigar. Watched the poplars in the afternoon breeze, the roses and lilacs which in the late light looked greener than during the day. There was his wall. There was his wife, in a silk gown from Armitage that had cost twenty-two guineas, taking the air along the path. He could hear the lowing of his cattle, waiting to be milked, and the shouts of his servants getting them in. Could smell the quality horseflesh in the stables behind the house. He had never ridden himself, but he had made sure his children were taught to sit a horse the way the gentry did.

Looking down at his estate it was possible to imagine it a version of England. The wall shone bright with its mortar and whitewash in the sunlight, so bright it was painful to the eyes. Foursquare, immovable, it was like a stately chord of music in this rumpled land. This was what he had worked for. He had lain awake planning, had burst his heart rowing and carrying, and here it was, given to him like the madeira: the good life.

But beyond the wall and the silver tray was another world, where the cliffs waited and watched. Above the roses and the rest of it was the forest. The harsh whistle of the breeze in the river-oaks, the rigid stalks of the bulrushes and the reeds, that hard blue sky: they were unchanged by the speck of New South Wales enclosed by William Thornhill's wall.

He watched Sal coming up from the garden, having paid her daily visit to the poplars, now tall enough to meet over her head. She turned to admire the drama of light and shadow playing out on the cliffs. When she caught sight of him her face softened. Her fine skin was worn and crepey now in the harsh light outside, but her smile was the same as it had been by the Thames.

Still watching? she asked and sat beside him on the bench. He could feel her leg, warm, solid, a comfort against his, and they sat in silence. Sometimes it felt as if their bodies could speak to each other, even if they themselves could not. Then she said, You'll wear out the glass, Will, the way you go on. He did not answer. He thought she knew what it was he was watching for, and wanted to hear him say it.

She spoke a sudden thought. You know, Will, I thought you was wonderful, when I was a little thing.

He could feel the air of each word separately against his face. He watched her, the smile on her face as she remembered. Why, pet? he asked. Why was I wonderful?

She laughed. Because you spit such a long way! she cried. I told Da, I says, Will Thornhill can spit such a long way!

Only Sal, in the whole world, would remember such a thing. He heard his startled laugh, the sound going around the verandah. I ain't lost the art, Sal, he said. Only in this dry place a man needs all his spit for himself.

After a time she got up, laid a hand on his shoulder for a moment, and went inside. He could hear the fire being lit in the parlour. In a while he would go in and sit in his armchair, enjoying the way the light gleamed around the room and shut out the night.

Watching the light on the cliffs was like watching the sea. Even after so long of living with them, their face was as unknowable as ever, new-formed each moment. Through the glass he would study a spot where gold and grey made a particular sort of pattern. While he looked at it, he knew that combination of rock and shadow as well as he knew the face of his wife. But if he glanced away and then tried to find it again, the light fell in a different way and it was gone. Like the ocean, it was never the same twice.

It was hard to judge of distance or size over there; the ramparts of rock could be just a little step, or a hundred feet high: the trees seemed mere saplings, crooked scrawls against the grey and gold of the cliffs. Without the advantage of a human figure over there, it was as slippery as a mirage.

Through the glass, the trees were flaked and cracked. The rocks were what seemed alive, something old and solemn out of the sea, their grey skins speckled with white lichen, creased and furrowed and ridged. Through the eye of the glass, he became acquainted with each one. He could see how those tumbled at the base of the cliff must have once been part of its lip, where the forest ended as abruptly as the edge of the table. One by one each had snapped and racketed down.

He had never seen part of the cliff fall away, although he sometimes held his breath, staring through the glass, to be watching at the moment it happened. Was it slow, the way a tree creaked away from the vertical? Or was it a clean break that sent the birds squawking up from the trees? He sat with the glass to his eye, resting his elbow on the back of a chair, until the landscape began to swim in his vision. But he had never caught a rock in the private act of falling.

There was a drama, every time, in watching the black shadow of the hill behind him—his own hill—move down across the garden, leaving everything behind in grey dusk. At the river the shadow seemed to pause in its progress. At last he would see a line at the base of the cliffs. Then it seemed only to take a few minutes to move up and engulf the fluid shifts of light.

Sometimes the top of the cliffs, where the forest stopped as if sliced off, seemed an empty stage. And if the cliff was a stage, he was the audience. He scanned the line of forest, back and forth, up there where the stage dropped away. There could still be a few of them living up there. It was possible. Scratching a living, the way they knew, out of bark and roots, possum and lizard. Lighting their fires only at night. They could still be up there, in that intricate landscape that defeated any white man—still there, prepared to wait.

If they had wanted to be seen, he knew that he would have seen them.

Sometimes he thought he saw a man there, looking down from the clifftop. He would get to his feet and go eagerly to the edge of the verandah, would lean out squinting to see the man among so many confusing verticals. Never took his eye off the one he was sure was a human, staring down at him in his house.

He knew they had the capacity for standing in the landscape and simply being. He stared back, and reminded himself how patient they were, how much they were part of the forest. Told himself that was a man, a man as dark as the scorched trunk of a stringybark, standing on the lip of the stage, looking through the air to where he sat looking back. He strained, squinted through the glass until his eyeballs were dry.

Finally he had to recognise that it was no human, just another tree, the size and posture of a man.

Each time, it was a new emptiness.

For all it was what he had chosen, the bench he sat on here felt at times like a punishment. He had never forgotten the narrow bench in the passage at the Watermen's Hall, where William Thornhill had sat with dread in his heart to see whether he could become an apprentice. That bench had been part of the penance a boy paid for the chance at survival. This bench, here, where he could overlook all his wealth and take his ease, should have been the reward.

He could not understand why it did not feel like triumph.

At that late hour the wind had dropped so the river was as still as a pane of glass. The cliff rose up from the water and its reflection dropped away into it. Far over against the bank, a breeze roughened the water and made a narrow band of light between the cliff and its reflection. It separated them, or perhaps it joined them. The two cliffs completed each other into something peaceful and perfect.

He put the telescope down with a hollow feeling. Too late, too late. Every day he sat here, watching, waiting, while dusk gathered in the valley, scanning the trees and the silent rocks. Until it was fully dark he could not make himself put the glass down and turn away.

He could not say why he had to go on sitting here. Only knew that the one thing that brought him a measure of peace was to peer through the telescope. Even after the cliffs had reached the moment at sunset where they blazed gold, even after the dusk left them glowing secretively with an after-light that seemed to come from inside the rocks themselves: even then he sat on, watching, into the dark. [*The Secret River.* Grenville, 2005, pp. 330–334]

3

The Australian patient:
traumatic pasts and the work of history

Bain Attwood

The history of the Australian nation, like most other nations, comprises traumatic pasts, and the darkest of these is the history of colonialism. The colonization of this country by those we can call "settlers" brought devastation in its wake. Prior to white settlement in 1788, Aboriginal people numbered between 750,000 and 1.25 million. Within a generation of "first contact" on the frontiers of settlement, hundreds of Aboriginal groups were destroyed. By 1900 only 100,000 Aboriginal people remained. This, quite obviously, is a cataclysmic event. It was once described (by Charles Rowley) as "the destruction of Aboriginal society" (in a book of that name). The story of this disaster has not been told adequately (and perhaps cannot be): this is my second premise. Indeed, the muted presence of this history in the nation's historical consciousness, as distinct from its historical unconscious, testifies to its profound impact (Rowley, 1970).

More then twenty-five years ago, Bernard Smith, one of Australia's leading intellectuals, suggested that Australian culture is haunted by the dispossession and death of Aboriginal people occasioned by the settler colonization of this country. "[T]he crimes committed against Aboriginal society", he wrote, "have been suppressed and removed from our nation's memory." Australian society had tried, by means of "psycho-cultural mechanisms" (by which Smith largely meant repression and projection) "to put the Aborigines out of sight and out of mind". Yet, Smith observed, like "a nightmare to be thrust out of mind", the dispossession and death settlers had wrought among Aboriginal people has continued to "haunt our dreams" (Smith, 1980, p. 17).

The problem Smith points up is the failure of the nation to remember a traumatic past. In "Remembering, Repeating, and Working Through" (1914g), Freud wrote of a certain kind of patient who "does not *remember* anything of what he has forgotten and repressed, but rather *acts it out*". The patient reproduces what he or she has repressed, Freud continued, "not as a memory but as an action", which is to say that the patient unknowingly repeats in action—"acts out"—what he or she is unable or unwilling to remember. In observing that this kind of patient was unable or unwilling to remember, Freud was arguing that this kind of patient resisted having a history—resisted constructing a history—and preferred instead to continue acting out a past he or she wanted to keep at a distance and so was unable to put a stop to the prescriptive power of that past, often at considerable cost to him or her self (1914g, pp. 150–151). Following Freud and Smith, I suggest that it is useful to consider the Australian nation as this kind of patient.

As readers will observe, I am presuming, as a professional historian, that both history and psychoanalysis—or both historians and psychoanalysts—have a common interest. As the English psychoanalyst and author Adam Phillips noted recently, "Psychoanalysis, like historiography, is about the re-presentation of the significance of events" (A. Phillips, 2004, p. 144), though I would prefer to put it like this: historians and psychoanalysts have a common interest in *relating* the past and relating *to* the past (by "historians" here, I mean anyone who seriously attempts to make meaning of the past).

In this chapter, I shall not consider the ways in which the Australian patient has continued to be unsettled by the telling of stories about the traumatic history of colonialism. (The so-called history wars of the last several years testify to this unsettlement. For a discussion of this, see Attwood, 2005, chap. 1). Rather, I want to focus on how we might relate the history of disaster in the Australian nation, and how we might relate *to* this history of disaster, in order that we might be more able to come to terms with this country's traumatic colonial past and work through this rather than merely act it out. This entails asking, in Freud's terms: what is required for us to become successful historians, or more successful remembrancers, of ourselves?

How we tackle this task, I contend, largely depends on how we tackle what we might call the matter of distance. (By "distance" I mean the continuum that has intimacy at one end and dissociation at the other.) I shall argue, after Freud, that the problem of the Australian patient has been caused by the fact that we have both too much and too little distance from our traumatic pasts. It is worth noting that the task of relating and relating to traumatic pasts has been complicated by the fact that we live in what has been called the age of testimony or the era of the witness: a world in which a concept of intimacy has come to dominate how our society and our media function. This puts experience on display and privileges affect rather than analysis. Today, the person who has experienced an event—particularly a traumatic event—and bears witness (testifies), rather than the professional historian, is regarded as the most authoritative bearer of truth about that past. This has prompted historians such as Annette Wieviorka to ask: "How can the historian incite reflection, thought and rigor when feelings and emotions invade the public sphere?" (Wieviorka, 1998, pp. 142–44; see also Felman, 1995, p. 16; Winter, 2001, pp. 56, 66).

History and distance

To begin this consideration of distance I shall discuss the manner in which most practitioners of the discipline of history have conventionally gone about the work of relating and relating to the past. An English historian, Barbara Taylor, has observed recently: "The position the historian adopts vis-à-vis [his or] her objects . . . can be seen as a key element in what, in psychoanalytic terms, might be described as a historical scene, meaning a fantasy 'setting for desire' where the *relationship* among the elements in the scenario ('the historian', 'the facts') is as crucial as the elements themselves" (Taylor, 2004, p. 120, emphasis in original). Since the nineteenth century, at any rate, Western history or historiography has been preoccupied with issues of distance and proximity. Distance, of course, is inevitable in historical work, inasmuch as we always undertake it after the event. In other words, some degree of distance is necessarily present in all historical work. Having said this, though, it is also apparent that distance is not just a given; it is also a construction (on the part of both the writer and the reader, or viewer or listener), and a construction that has several dimensions. This is to say that "distance" has a broader meaning than its usual temporal sense; it has, most importantly, formal, affective, ideological, and cognitive elements, all of which are determined by the historian. Thus, one can speak of "a series of distances (or even distance-effects) that modify and reconstruct the temporality of historical accounts, thereby shaping every part of our engagement with the past" (p. 120; see also M. S. Phillips, 2004, p. 126).

In modern times—and by "modern" I mean the period since the eighteenth or at least the nineteenth century—history has actually insisted on making a distinction between times past and times present, and this has served to create a sense of distance rather than proximity in the relationship of our present to the past. In one sense historians have proceeded from the assumption that there is, and has to be, a connection between present and past in order to do our work, but in another sense this is disavowed as we have tended to disconnect the past from the present. As Michel de Certeau once famously observed: "Historiography . . . is based on a clean break between the past and the present. . . . Historiography conceives the relation [between past and present] as one of succession (one after the other), correlation (greater or lesser proximities), cause and effect (one follows the other), and disjunction (either one or the other, but not both at the same time)" (de Certeau, 1986, p. 4). In making this argument, it should be noted, de Certeau was explicitly concerned with the differences between how psychoanalysis on the one hand and history on the other represent or re-present time. "Psychoanalysis", he argued, "recognises the past *in* the present; historiography places them one *beside* the other" (p. 4). In other words, de Certeau makes clear, as the Melbourne historian and psychoanalyst Esther Faye has pointed out, that the work of history has rested upon "some version of the 'past/present opposition'" (Faye, 2003, p. 160).

Indeed, several characteristics of the discipline of history have long entailed what a British historian, Mark Salber Phillips, has recently called "distantiation", by which he means whatever has the effect of putting things at a distance (M. S. Phillips, 2004). Several aspects of historiography have entailed distantiation. First, historians have striven to articulate the ways in which the world of a particular past was different from that of our own, and this has inclined us to focus on the discontinuities or differences between past and present rather than on the continuities or similarities. Second, historiography has conceived of time as lineal and progressive, and we have told the story of the "modern" world continuously breaking with, or continuously moving away, from, the past. Third, our discipline has had an ideal of objectivity, which has emphasized the importance of historical detachment. Fourth, historians have long focused on examining historical events in terms of their causes, and this has tended to direct our attention away from the effects of those events. Last, in our practice we have had a tendency to subordinate experience and all this entails to the abstract, the conceptual, and the analytic (Novick, 1988, pp. 1–2).

The insistence on a proper form of distance in historical work has been such a marked feature of our historiographical tradition, Phillips has remarked, that this has been rendered almost invisible, so much so that "it has become difficult [for historians] to distinguish between the concept of historical distance and the idea of history itself". If this is an overstatement, there can be no denying the power of the ideal of distance in historical work. The commitment to it has been so strong that a failure to live up to this has been the grounds not simply for criticizing one's fellow historians (as presentist) but also of demanding that their work be excluded from the body of writing called history (M. S. Phillips, 2004, pp. 125–126).

This said, it should be noted that the nature of historical practice has changed considerably over the last forty or fifty years. The rise of what has been called "history from below" has, in the course of focusing on those peoples "hidden from history", paid considerable attention to experience, particularly the experience of loss and suffering of indigenous peoples, migrants, sexual minorities, slaves, women, and the working classes. This has challenged both the concept and the ideal of distance. This has been especially evident where oral history (or testimony) has been to the fore, rather than the written word that history traditionally emphasized. Oral history, by its very nature, has a very different relationship with the past than history has (or used to have). If the practice of history in modern times has rested in effect upon the absence of the past, the practice of oral history has required the presence of the past. Oral history's conjunction of past and present has, more often than not, led to a greater emphasis on continuity and similarity rather than the stress on change and difference between past and present. In oral history, moreover, time is not always a matter of succession or linear time—the past always before the present—but often a matter of cyclical or repetitive time, and sometimes past and present are effectively in the same moment as "then" and "now" become entangled with one another. As the historian Paula Hamilton has pointed out, doing oral history *changes* "the relationship between past and present in historical research" (Hamilton, 2003, p. 145). Another historian, Alan Atkinson, has asked: "Why should it matter whether the voices you hear as a reader, writer or listener are present or past, living or dead, immediate, orally recorded or transcribed?" Yet, it usually does. "Men and women experienced in Oral History", Atkinson observes, "often say how hard it is to listen with both sympathy and 'scientific' detachment. . . . Listening to another person is an activity so fundamentally different, so fundamentally humane", Atkinson argues, "as to confront the whole business of conventional scholarship." In the practice of oral history the degrees of distance and proximity of the past are radically changed, most importantly in terms of the relationship a historian has with his or her subjects or sources of information. As a result, oral history has proven to be not only another way of relating the past, but another way of relating *to* that past (Atkinson, 2002, p. 62).

Traumatic history, transference, and countertransference

The impact of oral history on distance in historical work has been all the more profound when the past being related is a traumatic one. Trauma, as we know, throws into question any distinction that might readily be made between an event on the one hand and its aftermath on the other, and it can diminish any sense of difference between past and present. In traumatic history, any distance between "then" and "now" tends to collapse. In other words, trauma challenges the very conception of time that has long informed history by placing the past *in* the present rather than putting the past beside, before, or behind the present. In short, trauma resists the attempt of historians to place events in (an)other time: the past rather than the present.

How, then, should historians approach a traumatic past? The challenge of relating and relating to such a past has been embraced most significantly in respect of the Jewish Holocaust, and here I am going to proceed mostly by drawing on the work of an American historian, Dominick LaCapra, who has long had an interest in psychoanalysis and who has been contemplating how best to relate and relate to the Jewish Holocaust (see LaCapra, 1989, chap. 3, 1998, 2001, 2004). Fundamental to this work, LaCapra argues, is an acknowledgment that we usually have a transferential relationship to the pasts we consider. This is to say that we have an emotional or empathic connection to something or other in the pasts we write about, and so we tend to be implicated in some way or another in our treatment of these pasts. Transference will be especially intense in the case of a traumatic history, particularly where historians work with oral history in some form or another and especially where we work with oral informants or interviewees. The very nature of trauma means that historians are working on matters that are highly charged, and this is all the more so when the past is a matter of contemporary social and political debate. As such, historians must consider how we will handle affect in any encounter or exchange with such a past.

Contrary to what many might recommend, professional historians should not try to deny or circumvent any transferential relationship they might have to traumatic pasts or histories. "[T]ransference occurs willy-nilly" and "the challenge is not how to escape it but how to come to terms with it", LaCapra argues (2004, pp. 192, 234). As I have been saying, the stance the historian has conventionally sought to take has been one of a distance, one that amounts to be an innocent bystander or onlooker. Yet, adopting this stance, LaCapra points out, runs the risk that one will repress or deny or dissociate from a traumatic past. Historians, therefore, need to work through their historical proximity critically.

LaCapra has recommended that historians adopt an approach in which they begin by accepting their empathic or empathetic response to the subject(s) in their object of inquiry with whom they are most compelled to empathize, whether that subject be, for argument's sake, a perpetrator, a collaborator, a victim, a bystander, or a resister. Indeed, LaCapra has insisted on the need for what he calls empathic unsettlement in responding to traumatic events or conditions: "one must ... undergo at least muted trauma and allow that trauma (or unsettlement) to affect one's approach" (LaCapra, 1998, p. 40). Empathic unsettlement is necessary, LaCapra argues, not so much because it can deepen a historian's understanding of a traumatic past, but because it provides the historian with an experiential basis for working through that past.

Allowing empathic unsettlement, however, is only the first stage that LaCapra enjoins upon historians who are seeking to relate and relate to a traumatic past. He insists that they must be careful not to confuse their self with the other, or to confuse empathy with identification. Rather, they must stop short of identification with any one participant and strive to work through their transferential relationship, not in order to dispose of it but to realize the differences between *their* position and that of the historical subject. In order to check any tendency to identify with one of their subjects, LaCapra urges historians to try to grasp the ways in which they probably have an emotional relationship to the other subjects of this traumatic past—the subjects other than the one or ones with whom they have originally empathized—and try to empathize with these (LaCapra, 1998, pp. 41–42).

In recommending this, LaCapra is suggesting that historians try to be both proximate and distant in relationship to the subjects of the traumatic past. Although he does not say this, he is suggesting in effect that historians should try to counter the original transference—to practise, in other words, countertransference. By adopting this approach, LaCapra suggests, the historian can attain a more complex subject position than many historians have adopted when they have sought to relate and relate to traumatic histories. He argues that this can provide for the critical perspective that is necessary for writing history, a perspective he has called historical objectivity, though not objectivity in any transcendent (third-person) sense. By adopting this approach historians can broaden and deepen their historical understanding of a traumatic past but also acquire a richer sense of their own relationship to this. Most importantly, this can help facilitate the process of working through the past rather than allowing dissociation, denial, or acting out of that past, as well as the process of mourning rather than melancholy (LaCapra, 1998, p. 206).

The Stolen Generations

I shall now develop what I have been saying by discussing a particular example: those Aboriginal children separated from their kin (the Stolen Generations). More especially, I shall discuss the historical narrative of the Stolen Generations that was manifest in the writing of the historian Peter Read in the 1980s and 1990s; the Human Rights and Equal Opportunity Commission 1995–97 inquiry into the separation of Aboriginal children, and its report, *Bringing Them Home* (HREOC, 1997); the championing of this by the political commentator Robert Manne between 1997 and 2001; and the reaction to the narrative by those who have been called "the sorry people". This narrative, I argue, had two noteworthy features: first, it was not the creation of academic or professional history but, rather, took the forms of other kinds of history we can call public history, oral histories, autobiographies, political submissions, legal briefings, and the like; second, it was presented in, or projected onto, forums that were not historiographical in nature but memorial, literary, therapeutic, and the like (though not psychoanalytic) (e.g., HREOC, 1997; Manne, 1998, pp. 23–36; Read, 1983).

The creators of this historical narrative took LaCapra's first step—of allowing empathic unsettlement, or transference—but they did not take the next steps LaCapra recommends. As a result, I argue, the outcome of this Stolen Generations narrative entailed, at least for most of its tellers, limited historical understanding; acting out of, rather than working through, the past; and melancholy rather than mourning. I also argue that this was actually the result of what Freud would have regarded as both too much and too little distance on the part of those relating and relating to this past.

Before going any further we should remind ourselves what the particular Stolen Generations narrative I have pinpointed comprised. It claimed that an enormous number of Aboriginal children had been separated from their kin during the twentieth century, indeed, perhaps as many as one in three; that most of the separations had been forced removals; and that the main purpose of the policy under which separation had occurred was the prevention of the reproduction of Aboriginality, and so amounted to genocide. This narrative, as I have argued elsewhere, had fundamental flaws both as a narrative that sought to relate the past and relate that past to the present, which meant it was extraordinarily vulnerable to criticism. First, it confused the separation of children with removal, and especially forced removal, and suggested that forced removal was more common than it was; second, it obscured the range of ways in which Aboriginal children were taken, and thus the different effects this had on children, parents, families, and communities; third, it obfuscated the fact that children were separated for several reasons, among which were neglect; fourth, it conflated government policy and government practice, or intent and implementation, and thus exaggerated the number of children removed; fifth, and most problematically, it claimed that the separation of children was primarily the outcome of a malevolent genocidal plan on the part of government to destroy Aboriginality (see Attwood, 2001, p. 210).[1]

At the centre of this Stolen Generations narrative was one historical subject—the victims of separation, or, to be more precise, a particular victim, the children—though another subject, the resisters, occupied an important place. The historians who were involved in the making of this narrative allowed the process of empathic unsettlement to occur in respect of these subjects and they sought to relate and to relate to their plight and/or struggle. In this, it should be conceded, they were very successful. However, their work by and large stopped there. There was little if any attempt to do the work of countertransference. As a result, the historians relating this traumatic past (many of whom were probably unaware of what had attracted them to it—i.e., the nature of the transference that had compelled them to do this work) did not merely empathize with the Aboriginal victim and the non-Aboriginal resister, but identified themselves with these figures, such that they fused, and so confused, themselves with them.

In this work there was little if any attempt to relate to the other subjects of this past—the perpetrators, the collaborators, and the bystanders—and almost certainly not in a way that allowed for much if any empathy with them, let alone for empathic unsettlement. As a result of their identification with the position of the victim and the resister, they treated those other subjects, especially the perpetrator, with enormous antipathy, accusing them of the heinous crime of genocide. Rather than an attempt to understand these historical subjects, there was, on the part of the creators of the Stolen Generations narrative, something of a rush to judgement. In this, they lost sight of the fundamental task of the historian, at least in the opinion of historians such as Marc Bloch. In his book *The Historian's Craft*, unfinished when he was murdered by Germans in France in 1944, Bloch wrote:

> When all is said and done, a single word, "understanding", is the beacon light of our studies. . . . "Understanding", in all honesty, is a word pregnant with difficulties, but also with hope. Moreover, it is a friendly word. Even in action, we are far too prone to judge. It is so easy to denounce. We are never sufficiently understanding. . . . A little more understanding of people [is] necessary . . . in the conflicts which are unavoidable; all the more to prevent them while there is yet time. [Bloch, 1954, pp. 118–119]

In relating and relating to the Stolen Generations, I want to suggest, the historians largely acted out or repeated a past by assuming the position of the victim and/or the resister. In other words, there was both too little and too much distance between the past and the present, and so there was little working through of this past. To consider this problem further, let us turn back to Freud's patient and move our focus to the Stolen Generations themselves. The problem in the case of trauma, Adam Phillips points out, is that survivors "do not have a history; there is history, but not for them; because they are too close . . . they can make nothing of their experience" (2004, p. 148). The problem is not merely that the patient is unable to construct distance from the past they repeat; it is that they have not noticed, to all intents and purposes, that this distance actually exists. At the same time, by re-enacting or repeating the past rather than remembering it, they could, paradoxically, be said to keep that actual past at a distance.

The problem this patient has, as Phillips notes, is that he or she is living in the past but is not living in history. In their being too-close, in too much feeling or affect being present, there is too little room for anything else, and so re-presentation of this past is hampered, a re-presentation that can provide the possibility of the ascribing of new meanings. This is to argue that it is the construction of distance, the construction of history, that allows the space for reflection, for redescribing the pain, and for working through, and so the prospect for psychic survival. In the work of the creators of the Stolen Generations narrative this was true of many of the Aboriginal narrators, but it can be argued that this holds too for the narrators of the particular narrative I have been discussing (A. Phillips, 2004, p. 142).

I shall now turn to consider the response of many of those who read or heard the narratives of the Stolen Generations, in particular those people who have been called "the sorry people". Here I want to present an argument that has been made by Haydie Gooder and Jane Jacobs, who are responsible for coining the term "the sorry people" to refer to the supporters of Aboriginal reconciliation and, in particular, the making of an apology to Aboriginal people, especially the Stolen Generations. Drawing on Freud's work on melancholy and mourning, Gooder and Jacobs (2000, pp. 235–236) argue that these settler Australians were suffering from the loss of a love object or ideal—the worthy nation—whose moral legitimacy had been drawn into question, had been unsettled, by the Aboriginal histories, particularly the history of the Stolen Generations. However, they refused to break their attachment to this lost object or ideal—they refused in other words to mourn their loss—but held onto it in a narcissistic fashion; they abased themselves, expected to be punished, and sought to redeem themselves and their object or ideal by means of an apology. ("In the clinical picture of melancholia", Freud argued, "dissatisfaction with the ego on moral grounds is the most outstanding feature": 1917e [1915], pp. 254, 256).

In their response to the Stolen Generations, many felt compelled to empathize with the Aboriginal subjects. In this there was probably some confusion on the part of the sorry people between absence on the one hand and loss on the other. (Arguably, absence refers to a transhistorical or general phenomenon, loss to a historical or specific one.) Most importantly, the sorry people, and settler Australians more generally, had very little historical understanding of the reasons why Aboriginal children were separated from their kin by their settler predecessors. This is a serious problem because it diminished the prospect of being able to work through this past in the present. A properly historical approach would have pinpointed that Aboriginal children were not separated because of a policy of genocide, which was something the sorry people could readily consign to a distant past that had little to do with them, but, rather, because of a policy of assimilation premised on the assumption that settler modernity was "for their own good", which is an assumption that is probably still dominant today and so one with which settler Australians are intimately familiar and thus implicated. Grasping this would have been both more unsettling and more helpful in relating to the past. Settler

Australians might have realized that the past was in the present not only in the form of the Aboriginal people affected by the practice of separating Aboriginal children from their kin, but also in the form of a white mentality we can call assimilationist. Understanding this would provide a means of working through this past as it would address the role of the very ideas and attitudes that have contributed—and continue to contribute—to the destruction of Aboriginal communities and Aboriginality, or at least their diminution.

The work of mourning

To turn to the question of how the nation might really do the work of mourning: Death, it has been remarked, lies at the heart of national formations. "States can be set up as political entities, but they only become nations through the magical or spiritual agency of death," Stephen Muecke has observed. "A people recognises itself as a people ... through the symbolic treatment of its dead" (1997, p. 227). In large part, Australia has become a national community by remembering and mourning those who have fought in wars "over there" (overseas) but not here. The nation has not remembered and mourned the victims of the wars here, particularly the Aboriginal people who lost the most because of those wars. The settler state has never acknowledged that their losses are worthy of recognition.

As a result of its failure to work through this and other such traumatic events, the Australian nation has been unable to grapple with the wounds of its past and the divided legacies these have left. Instead, it has repressed these. Consequently, historical discourse in this country has swung between two extremes, two excesses: overstating the amount of blood shed on the one hand, understating the amount of blood shed on the other. To come to terms with this traumatic past, I have argued elsewhere (Attwood, 2005, pp. 194–196), a process of mourning this event and its aftermath is required. For this work, some rites of passage are necessary. What is required in Australia are appropriate memorials in the form of monuments throughout the land and appropriate rituals such as an annual day of mourning.

Writing traumatic history

Finally, I am going to consider the question of how one might best relate traumatic history in terms of narrative forms. In my last book, *Telling the Truth about Aboriginal History* (Attwood, 2005), I suggested that historians should give more consideration to the forms of narrative they might adopt in representing this past. Here, I want to relay an argument an American philosopher of history, Hayden White, puts in an essay in a collection entitled *Probing the Limits of Representation: Nazism and the "Final Solution"*. He argues that the traditional or classic realist mode of representation—that is, the form, that came into being in the nineteenth century, whereby both novelists and historians have sought to represent reality "realistically"—is inadequate to the task of relating events and experiences such as the Jewish Holocaust because of their nature, and that consequently another form of representation is required—namely, that of modernism. More particularly, White (1992, p. 50) argues that a form of representation Roland Barthes (1989) called "intransitive writing" fits the bill.

Barthes, White tells us, considered "intransitive writing" in order to characterize the differences between classical realism and modernism. In the context of a discussion of voice, Barthes sought to focus attention on the different kinds of relationship someone can be represented as bearing in relation to action, and he pointed out that whereas modern European languages offered two possibilities for expressing this relationship, the active voice and the passive voice, ancient Greek offered a third possibility: a "middle voice". "Whereas in the active and passive voices the subject of the verb is presumed to be *external* to the action . . . in the middle voice the subject is presumed to be *interior* to the action," White notes. It is a form, Barthes observes, in which "writing becomes itself the means of vision or comprehension, not a mirror of something else" as it is in realism. Intransitive writing is, then, "a distance-denying discourse" (Barthes, 1989, p. 19; White, 1992, pp. 47–49).

In making the case for this as way of representing traumatic pasts, White spells out the differences between realism and "middle voiced-ness" by referring to the characteristics of modernism (at least as they have been identified by the critic Erich Auerbach discussing Virginia Woolf's *To the Lighthouse*). First, the writer as a narrator of objective facts disappears, and instead almost everything appears by way of reflection in the consciousness (and/or unconscious?) of the *dramatis personae*; second, there is a dissolution of any perspective or point of view outside the text in which the people and events within it are observed; third, in the narrator's interpretation of these "events", the predominant tone is one of doubt and questioning; fourth, there is an employment of devices such as stream of consciousness (or should that be stream of unconsciousness?) that obliterate the impression of an objective reality completely known to the author; fifth and lastly, the use of new techniques for the representation of time and temporality, such as those that counter the notion of time as lineal or successive, those that use "the 'chance occasion' to release 'processes of consciousness' which remain unconnected to a 'specific subject of thought'" (White, 1992, pp. 50–51). It seems to me that in order to tell the traumatic story of colonialism in this country, it might be necessary to adopt forms such as this.

Conclusion

In this chapter I have argued that the task of relating and relating to Australia's traumatic colonial past primarily depends on the way historians tackle the matter of distance. I have suggested that at least two moves are necessary: we historians must allow empathic unsettlement, must allow ourselves to be unsettled by an empathetic relationship to this traumatic past, and we must try to empathize with all the subjects of a traumatic past (not only the victim and the resister but the perpetrator, the collaborator, and the bystander), in order to recognize our relationship to them and to attain a complex subject position. This approach enables both proximity and distance, and by integrating affect and analysis it offers the possibility of constructing a history and mourning the past. It thus provides the basis for working through rather than merely acting out the past. By these means, the traumatic burden of the past can be mitigated, and there can be a re-investment in life in the present.

Note

1. Significantly, some academic commentators working in disciplines other than history and psychoanalysis have apparently failed to grasp the

need to test the reality of this Stolen Generations narrative. Having reminded us that it is impossible to gain direct access to historical reality (or,
indeed, any reality), the historian Carlo Ginsburg (1999, pp. 17, 36) would
remark, they seem to infer that reality is unknowable, rejecting "the possibility of analysing the relationships between these representations and the
reality they depict or represent ... as an unforgivable instance of naïve
positivism", and implying that we can discard the principle of reality in our
consideration of historical representations. These critics seem to overlook
a major source of danger when they denigrate the role played by empirical
research: unless historical narratives are tested and altered or even abandoned where they are contradicted by the known facts, how can one avoid
historical error, and how can one mount a critical case against opposing
historical narratives, most importantly denialist ones?. One of the offend-
ers I have in mind here is Rosanne Kennedy (2001), who, in my opinion,
reveals a limited grasp of my essay on the Stolen Generations narrative and
of psychoanalytic practice.

4

Lost children

Eve Steel

This contribution is like a small pebble in a vast arid landscape. I hope it may be like a pebble in the Aboriginal custom, which is taken somewhere else and develops significance not initially envisaged. The issues under consideration are complicated. They also belong in our inner worlds, in our consulting rooms, as well as in our social and political environment. As clinicians struggling in the minutiae of intricate intimate connection and disconnection with another, in the microcosm of the fifty-minute hour, we have profound experience to bring to a more public discourse.

When I agreed to give the talk[1] from which this is a written version, I did not know what experience would follow. When we agree to work with someone psychoanalytically, psychotherapeutically, we also have no idea where it will lead us, what we will hear, learn, or discover—not only about the other but also about ourselves and about the two of us together. It can be a transformational journey. My reading and explorations in relation to the Stolen Generation led me into unexpected areas and directions. One primary focus emerged: the history and role of the Christian church.

Reading the 689-page *Bringing Them Home* report (HREOC, 1997) is not the same as reading literature. There is not the transformation of tragedy related through a story. It is raw. We know that a work of art can enable the reader, viewer, or listener to experience terrible tragedy, because it is contained within the work of art that has gone through a process of transformation. There is a difference between feeling violated and repelled by a work of art that wishes to shock the other and drawn to another work that moves one to be amazed at the capacities of human experience (however terrible) and that enriches one's understanding.

Bion said that to hear one baby crying is difficult, but to hear a ward of babies crying is intolerable. Our minds shut out what we cannot bear to hear, see, or know. The content of this report is not just about crying babies; it is about knowing of violence perpetrated upon innocent children and human beings. To admit the significance of what lies behind this social document is to let it penetrate one's consciousness, to allow other states of mind be known to us. These states of mind do not belong just to the traumatized victims, but also to the perpetrators. I would see both as Lost Children.

As I read the report, the children's game of "Who's the King of the Castle, Who's the Dirty Rascal" rang through my mind. The "I'm the king of the castle and you're the dirty rascal" view is very much what the foundation of Australia was based on. It was founded as a penal colony, a place to send unwanted rascals at the bottom of the social scale, convicts. The cruelty and deprivation imposed by the kings of the castle on the so-called dirty rascals was horrendous.

Others came to Australia to seek a better life, many having suffered from the Highland clearances in Scotland or the potato famines in Ireland. These are terrible histories. The clearing of people off the land in the Highlands by those with power to fulfil their own purposes has qualities of the similar clearing of indigenous peoples from the land in Australia. Being aware of history, it is possible to see the patterns from the past being repeated. When opportunities arise it is easy to slip, for instance, into becoming like the lairds who kicked out the Highland Scots; this time it was the Aborigines who were kicked out. We have intimations of the origins of the fantasy of creating one's own little kingdom to be lord over. When such land is called God's Little Acre, I wonder what kind of God it is dedicated to. Veronica Brady (Honorary Research Fellow at the University of Western Australia) said in a radio programme, "perhaps it is because the gods or God we worship is the God of the winners, who has little mercy for the losers".

Who is one identified with when this happens? We are identified with the aggressor, the one in power. We never want to experience being helpless and humiliated again but will give someone else that experience as we were given it. This may not be a conscious thought at all, but it is enacted. Do the dispossessed inevitably become the oppressors? Not always, but when there has been no working through, the pain is passed on, in various ways, which include an intergenerational transmission.

This was something Freud understood when he wrote to Fliess on 2 May 1897, "everything goes back to the reproduction of scenes" (in Masson, 1985, p. 239). And later, in "Remembering, Repeating and Working Through" (1914g), "Whatever is not remembered and worked through will be repeated, whether we like it or not." On p. 150, he wrote, "the patient does not remember anything of what he has forgotten, but acts it out. He repeats it, without of course knowing that he is repeating it." He adds, on p. 149, "These are experiences of very early childhood." And: "He cannot escape his compulsion to repeat; and in the end we understand that this is his way of remembering." Freud's realization of this way of remembering is profound, as we see in areas beyond our consulting rooms in our social and political worlds.[2]

In the twenty-first century we no longer have anywhere to send unwanted people. We still talk of sending our rubbish, like nuclear waste, to the sun or outer space. Recently it has even been suggested that we "Down Under" can take the world's nuclear waste! Without a way of dealing with unwanted feelings we suffer in our world from what is done to un-metabolized experiences inside ourselves. This is the stuff of psychoanalytic work.

When I have spoken about what I was encountering in my reading and meeting of people and said that I felt traumatized, I have often met with glassy-eyed dismissals and a turning away. One friend said to me, "There's all this sentimentalizing of Aborigines." There is a danger of making us the monsters. That is just tipping the see-saw, within that vertex of idealization and denigration, accusation and blame, attack and counter-attack.

The *Bringing Them Home* report has documented many stories about what we have done to Aborigines, but the implications of what has happened are wider and deeper than that. It is what we do—and continue to do—to those without power, those without a voice: to children, to women, to animals and nature. It is about what we do to ourselves. It is what we do to our own knowing. The English language does not have the different words for "knowing" that European languages do. For instance, in the German language, the language of Freud, there are two words for knowing, *kennen* and *wissen*, the difference between "being acquainted with" and "having experience of", thus conveying different levels of knowledge that penetrate our inner knowing. To be aware of what is happening around us and within us, to be able to acknowledge what is right and what is wrong, requires an effort. The results of this can be uncomfortable, distressing, and isolating. In mentioning what is right and wrong, one is in danger of being seen as taking the high moral ground. There is also the danger of intellectualizing and using theory as another way of distancing and protecting oneself from truly knowing the pain, suffering, and helplessness of the experience; taking safety in an ivory tower, the tower of the castle of the king. There are no simple solutions in relation to the effect of colonization and the particular results of the past government policies that led to the taking of so-called half-caste children away from their Aboriginal mothers, families, and communities.

Ideology, superiority, and prejudice

We are all enculturated initially within our primary familial relationships. How we experience these colours our experiences as we grow up and relate to a wider social network. At the time of the British Empire, white supremacy was taken for granted by those in power. If we belong to the ruling group in any part of the world, it feels different from belonging to the underdog group. This affects our feelings about ourselves and our sense of who we are. It is relevant in relation to the sense of belonging that the so-called half-caste children felt when the white community did not embrace them as belonging to them. Being looked down on and cut off from their families, language, and culture affected their sense of self.

I would like to focus attention beyond the individual and his or her inner world to embrace the reality of the group and culture that the individual belongs to. We know from our psychoanalytic work how the phantasies and beliefs of our inner world affect our functioning in external reality. We also know from experience of

infant observation and child development that our inner worlds
are fed by our earliest interacting relationships. These occur within
a wider group and culture. We may believe we have a mind of our
own. We may be so enculturated in our group and culture that we
are unable to be aware of anything different from the view we hold.
In our psychoanalytic work we endeavour to create a setting where,
with time and sensitivity, encrusted layers of protection of a vulnerable self may be shed. The fear of annihilation and disintegration
can be overwhelming. This is a danger zone. The fears may be valid.
This is a topic I shall return to later.

In thinking about Lost Children and the many examples that
have been gathered, I have chosen to focus on the use of ideology,
related to the Lost Children in the perpetrators. The assumption of
superiority is one that white people automatically took upon themselves. This assumption was and often still is deeply held and taken
for granted. This is what I mean by being embedded, being part of
a system that cannot be questioned or thought about. One way of
achieving this belief of superiority is to follow an ideology.

For instance, a belief that being white is superior allies us with
a certain group of ancestors who acted upon this belief. The same
can be said for those who follow a belief that Christianity is superior
to other religions. Acting under such a banner, we are in projective
identification with a superior being that cannot be questioned. To
question such a basic assumption endangers the individual's position
in the group. In relation to the church, heresy has a long history,
where excommunication and death were not uncommon results for
heretics.

At the time of colonization, the scientific notions of evolution
and eugenics enhanced the belief that white industrial peoples
were obviously seen to be a superior species to those who had not
achieved the same development in these areas. In pursuit of ideologies, we see the scapegoating of others. The Aborigines at the time
of settlement were described as lesser beings. The land was "terra
nullius", therefore uninhabited. These non-people, dark-skinned
hunter-gatherers, could therefore be easily got rid of. The land
could be used as the white settlers wished. To imagine how the inhabitants perceived the white people arriving on their large sailing
ships and not simply to visit and go away requires a desire to think
about this and use one's imagination. If the inhabitants are seen as
lesser creatures, it is easier not to think about their experience. In

such circumstances people are dehumanized and projected onto. We see this happen in war.

The Christian church grew out of the Judeo-Christian tradition. In the Bible, in the first book of Genesis, we hear that God explicitly gave human beings, particularly men, dominion over the earth, nature, and what are seen as lesser creatures, to subdue and multiply. It is easy to see how such a belief becomes an unquestioned mindless sense of entitlement. The other does not exist except for one's own use. There is not a reciprocal relationship when the other is used as a part object. If the other is alive and a human being or many human beings, one can use them as you wish and get rid of them without impunity. We see the projections of one's inhumanity, due to an incapacity to identify with the defenceless other. The other is despised, and often it is not difficult to recognize what has been projected and disowned. We see these levels of functioning not only in the past in those who followed Hitler or Stalin. We see it also in the ideals of "the promised land" arising out of depression and exile. I think these searches are relevant to aspects of colonization. Such pioneers, identified with their ideal and dream of making God's kingdom on earth, suffered from concrete thinking and a questionable sense of entitlement. The belief in utopia links to what Janine Chasseguet-Smirgel (1985) called one of the narcissistic yearnings for perfection: to follow an ideology. Christian ideologies feed such yearnings, but I think it is food that does not help one to grow.

However, the force of group pressure can be terrible to withstand. Individuals and groups who feel empowered by a dictator demonstrate an absence of thought and compassion. Those who do not agree are seen as weak or dangerous. The individual is pulled along by the tide or by the fear he will be killed. This may be a valid fear. Nevertheless, Vaclav Havel, an independent writer in Czechoslovakia at the time when it was under the yoke of Russian Communism, said there were some things more important than life, and he continued to write even in prison. Teilhard de Chardin, a Roman Catholic priest and geologist, would not cease writing, even though the Catholic Church threatened him with excommunication. He died before this happened, and we are enriched by his writings.

As I struggled with the task of clarifying this topic, I was reminded of the children, described in Bowlby's paper, "On Knowing What You Are Not Supposed to Know and Feeling What You Are Not Supposed to Feel" (1979). John Bowlby wrote about children in families. We also feel like children when we see and voice what is known but not mentioned about institutions that pride themselves on their good image.

When some politicians confessed in parliament that they were moved to tears when reading the *Bringing Them Home* report, they were met with scorn and derision. This seems a clear example of the fear of being sad, moved to tears, and open to feel pain. If this open expression of these emotions is only seen as weak and humiliating, as putting one in a vulnerable position, there is a barrier in relation to providing a possibility that could lead to fresh thinking and new perspectives.

The Christian church and colonial power

In relation to the history of the Christian church, I would like to quote from *The Kindness of Strangers* by the historian John Boswell.

> Christianity was itself a foundling in a way: born out into Judaism but rejected by it, it was adopted by Rome and grew up to be more part of its foster than natal family. [Christianity became the dominant religion in the Roman empire.] The Romanizing of Christianity resulted in the Christianizing of the Roman world. . . . Like other abandoned children, Christianity had come with tokens, most notably the Jewish scriptures. . . . Three aspects of the Hebrew scriptures in particular may have affected attitudes among Christian cultures where they were studied as the Old Testament:
> 1.   a startling matter-of-fact attitude towards parental sacrifice or execution of their children;
> 2.   the definition of guidelines for selling children;
> 3.   the implicit acceptance of abandonment in general. [1990, pp. 138–139]

Children were taught to honour their parents, but nowhere were parents told how they should treat their children. In the story of the sacrifice of Isaac by Abraham, we see a God who demands a sacrifice as a test of submission. Joseph was sold. Moses was saved from death by being hidden in the bulrushes. The theme of a person's sacrifice affecting a whole people is a theme in both Jewish and Christian traditions. In the Christian tradition there is the theme of being loved by God, not by parents, of being adopted into the Christian church by baptism. "Jesus loves you, suffer the little children to come unto me." Militant Christianity supported conquering and saving those who did not belong to this superior religion. Those who were not saved and called infidels and heathens were seen as lesser beings and destroyed. They joined the ranks of "dirty rascals" around the world.

Relevant to this is the story of the kidnapping of Edgardo Mortara, written about by David Kertzer (1998), which is an example of the church and the Pope supporting this in Europe in 1858. Edgardo Mortara was a 6-year-old Jewish boy in Bologna, Italy. He was seized from his family and taken to Rome, because he had been baptized by a servant. Baptism was seen as a magic act. Thomas Aquinas had said children should not be baptized without their parents' consent. Despite this thirteenth-century teaching, Catholics in Italy were forcibly baptizing Jewish children in the nineteenth century, during what was called the Enlightenment. The Papal newspaper of the time wrote that the child Edgardo must be protected by the Pope as his Jewish parents would torture him into giving up his faith and even kill him if he did not. The parents were told they could have their son back if they agreed to be baptized into the Christian church. When they refused, it was seen as more proof of how unfit they were as parents. The Pope said, "Both the powerful and the powerless have tried to steal this boy from me." And he added: "I am his father." Six years later a 9-year-old Jewish boy, Giuseppe Coen, was baptized in Rome and taken from his parents. The Pope complained that so many were against him and that "no one showed any concern for me, father of the faithful".

The beliefs revealed by these contemporary stories are relevant to what was happening in Australia in the nineteenth century and was to continue into the twentieth century. Those who have power over others justify what they do as only being for the others' own good, and they *believe* it. Stealing children was not new, and the powerful have always taken what they wanted from the weak. The history of the slave trade to work the plantations in America is a particularly large people-stealing enterprise. The desire to own appealing black babies—for instance, when they had come to hospital—was easily catered for until comparatively recently. "I do but beg a little changeling boy to be my henchman," asked Oberon of Titania, in Shakespeare's *A Midsummer Night's Dream.* An attractive black child was special and used as a pet and token then, but still was stolen.

I am focusing on this aspect of the church, rather than on other aspects of Christianity: the side of compassion, mercy, and love. Henry Reynolds in his book, *This Whispering in Our Hearts* (1998), gives detailed examples of those who represented a different position from the beginning of colonization of Australia. They had different internal kings and interior castles. There have been many books written about church history and the change to a Roman patriarchal institution. I do not wish to dwell on that but, rather, indicate the origins of these traditions. In my opinion we need to know the history and context of socio-political occurrences in order to understand how they have arisen. Psychoanalytic understanding of human behaviour, particularly what is unconscious and therefore disowned, adds another dimension. I hope I may arouse the reader to think of other aspects in relation to this topic.

The Christian church in Australia saw the indigenous people as being without spirituality and in need of being saved for their own good. They did, in fact, need saving from the predations of their fellow white settlers. Those who saw Aborigines as God's people and deserving of concern and different treatment were, from the very beginning, seen as weak, not having the stamina needed for colonization, and told to take the next boat home. I am not denying that there was enormous courage in facing the unknown and that remarkable things were achieved by many early settlers. We are all here as a result of their actions. Those who did support the Aborigines were attacked, and some received death threats. For instance, the Anglican Reverend Gribble: "Following a concerted campaign of vilification and persecution in Western Australia, he fled across the continent to Queensland in fear of his life. His crime? The exposure and prosecution of police atrocities against the Aborigines" (quoted in Kidd, 1997, p. 39). This was in the 1890s. The Government men were against the intrusion of missions, who would take away their cheap labour. The institution of the church supported the vested interests of colonization, first the pastoralists, then the establishment. Might was seen as right. An individual, like the Reverend Gribble, who believed in a different Christian ethic and acted according to his conscience, was said to be mad. Others like him, who saw the Aborigines as human beings, not to be killed, treated cruelly, and exploited, were reviled and ostracized by those with power. Thomas Backhouse, a Quaker who settled in Tasmania said that people who would behave like gentlemen at home, behaved in unrecognizable ways in this new land. I think the fears that arise in a strange place and situations certainly can lead to unrecognizable behaviour.

The power of the colonizers was aligned with the institutional church. This church suppressed the feminine and all that it stood for. This was seen in attitudes towards nature, the body, and sexuality, all to be subdued, according to the priests. There was a disconnection between heaven and earth. Heaven was distant, not of this world; the spirit was disembodied. For the Aborigines, as with many indigenous peoples, the spirit was within the earth. They belonged to their part of the earth, and their own spirit was revived as they revived the earth, with song, dance, and ritual. Different clan groups have links to different constellations of the stars, and as well as believing they come from there, they also believe they return there. The desert peoples have stories and paintings depicting their link to the Pleiades. Each clan group holds a part of the story, which connects across the land on the Song Lines. The beautiful feathered mourning poles from Elcho Island are made to help the spirit, when one dies, to fly back to the Morning Star whence they came. The loss of their spirit experienced by Aborigines, with their severance from their specific place on this earth, was not understood by the white colonizers.

The earth and the human body

For hunter-gatherer people to meet post-industrial and agricultural people would inevitably lead to change. The white colonizers' relationship to the earth was different. Their right to possess and use as they wished was taken as a given. We can see similar clashes of belief in the attitude to the earth and nature with the white colonizers and the indigenous peoples of North America. The god of the colonizers came with the exhortation from Genesis to subdue and have dominion over nature. The pagan god Pan was made into the devil. We can see the split between the body and spirit, between heaven and hell. We see the continuation of this split in the Church's attitude towards sexuality and the pursuit of purity. There was also a split in the view of the pure woman and the sexual woman. The madonna—mother breastfeeding the baby—could be seen as pure. The mother making new babies, who is seen as a sexual being, whom it is natural to hate, was seen as a whore. We can see the primitive splitting between the top and bottom of the woman's body, clean and dirty respectively. We understand such splitting in the consulting room and see it clearly in child development. When a 3-year-old looks down on a new baby and calls it a dirty pooey baby and sees itself as clean and grown up, we consider this natural and amusing. A little girl whom I saw in a hospital outpatient department vehemently denied she had a bottom, although she was wearing nappies and had problems with toilet training. When distorted views and accompanying phantasies become stuck in adulthood, we would call it arrested development. The Catholic Church demands that priests and nuns be celibate. They are expected to subdue and sublimate their sexuality. Often the turbulence of puberty and anxieties about adult sexuality have not been negotiated. Grown ups in adult bodies can still feel emotionally like latency children. I have known patients educated by religious orders who have said they were convinced that the nuns, or priests, did not have bodies, certainly did not have bottoms or genitals. These children were shocked when they saw that they actually ate food. We can see the primitive oral phantasies that cannot allow a holy person to devour, have teeth, and have a physical reality. This says something about the children, but also something about the attitude of the religious orders towards their own bodies and their feelings.

The hardship and deprivation amounting to what we would see now as cruelty and sadism was inflicted by the religious orders on themselves and their own. In Karen Armstrong's *Through a Narrow Gate* (1993), her description of the way the young novices were treated was accepted as natural by the institution of the church. In giving themselves to be brides of Christ, they shunned and were shut off from the outside world and previous familial connection. Their training in physical hardship and emotional coldness was seen as part of the ascetic spiritual tradition: obedience, poverty, chastity—all Christian virtues. They were in the tradition of oblation, a gift to God. The self-flagellation could become eroticized, as Karen Armstrong realized before ceasing the practice. Rules, regulations, group confessions, power over the young, how easily all this can become perverse. The treatment the nuns and priests themselves had undergone was passed on to those in their care. At that time, it was not seen as we see it now.[3]

Not everyone in religious orders was able to rise above the harsh deprivation of the senses to become loving and charitable. Often the punitive depriving experiences were simply passed on. If you are fused with an object, there is no space to work through your experience. If you are looking for somewhere to put yourself, or stick to, like a belief system, a group, an ideology, or to simply honour your parents, in various forms, there is primitive identification. There is no inner space to recognize how you feel and what you are experiencing. There is no space for developing a mind of your own to think. The separation that the Aboriginal half-caste children experienced was such a severance that the possibility of "reclaiming your own spirit", in the way that was practised in the past, was not possible.

The spirit was closely linked to the earth and place of personal totem and clan group. The Aboriginal children belonged to close family networks. There are many stories of cruel separation against their mother's will. Children were often taken far away and not allowed any contact. Their names were changed, and they were forbidden to speak their language. This was then forgotten. The children were lied to and deceived to avoid contact between mothers and children. No personal relationship was fostered as a substitute for the loss. They were put in alienating institutions, bereft of affection or physical contact. Except when they experienced abuse. The abuse was also sexual. This was emotionally devastating. To be put in these institutions was said to be in the child's best interests. The Aborigines were thought to be a dying race, and at least those with white blood should be rescued and given a chance. It is difficult to let ourselves know the truth of what was experienced.

As many as 150,000 British children were shipped to a new life in distant parts of the Empire from children's homes. The last group came in 1967. The first of these children arrived in Western Australia in the late 1930s. These children were said to be orphans, but often they were not. The children and parents were deceived. They were sent to the Christian Brothers orders in Western Australia and elsewhere. They were exploited like slaves to build churches and buildings. They were also subjected to violence. One of the grown-up child migrants said in a radio interview ("Innocent Exiles") that the violence that he experienced in the home run by religious orders was worse than anything he later experienced in the war in Vietnam. He described the sense of foreboding he felt as a young boy arriving in Australia and realizing he would never be able to return to his family, or his country. "I had been stripped of my personality.

We were treated in a degraded way, which was a mockery of human dignity." They were also exploited sexually. It was said that the British children were depraved. They were accused of tempting the priests. Another of the child migrants, still stuttering as a result of the violent treatment he suffered, said: "I believe we were seen as Satan's children, second-class citizens, they knew best." There is a tradition in some sects to see children as full of original sin and devilish instincts. Beating it out of them is part of the "poisonous pedagogy" that Alice Miller writes about in her book *For Your Own Good* (1987). She uses the term poisonous pedagogy referring to the manipulative and emotionally blackmailing ways in which parents and educators overtly and covertly make children obedient.

Aboriginal women were also seen as depraved seducers of the white men and blamed for the rapes inflicted on them. Many of the early settlers and seekers of fortune were without women. It was taken for granted they could forcibly take young Aboriginal girls and young women and use them as they wished. Projecting sexuality into the Aborigines, the black, the primitive, is to deny the sexual exploitation of the girls and women. However, the existence of the so-called half-caste children, who were the result of the sexual encounters between white men and black women, could not be denied.

Brian Keenan, in his book *Evil Cradling* (1993), mentions the violence of the Jihad and how the young men who had been sexually repressed became sexually aroused by their use of violence. A similar charge could be made against those from the Missions, who beat children's bottoms.

Child abuse is always a three-person affair: an abuser, a victim, and someone who is a bystander and turns a blind eye. Child abuse cannot happen if the third person sees what is happening and protects the child. Prejudice and inner blindness protect the abuser. We need to create the third party in our own minds to first of all see and be aware of what is going on. Justice is proverbially shown as blindfolded, with unbalanced scales, like the see-saw. The imbalance is within us. The primitive justice of revenge perpetuates the same system. It is vital to name the injustice, so it can be acknowledged. The defences against persecutory and depressive guilt can be huge. We know this from our work. Holding on to a manic defence keeps the depressive feelings at bay. Mourning for what has been done and facing the grief and loss cannot start until this is known. We need a threesome rather than a twosome (the triangle rather than the see-saw), a different kind of healthy couple looking after the child, with a capacity to hold a parenting function. The adults need to remember what it is like to be a child.

The Catholic culture of the *mater dolorosa,* a mother of suffering for our sins, seems to be echoed in the wailing of many mothers, suffering, crying where are our children? The Aboriginal mothers and grandmothers (also those of the Plaza de Mayo in Argentina and elsewhere in the world) were met by SILENCE. This silence has gone on a long time.

The significance of acknowledging tyranny

In this context, the wish to be said sorry to is to do with needing the genuine acknowledgement of the pain that has been inflicted.[4]

A patient who had been badly treated by a group he admired said to me: "If only they'd say sorry, I would have my dignity back." Otherwise he felt unnoticed, "like dirt under their shoe". I realize that to say sorry is not enough to repair the damage, but it can be a beginning to acknowledge what has happened and to be a witness to that reality.

A genuine wish and concern to protect the girls and women from white exploitation led to the setting up of the Protection Boards. A letter to *The Queenslander* newspaper in 1883 stated that "the Aboriginal inhabitants are treated exactly in the same way as the wild beasts or birds the settlers may find there. Their goods taken, their children forcibly stolen, their women carried away, entirely at the caprice of the white men" (HREOC, 1997, p. 71). The Missions were given the responsibility of protecting the Aborigines. Later it was alleged that what was concealed was the wish by the Mission to have cheap labour and that this became a protection racket. The Missions treated the Aborigines as they treated their own novices, who experienced the same harshness and deprivation in their initiation to their orders. In her book *Over My Tracks: A Remarkable Life* (1993), Evelyn Crawford wrote: "No one from the Protection Board gave a damn for our culture or anything we valued."

In relation to how the Aborigines were treated, I quote from the report:

In the name of protection indigenous people were subject to near-total control. Their entry and exit from reserves was regulated as was their everyday life on the reserves, their right to marry and their employment. With a view to encouraging the conversion of the children to Christianity and distancing them from their indigenous lifestyle, children were housed in dormitories and contact with their families strictly limited. [HREOC, 1997, p. 29]

The speaking of their own language was forbidden.

In 1938 William Ferguson and John Patten forcefully denied the white myth of benevolence: "You hypocritically claim you are trying to 'protect us', but your modern policy of 'protection' (so-called) is killing us off just as surely as the pioneer policy of giving us poisoned damper and shooting us down like dingoes!" (HREOC, 1997, p. 46). *The Way We Civilise* by Rosalind Kidd (1997) makes chilling reading, but I recommend it to anyone who actually wants to know the history of Queensland's governing of the Aborigines.

One wonders what the sexual phantasies were in relation to what are variously referred to as half-castes, quadroons, or octoroons—bizarre zoological labels conjuring up fear and contempt, perhaps seen as a sinister third race in Australia. In the wish to get rid of the "black", there is a wish to get rid of aspects of the self that are disowned. The belief in a superior God, linked to a belief in themselves as a superior race, led the settlers to see themselves as ordained by God to bring better ways to the world. The Presbyterian minister John Dunmore Lang, in a speech to the Moreton Bay Friends of the Aborigines, justified the British expropriation of the original inhabitants by saying that:

God in making the earth never intended it should be occupied by men so incapable of appreciating its resources as the Aborigines of Australia. The white man, indeed, only carried out the intentions of the Creator in coming and settling in the territory of the natives. [Webb & Enstice, 1998, p. 38]

In 1938, the Archbishop of Perth welcomed children shipped in from Britain as supporting the White Australia policy: "If we do not supply our own stock, we are leaving ourselves all the more exposed to the menace of the teeming millions of our neighbouring Asiatic races" (Humphreys, 1995, p. 11). An added purpose of these human imports, according to a leading Catholic, was to ensure the increase of Catholics in Australia, which should not be outstripped by the growth of Protestants. (Colonies also transport feuds from their mother countries. There was a schism between primarily Catholic Irish and Protestant English that permeated early Australian society and education and continued into the 1960s.)

My reason for bringing in this aspect of church ideology of that period is that it was perverse and created a poisonous climate. This can so permeate an inner and outer culture that one is unaware of it. We are embedded in our surrounding culture, unable to see it as separate as we have grown up with it—the good public image, the good mantle, under which evil can hide, as well as a place where good people can gather. This is part of all of us. We do not all see, as Bowlby's children saw, "what we are not supposed to see and know what we are not supposed to know". If we do see such things, it is uncomfortable, distressing, and shameful. We are changed by this.

I have found in my work with some patients a predominance of a harsh, cruel superego rule that has imprisoned a frightened, confused child. This has been clad in the language and experience of a "primitive" religious upbringing, to which they were subjected. (In relation to a deeper exegesis of primitive and mature religion, I recommend Neville Symington's 1994 book, *Emotion and Spirit.*)

Two of my patients were brought up in different churches: one an extreme puritanical Protestant and the other extreme Catholic. The puritan held terrible sway in the mind of my patient. The male elders were still tyrannizing internally. I felt I was not allowed to speak to my patient, with these severe elders ever present, keeping her imprisoned. It was tragic to see how they restricted her from making any move for freedom. Such vehicles for an inner harsh crippling superego are not uncommon. The Catholic patient had turned against the church with venom when he went to university. However, it was disturbing to see how he found a belief in psychoanalysis as a saviour. He found a substitute sect, clambered inside it, felt superior, and vented his spleen on anyone who was fool enough to be religious, calling them despicable. He was, at that stage, still in the king-of-the-castle see-saw position under a protection racket. Such a two-dimensional position has not yet allowed any development of an internal third position, which is able to observe. The insistence on being in the right and superior position is still clung to. I wondered how much these religions were clung to by the earlier migrants, in the face of the strangeness of an alien place. As they made fences in the unknown land, they also fenced-in their minds, shoring up insecurity.

I mentioned earlier Veronica Brady who said that the "God we worship is the God of the winners, who has little mercy for the losers". What kind of god is that? What fear and vested interest of our own do we align with so that we may also by association stay close to such a king of the castle and be protected from the fate of the dirty rascal? In a social climate of growing fear and insecurity it is not surprising that this way of being and behaving grows. Donald Meltzer writes the following about tyranny in his 1973 book, *Sexual States of Mind*: "May it not be that the tyranny and the ultimate perversion, war, is forced upon us by accumulations of unconscious terror and depressive anxiety constantly generated by activities which appear innocent to common sense, where we 'know not what we do?' We continue to be ignorant of our ignorance. In our inability to imagine ourselves in someone else's position, we defensively project onto them. To get to know how it is for the other could be distressing, painful, guilt-inducing, depressing, overwhelming" (p. 150).

The case of Rob Riley

At this point, I would like to bring in the much publicized story of Rob Riley, from Perth, Western Australia. It is tragic and is an example of what many of these half-caste children experienced. It also brings up issues about how delicate people who have suffered trauma and displacement may be, underneath the persona of a professional role. Education and adherence to the white system is not sufficient to hold a fragile self together when old wounds are opened up and there is a break in the usual support system of daily life. I shall return to this issue when I have reminded you of Rob Riley's story.

He worked with Jerry Hand (a politician who held the portfolio for Aboriginal Affairs) on behalf of Aborigines. He came into the headline news when he hanged himself. It is a tragic story and an example of how his early experiences could not be dealt with when he tried to face them in adult life.

In 1955, when he was 8 months old, Rob Riley was taken away from his mother to Sister Kate's Children's Home (in Perth). They did not see each other again until he was 9 years old. He had a white father, so was taken away to be assimilated. "If I had a bit of white blood, I had a bit of a chance." His mother was 18 years old, with no means of supporting herself. "The Welfare lady came and took him and that was the last I saw of him. I'd try and get a glimpse of him at the home and was sent away and told not to go" (ABC, 1996). Similar things happened at this time to poor white girls who had illegitimate babies. Irish girls who worked in a laundry were treated in a similar way before and after their illegitimate babies were taken away. The 1950s was a different time from the 1990s. This was before John Bowlby's seminal work on attachment had influenced institutions such as hospitals and children's homes.

Rob Riley was told he was an orphan found abandoned, on a track. He said Sister Kate's Children's Home was a sterile environment, with no love or affection. The boys in the home were to be trained as farm hands and the girls as domestics. This was the usual purpose. This was so for poor white children as well. When Rob Riley was 9, an uncle visited the home and recognized him as related. Rob was "confused and ecstatic". The tug of war over him lasted for more than two years. His mother was told to stay away and not visit. In the 1960s the official policy changed, so children could be kept with their families. At the age of 12½ years, he went to live with his mother and her new family. He was shunted around the extended family as his stepfather was violent towards him. The town where they lived was very small, with "back-blocks racism". He moved to Perth in 1972, and two years later he married. He went into the army—a well-worn path for children from institutions, "where you got fed decently". In the late 1970s he went to university at the age of 25, studying psychology and becoming a political activist. He became a spokesman for Aboriginal land rights. He had learnt to be articulate. This is not usual for many Aborigines, who say they are not "big talkers, and white people talk all the time". The National Aboriginal Council consumed his life, to the detriment of his marriage and family. His work was totally demanding; he had a cause to fight for.

Under the new Freedom of Information Act, he was able to read his file from Sister Kate's Home. He was devastated to read how often his mother tried to visit and was turned away. He'd been told he belonged to nobody at all. At the time of the Human Rights and Equal Opportunity Commission Inquiry (HREOC, 1997), the impact of telling his story was too much for him. For the first time he confessed how he had been raped at Sister Kate's. "Who wants to hear?

It is too painful, no one wants to know and no one can say sorry."
This was quoted in the television programme about Rob Riley's life.
At that time there were fifty "take-away children" who told of sexual
assaults, and the blinds had to be drawn down before they could tell
anything. They could only speak of their horror and shame in the
dark, where they could not be seen and feel looked at.

"The whites would come and take us out for the weekend or a
holiday and we didn't want to go, because it was so bad." (British
children in other Homes described similar happenings.) Some of
the staff were involved. Rob Riley broke down at the launch of the
Inquiry. He got drunk and drove his car, refusing to be breathalyzed.
Despair leading to drinking is common. Rob Riley lost his licence.
He booked into a psychiatric unit, suffering from clinical depression.
He was said to be "driven by unbearable life experiences". He was
sacked from the legal service and became dispirited. He felt a need
to belong and needed to identify with the Aboriginal people. He
went to work as a consultant at the Mangoori centre, which was in
the old Sister Kate's building. He was drawn back to the place of his
misery and abuse, where he hanged himself. He had held himself
together by finding a cause to fight for. His overwhelming despair
finally broke through.

From storytelling to working through

Rob Riley's is a tragic story, about just one of the 30,000 children
who were taken away from their parents. It also alerts us to the dangers of thinking that telling one's story is healing in itself. Earlier
I mentioned Freud's understanding of repetitions in our lives and
through generations, with a need not only to remember, but to work
through. Freud knew long ago that catharsis alone is not sufficient
to heal. Psychoanalytic work is based on the knowledge that it often
needs time and skill to enable working through to take place. Intellectual education without emotional education does not strengthen
the ego from within. It can provide a false self, an armour, that in
circumstances as have been described here are not sufficient to hold
a person together. The severe problems with addiction in Aboriginal
communities are related to this. The pain and the guilt are tangled
up with the perpetrators. We cannot bear to see what has been done

to us ourselves, when those who cared for us in many ways also abused us. Often the people who were the carers and abusers had not been cared for themselves. It is not surprising that the unbearable pain is blotted out with alcohol or petrol sniffing. The vicious cycle continues, as those who become addicted are blamed for their situation, without thought about why it has arisen.

Well-meaning officials and helpers from various backgrounds have observed that Aborigines with such past "stories" repeat them through the generations. In despair after telling their stories and seeing the perpetuating troubles, Aborigines withdraw from schemes set up to help. The helpers, who desire to repair the tragedies of the past, which affect the present, are distressed and feel let down. Professionals from various fields need to link together to bring their different understandings and ways of thinking to the problems and issues. There has been a great development, particularly since the Vietnam War, in understanding trauma and how this can be met in individuals and groups. Emotional pain needs time and attention with someone who can bear the pain and allow gradual unfolding of the person's narrative at his or her own pace, in a safe place.

There have been and still are questionable political agendas, empire-building, and vested interests in various professional and political groups. Human frailty and corruption do not belong to any one group, whatever colour our skin may be. The question of continuing dependence on white people to run even a shop in an Aboriginal community raises more questions. Looking at group co-dependency and the interweaving patterns that have become habitual is another challenge. In these areas there is also a need to get beyond the polarization of two positions and create a space that could allow a different kind of exploration to take place.

The woeful history of attachment in these institutions, where, instead of substitute healthy bonding, often deprivation and abuse developed, was brought to light in the "Deaths in Custody" inquiry. (Reconcialiation and Social Justice Library, 1991). Richard Franklin's 1996 film *No Way to Forget* showed us the plight of young Aborigines in prison. I have heard him speak of the agony he went through during the investigation and film-making. He conveyed a clear sense of belonging to the Yorta Yorta people of Victoria. He speaks the language and knows where his family and ancestors came from, describing where his land is. Therefore, he does not feel uprooted, and he has also done creative work in music and film-making. He conveyed a sense of self linked to these factors and his meaningful work, which is valued in the white world (his film received an award in Cannes).

Our understanding of attachment theory as it has developed since John Bowlby's post-war work helps us to see how damaged many of these separated children became. There were no internal resources for enough resilience to develop. Neither was there a helpful external culture for them to belong to. Similar stories were told by the British children who were brought out to Australia as child migrants. But they were not caught between two worlds in the same way as were the Aboriginal children. White established society did not embrace the part-Aboriginal children with a desire to accept them. Aboriginal families accept anyone—including those from the Stolen Generation—who can establish a connection, however white their skin may be. They are often welcomed with an affection that they did not find in the institutions. Where white children had been brought up by Aboriginal servants, they also were embraced with this connection.

There were some situations where there was a different kind of foster care, which was not cruel, and these children then went on to experience different familial connections. A positive belief in a Christian religion also gave to some a sense of belonging. As with black Americans, sport and music remain areas where one can find acceptance and appreciation. The difficulty is that the Aboriginal assimilation policy was aimed at their performing the labouring and domestic work of a poor white class. However, they often were not accepted by the white community even at school. It affects one's psyche when the group culture and the country look down on you and treat you badly.

Concluding remarks

I have drawn attention to the King of the Castle and Dirty Rascal game in relation to history. It has value when played as a child, with a sense of excitement and gaining control. It is different when, as adults, we maintain these positions internally and externally. I am keenly aware that this is present today. I believe that psychodynamic understanding has valuable offerings to make to our social situations and systems beyond our consulting rooms.

Valerie Sinason (1994) talks of the invisibility of the survivors of abuse and traumas. No one really wants to know what they have gone through, no one can bear it or believe the reality of what has been experienced. There seems to be a fear of contamination. This even happens when people have life-threatening illnesses. This invisibility to those of us who live in middle-class white suburbs of cities on the fringes of this continent is real. Is it real in our consciousness? Alice Miller reiterates the theme in her books of how our social community hides the suffering of the humiliated and manipulated child." We cannot bear to be in touch with this in ourselves.

There is a history of black people being treated like children by white people—not just here, but also in America and Africa. When Nelson Mandela left prison, he was given short trousers to wear, because black people were treated like children and called boy. In Mandela we see an example of someone who, after years of resentment at his treatment when he was in prison, realized that in maintaining this state of mind he was imprisoning his mind, which gave power to those who put him there. He was able to make a choice to be free. His example of creating a third position in his mind, able to witness what he was doing and do something differently, shows a maturity where a different aspect of himself rules him from the one before. It also shows maturity in a group to choose this quality of leader, one who does not seek the justice of revenge but, rather, gives hope for something different that inspires, instead of fostering fear. The truth can also set you free; yet, if we use this as a quick-fix slogan, it can be destructive in the extreme. Defences are built to protect, and to try to break them down prematurely is not helpful. Without the right timing, unwelcome knowledge is repelled.

However, the tragedy for victims, who have suffered personally and within a culture and society, is that the destruction often turns on themselves. We see this with Aboriginal self-destruction in various forms, one of them being alcoholism and the ensuing violence. There may be some understanding of this as a symptom, that we drown our sorrows in drink. The same clouding of the mind happens with petrol sniffing, which destroys the brain. The frequent response is contempt. The behaviour is seen as added proof of their being dirty rascals beyond the pale.

The perpetrator who disowns the unwanted lost child within prevents the working through of the repetition of behaviour. The patient who became an adherent to the cult of psychoanalysis had a disgust for anyone disabled or black. He had dreams of his Aboriginal self showing his impoverished emaciated state. He could not bear to think about his dreams and deposited them into my mind for me to bear. The psychoanalytic work and the meeting with these aspects of himself, as seen through his dreams, enabled gradual awareness to develop. A minority of successful kings of the castle who need dirty rascals to maintain their position find themselves undergoing such personal inner work. The Lost Children in the perpetrators remain immured, not known within themselves, staying ignorant of their ignorance. The defences are kept strong and the fear of contamination is high. One can only imagine the degree of pain and guilt that causes the continual dumping of blame and disowning of such unwanted aspects of the self onto others.

We know that perpetrators, when they begin to face what they have done, can die because the mind cannot bear to know what they have done. Arthur Hyatt Williams, a doctor and a psychoanalyst, told me (in a personal communication) that when working with murderers in Wormwood Scrubs Prison in the United Kingdom, he found that at this point of realization some of the men died of a heart attack. Gitta Sereny (1974) in her interviews with Franz Stangl, the commandant of Treblinka concentration camp, had a similar experience. It is understandable that there is such resistance to the truth. The guilt at what one has done is unbearable. The mind cannot hold it. The body carries the brunt of it. Nowadays, I believe, there is a danger that our fears can make us all bystanders in our social realities.

The history of ownership and misuse of children is universal and ancient. Perpetrating these abuses can be seen as belonging to arrested and perverse stages of emotional development. Aborigines viewed themselves as connected to all life forms, a different way of belonging to the earth and its creatures than possessing them. Such beliefs are interestingly akin to new scientific theories of an interconnecting web and of the earth as a living Being, which the scientist James Lovelock (1987, 1988) has named *Gaia*. Perhaps, like Rainer Maria Rilke in his *Duino Elegies*, "we don't feel at home in our interpreted world". Before we interpret we need to give time and be present to the other. When the other is utterly foreign, it can be alarming to the point of feeling mad. It is very difficult to be truly present without trying to impose one's own ordering prematurely in one form or other. I hope that by bringing some psychoanalytic understanding to this theme, I have been able to be present with you in thinking about human suffering, which is part of our history.

I would like to close with the following quotations from Bion (1978, pp. 290, 291): "The fundamental problem is, how soon can human beings reconcile themselves to the fact that the truth matters? ... The fear of knowing the truth can be so powerful that doses of truth are lethal. ... Our fear may be just as great as the client's."

In relation to this vast and painful subject, we know this to be true: children lost between two worlds, often holding terrible grief, mirror our out-of-touchness and need to embrace the dark, where we may indeed begin to see.

Postscript

Since the time of presenting this paper, I have had further thoughts and experiences relating to this theme, which give rise to additional perspectives.

Notes

1. The talk was given at an Open Day for the public at an Australian Psychoanalytical Society annual conference in 1998 in Adelaide. The theme for the day, "The Stolen Generation", was a response to the "National Inquiry into the Separation of Aboriginal and Torres Strait Islander Children from Their Families." The report was entitled *Bringing them Home*. This inquiry was undertaken by the Human Rights and Equal Opportunity Commission. The inquiry was requested on 11 May 1995, and the Report was published on 5 April 1997. The two other speakers on this day were Judith Brett, Associate Professor in the Politics Department of La Trobe University, Melbourne and Raimond Gaita, Professor of Philosophy at the Institute of Advanced Research, Australian Catholic University, Melbourne, and King's College, London.

2. It is important to draw attention to the work of Vamık Volkan and others on transgenerational transmission of trauma (e.g., Volkan's 2004 book, *Blind Trust*), which has been extensively written about subsequent to the presentation of this paper in 1998.

3. Karen Armstrong was a young novice in the 1950s, before the Vatican Council began in 1962. The Aboriginal children were removed and taken into the care of religious orders and government homes after 1911, when

"protectionist legislation" existed throughout Australia, except Tasmania. "The Protection Board was given power to control Indigenous people. . . . The Chief Protector was made legal guardian of all Aboriginal children, displacing the rights of parents" (HREOC, 1997, p. 28). Tasmania insisted until the 1960s that they had no Aborigines, "just some half-caste people". This went on until 1967 but only really began to change after the Whitlam Government was elected in 1972. The forcible removals went on between 1910 and 1970.

4. At the time of presenting this paper, there was an upsurge nationwide, following the publication of the *Bringing Them Home* report, urging the government to apologize to the Aboriginal people for the Stolen Generations. The capital cities of each State were filled with marches and banners saying "Sorry". There were Sorry books all over the country, which were signed by thousands. It was called "Sorry Business" by the Aborigines. This is a name for mourning loss with ensuing rituals. The prime minister and government refused to say sorry. This refusal was said to be for fear of compensation demands.

5

Coming to terms with the country: some incidents on first meeting Aboriginal locations and Aboriginal thoughts

Craig San Roque

This is a narrative. It follows a somewhat loose, associative track, which may be familiar to those who appreciate those storytelling styles of remote areas where a story may, on the surface, ramble a little and even obscure as much it reveals. The essay is constructed around seven incidents but includes some introductory history with retrospective commentaries on the incidents. It may be read as a reflection upon experience in indigenous Central Australia by a psychoanalytic practitioner reorienting his craft to accommodate to contemporary psychosocial situations in an unfamiliar cultural milieu. It makes no pretence to certainty.

The seven main incidents, which are summarized in the last section, each have associations and implications or add, in a cumulative manner, something to the interwoven themes. An attempt is made in the last section at an overall formulation of what may have been going on, but this is tentative and begs questions.

The author deliberately "gives himself away" in a bid to learn from experience and show a process that, while perplexing, may help to reveal something of little-understood procedures of cultural transference and countertransference, as the author tries to come to terms with living and working in a country that is impregnated with the Aboriginal mind, experience, and consciousness.

A word of caution

Readers should note that the fragment of the Warna Tjukurrpa reported herein is not the complete saga and is reproduced, in response to the long-established desire of the traditional custodian, to educate and inform non-Aboriginal doctors and therapists and stimulate interest in appreciating how indigenous healing procedures work. The purpose is to promote a recognition of indigenous methods and thinking about therapeutic practices and demonstrate how black and white practitioners try to reach some reconciliation in the current fraught situation of rapid change and de-integration of culture. This work is offered in a spirit of exchange between practitioners. In order to protect the integrity of people or places, some details of sites and story have been obscured but not so far as to substantially alter the value of the discussion and the point of the exercise.[1]

Between the European dream and indigenous Australian dreaming: psychic pain

This chapter is a segment of a larger project, a personal and professional preoccupation with the problem of psychic pain—in particular, with the peculiar way in which we fashion psychic pain in the Australian milieu and how this affects the way psychotherapists train and practise. I invite the thought that Australian psychotherapy should be oriented to the specific psychic realities of the Australian milieu, that psychotherapeutic methods must be developed to meet contemporary Australian psychocultural states. I sense that we must study the Australian culture, its psychic history, and its contemporary distress in order to arrive (continually) at diagnostic positions that recognize the specific nature of the "national psyche" as well as the individual disorders of psyche. We have to attain a cultural meta-diagnosis and redevelop (perhaps) our practice methods accordingly. The psychological dynamics of Australian social systems are not simple. Many institutionalized assumptions about the causes and cures of contemporary psychic ills may require rethinking.

I suggest that psychotherapy training and practice can become a "false-self" enterprise when carried unchallenged from the cultural cradles of Europe, the United States, and spiritual Asia. This is a matter that must concern those who inherit custodianship of the psychoanalytic tradition. The mind stuff of Australians is patterned, of course, by the European/US/Asian heritage grafting into the Australian space; I am not advocating isolationist psychic protectionism but, rather, reflective discrimination about the use of our therapeutic craft in the service of a polymorphous Australian psyche.

For instance, there must be specific qualities to psychic pain as experienced in Australia. What are these qualities? How unconscious are we of the nature of this pain—collective and individual? What symbolic forms does it take? How might this differ from the psychic pain created in the historical matrices of the northern hemisphere, or to the east and west of our surrounding oceans?

I suggest that the nature of antipodean psychic pain begs to be studied as a professional, psychoanalytic enterprise. The matrix of pain is formed, no doubt, partly from physical and mental disturbances in the relationship between the original inhabitants and the eighteenth-, nineteenth-, and twentieth-century settlers—the period of the "the displacements". But the detail of that psychic impact is still crude: it is debated, for instance, in court through the Stolen Generation cases and is referred to by expert witnesses for various reports and Royal Commissions, but it is still not adequately included in the acknowledged repertoire of therapeutic procedures. Since we rely upon an American-generated guidebook to the psyche (*DSM-IV*), it may be some time before a way is found to include local detail of psychic pain into the mainstream therapeutic procedural manuals. Subtle detail becomes trivialized, for instance, as "the black armband version of history". Truthful details of the nature of mutual distress sparked between the clash of the European dream and the indigenous dreaming hardly get a chance to be held and attended to before desperate reactive defence systems are brought into play, on both sides of the border.

The revolutionary element that characterized early psychoanalysis seems to have been lost. Over time, psychoanalysis seems to have become no more and no less than the handmaiden of the Caucasian psyche, a self-reflective meditative method to help ease "discomfort", a mental playground of the intellectually cultivated. Is that the end of the psychoanalytic revolution? I believe, though, that we have a challenge yet to meet at home, not as handmaidens of the European psyche, nor worker bees for the North Americans, but as therapists to an active Australian national condition, a psychic pain of our own, the shapes of which are prefigured in the themes set out in the 2000 Australian Psychoanalytical Society Conference and signalled through its title, "This Whispering in Our Hearts". For me, "This whispering . . ." has a double meaning. It includes the intimations of inner distress about the indigenous–settler relationship, which Henry Reynolds (1999), Peter Read (1999), and their companions research and articulate in their histories of Australia. These investigators, along with the late Mr Eddie Mabo, have performed an authentic psychoanalytic act, making the unconscious conscious.[2]

"This whispering . . ." also refers to intuition. Disciplined use of intuition has been useful before in reading the entrails of a collectively unconscious political state. Mythological Teiresias was particularly good at it, helping Oedipus sort out a few home truths. Jung, Freud, and comrades helped to systematize intuitive skill while deciphering some psychic complexes of their own Europe in turmoil. I anticipate with pleasure the challenge of making systematic attempts to develop intuitive capacities to apply within our peculiar milieu. Perhaps our joint Teiresian psychoanalytic project could be named, "Reading the entrails of Australia".

A fearful thing, my country

"It is a fearful thing to fall into the hands of the living god;
but it is a much more fearful thing to fall out of them."

D. H. Lawrence

I am concerned with a question. It is a kind of Winnicottian, immigrant question: "This pain, did we find it here or did we create it?" The history of Australia has concerned itself with progression in the uses and abuses of the country's spaces; a country apparently open for discovery, for impingement and exploitation. Perhaps it is also a history of people who have been falling into the "hands of the living God".

The avuncular Devonshire doctor, Donald Winnicott, inheritor of English enclosures and displaced children, wrote, in his technical papers on psychotherapy, about a "space" that is created between parent and child. Winnicott calls it "potential space"—a mysterious, invisible yet utterly palpable space of interaction between one human and another. Between a mother's breast and a child's per-

ceptual system a mental space slowly forms itself wherein psychic
adventures begin. In this space, play begins and continues until it is
transformed into shared culture. People of a shared culture form us
and inform us. The "potential space" between intimate people is full
of imagination and psychological transformation. Sometimes a cultural group attains, by joining "living hands", a "potential" space that
holds hearts and souls, feeds imagination, and sustains psychological
transformation. This is a maturational environment. Sometimes a
cultural group creates such spaces that are destructive and attains
self-destruction.

We have to ask ourselves about the nature of the "potential space"
that is being formed here, in Australia. There is an optimistic fantasy
generated that, between us, we can create Australia as a place to
play—with money and land, sun and sand, freedom and opportunity,
and so forth. Well, why not? But there is another dimension to the
space we are making.

In the dark matter of the Australian universe, there has been
shaping itself, over these same years, a culture of psychic pain. Certainly, something less than promising has formed between the original inhabitants of this country's spaces and those who are coming
later. It has been stunningly difficult to construct a "potential space"
between the indigenous and non-indigenous cultures. We have not
reached a stage where a "space for play" has been established. Un-
ease about how and what to create as an authentic "potential space"
between black and white manifests in the ambiguities and ambivalence about the use of the country. "Country" is a third element in
the equation of "black" plus "white".

The "hands of the living country" and "the hands of the living
God" may be, for some, somehow, indecipherably, synonymous; or
there may be category confusions whereby people's feelings for what
is sacred and what is not are muddled and contradictory. Sorting out
these muddles is, in my opinion, a psychoanalytic enterprise because
psychological manoeuvres are so much a part of our way of dealing
with the triangular equation: Black + White + Country. To fall into
the country's presence is one matter; to fall out of its living presence
is another.

Themes of being lost and found, being present and absent to
the country, are consistently expressed in various modes by envi-
ronmentally attuned Australian artist/poets, black and white. Our
history, stretched along the 50,000-year-plus Song Line, celebrates

the symbiotic participation with the spirit of the country, and yet so many of us, so oblivious, stumble into and out of each other's "countries", fall into and out of each other's "gods", tumble in and out of each other's mental worlds, and in the process we do strange things to each other. Having the poetry here and ignoring it is one of the "strange things we do".

If one is an Australian, one becomes a party to doing these strange things. You and I participate in finding and making the psychic pain of the region. If you are an Australian therapist you may be developing a therapeutic response to the local condition, to that specific complex of psychic pain that you and I help to make, simply by being here. It is this problem that the work in this essay is directed towards.

If psychoanalysis was formed out of the catastrophes of Europe, in Australia psychoanalysis may need to reorient in the light of our own peculiar catastrophe. I suggest that it is our job as psychoanalysts to think deeply and act transformatively within our own cultural milieu. I suggest that thinking begins with frank analysis of our own very personal primal experiences of the country. I mean a careful analysis, not only of object relations and family dynamics and individuation politics, but also of what has happened to us ourselves, as we have come to engage with the environmental and psychic conditions of the country.

White chook and Menzies' eggs

A little history

Since our personal histories are implicated in the collective psychological history of Australia and none of us can claim an exemption, each history must contribute to describing the strange region of psychic pain and pleasure that swells between the indigenous Dreaming and the Caucasian dream. Even absenting oneself from that between-space has its impact. My story is, basically, a story of trying not to be absent.

I came on a visit to Central Australia in 1988, two years after returning from London and the completion of my psychoanalytic apprenticeship. I recall now with some nostalgia the linoleum sobriety of the Tavistock Centre, the gritty alleys of Kilburn, the leaf-strewn avenues of Belsize Park, the ivy frontage of Freud's refugee house, the hushed domains of Analytical Psychology—all those subdued enclosures, Socratic academies of the psyche. And those endless bee-line travels across the city from consulting room to consulting room. Twenty years under northern clouds of unknowing doing what? Suffering the archaeologies of the couch? Delicately brushing layers of illusion? Learning to use the traditions? Escaping Antipodean reality? Who knows? It happened. It was useful, and it's over.

Now I spend hours in a yellow Toyota truck. My landscapes are long red ranges and endless skies. My "consulting rooms" are strewn with sand and detritus. I am familiar with dark eyes, sidelong glances, and designs in red dust. I work in no visible enclosures. I have distances, and I have intimate conversations with traumatized black-skinned youth and old men lamenting patiently. I am alert for violence from unexpected quarters, and for beseeching humour. I act yet apparently do nothing, powerless, each day a witness to passive calamity. I perform my therapeutic duties of care a long way from sobriety, from the academy and the couch. I am rethinking how we came into being and why.

In 1967, I left Australia for the first time, struggling (at 24) to shake myself free from an oppressive cultural somnolence that, throughout the Menzies Government era, had settled its great white breast of chook upon the soul of the country. The pervasive stifling experience was probably some almost unconscious, nationally sanctioned, attempt at reassurance after enduring the predations of those "civilized" beings of Europe and Japan. That outbreak of collective psychotic omnipotence so effectively activated in ordinary folk the primal horror of being human and being eaten that we withdrew into "freeze" behaviour for a bit. In retrospect, the nesting of the Menzies era may have been a necessary period of incubation that Gough Whitlam's flamboyance brought to an end. In England the reaction to the horror and subsequent reparative attempt was more variedly different from the suppressive manoeuvres undertaken by the Anglo–Australian establishment. In England I encountered intense disciplined introspection (psychotherapy flourishing) and extraverted cultural deconstruction and revolution (the youthful spiritual/political explosions). I found benefit, stimulation, and direction. I recall a contradictory detachment from the preoccupations of Australia as well as a restless desire to bring back home some of the introspective discipline and some of the cultural revolution.

Senior members of my family circle were actively engaged in the politics of indigenous issues. However, having entered the labyrinth of psychoanalysis around 1972, I had no choice but to serve my internal time. I emerged from that labyrinth fourteen years later, in 1986. I may have learned to deal with some kind of minotaur, but I also had a feeling that half my substance was still missing. Nevertheless there was much psychotherapeutic tradition to expound and practise, so back home in Sydney I unpacked my basket and began handling Menzies' chicks, grown up now, but many—the women particularly—still feeling stifled, addled. It was good-enough work, and I had the good fortune to be of service to a number of remarkable people, some of whom were also distressingly aware that a part of their substance was missing. There was also among us this undertone of elusive distress, this "whispering in our hearts".

Hearing voices

"Are you hearing voices? Yes, I am hearing voices. Clear voices? No, voices of distress. Whose voices? What voices? Ancestral voices . . . something trying to be born . . . something buried. A woman buried . . . I don't know. . . . My life is in ruins. . . ."

As I listened to folk murmuring their discontents about our civilization, I began to differentiate dimensions in the whispering. These are four of those "voices" that are relevant to the themes set for this chapter:

1. *Voices of women:* There was a woman's voice or, rather, the symbolic voice of a culturally "buried woman", a kind of Australian Antigone, emotionally suppressed and walled up, whose suppression generated rages, depression, and laments for a lost feminine self and a lost authentic erotic life. The rage of sexual-abuse accusations and feminist terror during the 1980s was a part of this drama in Australia of Antigone breaking from confinement. Many therapists in Australia have done and are still doing deep and vibrant work with this "voice".

2. *The refugee/immigrant voices:* There was a voice of immigration, the "suitcase stories", the grief of families, countries, and cultures lost and left behind; the residue of trauma from overseas. The phase of serious psychotherapeutic attention to the immigrant/refugee

"voice" in our multicultured forming nation is only just beginning. A psychoanalytic congress could be devoted to this theme
alone.

3. *Indigenous voices:* There was an indigenous "whispering" (and a
   whispering response to it), a request for recognition, visibility,
   and justice, not only by indigenous people but also by those who
   felt and knew that the suppression of the indigenous was a crime
   in the national psyche for which eventually everyone would have
   to answer.

4. *The voice of the country:* There was a voice of the "country" itself. It
   speaks in "country tongues" and the language is hard to decode,
   but it is there, affecting the being of the humans in ways that are
   still waiting to be deciphered.

It may be necessary to comment on the latter theme a little. For
instance, you may have a feeling for the pattern of the countries of
your family's origin. You may know the vocabulary and history of folk
who dwelt within the boundaries of northern climes, mountains, val-
leys, ditches, plains, heaths, fields, beaches. You may know the mood
effects of granite, basalt, mud; the response to forms of flora and
fauna; the poetics and the pragmatics of bird-flock and fish-school
movement; the impact on language of the presence of cattle, sheep,
goats; the implicit psychic formations patterned on enclosure, road,
and streetscapes—architecture shaping itself around the human psyche. Psychoanalysts use this implicit knowledge in the interpretation
of dreams, decoding symbolic communication or detecting when an
inner landscape is psychotic by scanning the detail against a taken-
for-granted background knowledge.

Among some of the people seeking analysis I found a preoccupation with the Australian environment and the effect of the specific
local character of the ecosystems upon the people. Some were aware
of Aboriginal language and symbolic forms woven with the geography of the country. In the Tjukurrpa texts and diagrams one can
see clearly how the country forms the mind and the mind forms the
country. It does not take much intelligence to see that there is an
entirely different sensibility at work in the indigenous perception
system. We have stumbled into a field of "environ-mental" relativity.
A European-trained analyst scanning his/her own taken-for-granted
environ-mental background may be in dissonance with a reading of

the symbology of the internalized environment of a Southeast Asian, a South African, or an indigenous Australian.

The subtexts of some of the questions, or "voices", I was hearing were, I think, these: Is the Australian environment re-forming my mind? Is the Aboriginal mind leaking into my own? Will it cause me pain? Is the country alive or dead? Am I missing something? Will I ever feel at home here?

In acknowledging that the country has a "voice" I began to wonder if one could find a way to attend, in a systematic manner, to the effect of the country on the mind, the body, and the heart. So I began travelling around.

A first go at the centre

In 1988 I came to Central Australia for the first time. My grandfather had been here in the 1930s looking for the missing gold miner Harold Lasseter and had worked a medical practice in Meekathara, in a remote area in Western Australia. There was a folkloric family connection to the region. For me the entrée was a brief visit to the Pitjanjatjara Lands, a brush against the membrane of Aboriginal Central Australia, still feeling light and half myself, yet attuning to the place, the people, the voices, the gestures, the smells, and the colour. There was a shock of recognition. I found myself inexplicably excited and soothed by the cadence of Pitjanjatjara singing, strangely moved by the patterns of Pintubi central desert art. Moved also by the gracious diplomacy of indigenous older people, and wryly amused at how I was quickly converted into a usable resource.

To convey some sense of the initial experience of entering the psychic grid of this part of the world, I would say that it was as though entering the realm of Bion's beta elements. I encountered in myself, daily, the impact of puzzling unprocessed bits of feeling and perception, primal states and images, loosely bound and unbound, disjunctions, unconnected dream thoughts and myth thoughts; intuitions, fantasy, and delusion muddled with projections of the most naïve and crude kind.

Coming to Central Australia, in 1988, I carried a very specific question that had been troubling me for several years: "If I am to work in Australian reality, what specific psychological experiences must I pass through in order to qualify as an Australian therapist, capable of engagement with the specifics of an Australian psychic pain?"

I believed I would find an answer to this question by placing myself, deliberately and vulnerably, in areas of actual overlap between the European and indigenous reality. I sought a way to do this because I believed, at the time, that the guts of the Australian national psychic problem was to be found where psychological and political tensions about the possession of the country were most acutely felt. The heart of the matter, if you like, was to be found where black blood/mind and white blood/mind most poignantly and vividly mingled. This abrasive and often joyless mingling happens in every city and most country towns, but, geographically, Central Australia is an actual and symbolic locations of overlap. It is a place where things happen.

As one step towards answering the question, I wanted to know, first hand, how a traditional Aboriginal healer was "made", "qualified", and practised. I wanted to see if some kind of partnership between the two differently developed therapeutic methodologies could be achieved. Why? In order, eventually, as a therapist, to be able to handle the psychic conditions and psychic pain that develops from the entanglement of the cultural and racial blood lines. I set about doing this.

Growing small

I recall a dream from early 1988, when these thoughts were emerging but well before setting foot in Central Australia. In retrospect, it seems that answers to the question were beginning to emerge, but these answers were premonitory intuitions, well ahead of my rational comprehension. Were they answers? Well, not really, more like a connecting series of experiences to which I responded in an idiosyncratic way. The cumulative effect was like that of being nudged by a directional wind, led along a track by a wilful companion. A dream I had at that time captures this:

> *I saw myself in the streets of London, witnessing the traditional children's game of "Oranges and Lemons", the tune ringing (nostalgically) in my dreaming ear. Quite suddenly there was change in the set-up and the English rhyme gave way to traditional Aboriginal singing. It was a section*

of a ceremonial song, whose words I did not recognize but I found myself
painted up and on an Aboriginal dance ground, yet unable to make any
sense of the steps required, I still recall the sensation of being so clumsily
inept and disoriented. As a solution to the ineptitude, in the dream, I
transformed into being a small boy, about 10 years old, unmistakably
Aboriginal, and in that position began to learn the steps, as it were, from
the inside.

Some months later, at an event in Pitjanjatjara country, I found
myself on a dancing ground, painted with Emu designs, and being
instructed in the steps. Awkward and out of time, I glanced left and
right at other men for guidance, only to see beside me a small Pitjanjatjara boy, by whom I was humorously but patiently being shown
the steps. I remembered the dream and an influential comment by
Winnicott to the effect that the practice of becoming a therapist is
really about developing the capacity to survive "growing smaller".

In England I had, in a sense, grown up. Now, back on indigenous
land, I felt that to follow the steps of the indigenous/non-indigenous
"dance" I would have to survive "growing smaller". Or even more
likely, as the poet Les Murray (in Tacey, 1995) put it: "Sooner or later
I will have to give blood for dancing here." "Oranges and Lemons"
says it all, anyway. It was a prophetic dream. "You will not make five
farthings and here comes the chopper to chop off your head."

I took this incident as an indication that to pursue further immersion in the indigenous world might seem to be an adventure, it
might even be a psychic necessity with some elements of a romance,
but it meant in fact sacrificing further growing up into becoming a
solid member of the institutions of my profession. Recklessly, perhaps, I chose to continue to pursue the "indigenous-immersion"
option. Secretly, perhaps, I thought I would get away with it and,
within a year or two, would have extracted all the answers I needed
about intercultural therapeutic practice and could settle back into a
mainstream position. I was wrong.

After ten years or more in this place, I still feel as though I am
growing smaller, yet I feel heavier. I feel as though much of the missing substance has slid into place. I don't have that haunting whispering any more. In fact, the normality of my life has been destroyed.
Not much is hidden. I can see the shape of how an indigenous–European combined healing practice might operate, to the benefit of
both black and white "patients" and professionals. We have tried it

out at the Intjartnama rehabilitation centre, and I know how difficult it is to achieve and sustain. I understand something about creating a "potential space" between black and white. I have passed through "naïve awareness" and "magical thinking" and "critical consciousness"—concepts developed by Paolo Freire (1973)—and now operate in these three states simultaneously, some of the time. I enjoy "negative capability", some of the time. I am grateful to Keats and Freud and Jung and the riches of the European cultural traditions. Also, gradually, a specific quality of a "voice" (or communication system) of the country has come to permeate and inform my sensibility, and that of my immediate family, so I am not quite so deaf, dumb, and blind any more. This isn't much, but it is better than being a white chook. I believe that what has happened over those years is a psychotherapeutic act, a third stage in my training. I have been the patient. Who or what, you might ask, has been the therapist?

Like many of my compatriots I was once desperately unconscious of my Australian "real self", discontentedly colluding with a "false self". Nowadays the psychic pain is no longer the pain of obliviousness; it has intensified and has taken on quite discernible shapes. That might be an advance in consciousness. Now and then I experience moments of what tastes like an Australian wasteland. I know, now, many indigenous and non-indigenous "hollow men" who maintain the stream of obliviousness: they have given up holding on to the vitalizing moments, have lost the thread. Many are drunk or dead. I know a few heroic Aboriginal people who have maintained the stream of intermittent continuities, who endure the pain and attend mentally and sometimes physically to their country. These people are the national living treasures. They can be individually named. There are a few thousand such people. They preserve the country. They have no other proper job.

Tjukurrpa and intuition

Tjukurrpa, or Jukurrpa, is a term used in the Pitjanjatjara, Pintubi, Warlpiri group of languages to indicate that unique phenomenon of time and timelessness, story and ceremony, that is known in popular culture as "The Dreaming". Tjukurrpa is the rendition I shall use, for convenience. Altyrre or Alcheringa is the term in Arrernte versions. Tjukurrpa is the pragmatic voice, the geographical articulation, and the mytho-poetic dream thoughts of the country we are presently inhabiting.

The term "intuition" refers to "immediate knowledge or apprehension" or "immediate insight" (*OED*); it is built upon "in+tuition", derived from tutor–tuition, conveying the sense of protection as well as instruction that emerges from a source conventionally located as internal to the human psyche rather than from an externally embodied person or institution. The internal source is conventionally represented culturally as emanating from inner faculties of perception, sensation, thought, and feeling or personified as internalized figures, dream figures, artistic images, guardian spirits, angelic forms, or divine or semi-divine visitations. Von Franz (1999), in *Clearing of Enigmas*, a translation from Arabic of an alchemic text with a commentary, refers to this as a "tutelary spirit". I use this evocative phrase because it conveys the sense of a proactive internal guarding and instructing element that somehow or other manifests itself for the benefit of the recipients or their group, activity, or place. From the etymological definition, then, I derive two senses or activities of intuition that are helpful for our purposes.

The first refers to the arrival of images or elements of thought in one's mind or sensations or feelings in one's body, while in a state of special attentiveness. The images may well present themselves from "external" sources—for example, the flight of a bird, which catches the observer's attention and is read by him or her as conveying meaning. A definition based strictly upon the convention of locations inside and outside the psyche or body may carry confusion. Those of an animistic state of mind may not make a dualistic distinction between inner and outer realities and may read activities in the natural world and in the psyche world as being seamless or interwoven. Moreover, the cultivation of "special attentiveness" may involve specific practices, such as those based on the contemplative disciplines or professional skills. I suggest also that there is a particular mode of attentiveness that can be cultivated by non-Aboriginal people while in the presence of the Aboriginal mind and affairs. This specific Aboriginal-oriented receptive attentive state allows multidimensional communication between people and between the individual and the living environment.

The second aspect of "intuition" is the activity of a "tutelary spirit", in the sense that one seems to be directly shown something for one's learning and possibly protection. A request for such "tuition" as instruction or guardianship may have been passionately made, but it is uncertain as to whether such a request needs to be conscious and deliberate. Sometimes the interventions of a tutelary spirit come unrequested and involuntarily; nevertheless, there does seem to be a kind of semi-conscious receptiveness or attentiveness that pervades the attitude of those who receive such intuitive prompts. One could argue that there is also a possible psychotic faculty at work, but I am not particularly thinking here of more lurid instances of medium-ship that delight the psychic playgrounds. A therapist may regularly make passionate requests and receive intuitive "instructions" while caught up in the process of solving a therapeutic conundrum—that is, while trying to heal. I understand that "passion" can be a quiet and internal process. The operative element seems to be a particular quality of intensity of attention linked to a capacity for allowing a binding of psychic elements—which could be termed "therapeutic eroticism".

The experience of receiving messages from the activity of a "tute-lary spirit" while working therapeutically is not unusual. Indigenous and shamanic healers speak about the presence of and use of such tutelary spirits (*ngkar*) which are often personified and summoned while working with a patient. The *ngkar* spirit is frequently credited with making the diagnosis and directing the cure. Rational therapists might refer to the same experience of receiving "instructions" as mental operations informed by training, experience, and intuitive skills, dismissing the *ngkar* as animistic fictions. However, if *ngkar* exist as actualities, they might be a bit upset by this diminution of their independent and autonomous character.

The use of Bion

Turning now to Bion's well-known algebraic grid map of psychic processes, procedures, and transformations, I think of intuitive activities as involving the following: (1) Premonitory images or communications, likely to be migrating beta elements, which arrive in the container of one's consciousness and are awaiting the next stage in psychological transformation—through the operations of alpha function. (2) These arrivals from the domain of beta, which are pressing consciousness for transformation into conceptions, thoughts, and streams of thought, may be generated by a "passionate coupling of two or more beings" as part of the transference–countertransference binding. (3). The process of receiving, holding, transforming, and doing psychological work on intuitions is constantly vulnerable to "attacks on linking". (The passionate coupling of indigenous and non-indigenous minds may produce most unexpected "conceptions" because the coupling may involve trying to make links between quite different orders of mental reality and different ways of doing transformation work. The inter-cultural transference–countertransference reciprocity may have qualities that are unique to an indigenous–non-indigenous coupling. Furthermore, one needs to be alert to the peculiar and specific manner in which "attacks on linking" occur in the indigenous–non-indigenous coupling interaction.) (4). The activation of a "tutelary spirit" may be seen as "alpha function" being spontaneously activated so that psychological work and transformations can be carried through. (There is a quality of independent action or elusively anarchic wilfulness about the way in which "alpha function" operates, especially within the transference–countertransference milieu, which may give it the appearance of being an independent entity.) (5). I think of the primal active elements of psychic life and death (which may include beta elements and alpha function in Bion's language) as having a tendency to be organized into patterns that Jung preferred to name as "archetypal". The patterning orders may be relative to the uniqueness of a cultural group and the cultural group's experience over millennia. A grasp of psychological patterning process and mythological history and a respect for archetypal tendencies is helpful when working cross-culturally because it allows associative and amplificatory symbolic thinking to develop and mitigates against the fundamentalist tendencies of the monocultured-type brain.

Tjukurrpa and Bion's ordering system of thought process

I have an idea that Aboriginal people, over millennia, have organized the primal bits of human psychological experience into bundles of patterning, as links of story/myth thoughts, which are now codified in Central Australia as Tjukurrpa or "dreaming lines". The ceremonies are possibly where the alpha function operates and collective psychological work is done. The essence of the psychological work has to do with reaffirming a special kind of connectedness.

As I have come to understand it, the essence of Tjukurrpa is a multidimensional pattern of connectedness. The connectedness is a complex of linking lines of sites, lines of "song", lines of kin relationship, along lines of country. This adds up to being a systematic matrix of connections of algebraic complexity, or a multidimensional system of linkage that parallels the neurological patterning of the brain. The Tjukurrpa system is somehow very like the neurological system externalized and set into the geography of the country.

Tjukurrpa is a poetic calculus that serves as the basis for making deductions pertaining to protocols of extended-family relationship, the carriage of law, marriage, cultural and intellectual power and politics, as well as the location of food and water sources. This complex Australian deductive system is not literary, not mathematical, geometric, or scientific in the European sense, nor is it ordered to produce money, goods, and capital according to a European system; nevertheless, it is ordered, it is systematic, and it is organized to produce and sustain life, animal beings, food, knowledge, relationship—that is to say, the capital of a hunter-gatherer society.

Tjukurrpa is complex and internally logical and is represented in multidimensional symbolic patterning. It is artistic. Tjukurrpa can be thought of as revealing the way indigenous poet-thinkers have organized into systems their experience of the primal elements of being human. It is psychological.

Tjukurrpa is evidence of how indigenous people do mental work with inner/outer reality. The activity of ceremony provides a container for an interconnected group to do mental work for themselves, their families, their country, and their culture. Ceremony holds the fabric of indigenous mind together and allows it to be active. Failure to continue ceremony leads inevitably to a disconnectedness of the elements of life, an unbinding, and a dissipation of mental work. A loss of active engagement with a body-based participative symbiosis with the country leads to a failure of psychological vitality. Into this empty vitiated space comes a parasitic culture. Into the established collective "potential space", when absent of ceremonial enactment by which to do psychological work, there leaks the pseudo-intoxications of cheapened alcohol. A false kind of psychological work is done through drunkenness. Drunkenness encourages a pseudo-interdependence upon the drinking kin and the drinking ceremony. The parasitic alcohol culture initiates an "attacks on linking" operation that dissociates country from body and country from mind, a dissolution that is completed by the alcoholic derangement of senses. The absence of a strong Tjukurrpa to counteract this dissolution means that there is no strong mental system that can operate as a collective immune system. Resistance to the drunkenness is therefore left up to individual will and a hard-won individualized consciousness. So far few people have been able to consistently achieve this on their own.

It may become clear from this that I am proposing that Tjukurrpa has a psychological function, the significance of which may be appreciated only by those familiar with psychodynamic theory. Maintenance of Tjukurrpa, through progressive ceremony across country, is a psychological activity that maintains psychosomatic health not only of the people but also of the country and thus of the nation—black and white. Paradoxically, loss of Tjukurrpa makes us all sick.

The incidents I recount go a little way to opening up this idea. They are spoken about here in order to try to get onto the psychoanalytic agenda the fact that the psychosomatic health of indigenous people, of the country, and of non-indigenous people is somehow interrelated. Tjukurrpa—among its other functions—holds, presents, and directs the mental dimension of indigenous life. This is a far more complex matter than meets the eye, and it deserves serious and systematic attention. Ignoring the dynamic existence of Tjukurrpa is another equivalent of the "terra nullius" syndrome. The conversion of Tjukurrpa into a commodity for art money or land dealing is a perversion with psychological implications. In an Antipodean application of the prophetic words of W. B. Yeats, when the Tjukurrpa goes . . . "the centre cannot hold . . . mere anarchy is loosed upon the world . . .".

An incident report

In the following section, I describe six incidents. They are about intuitive processes. They are also about something that makes itself felt when one enters a region that is under the influence of the dreaming of the country.

In April 1990, after the little dancing episode, I visited Central Australia again, with Dr Leon Petchkovsky, a psychiatrist. In Alice Springs, we met up with a Warlpiri man, Andrew Spencer Japaljarri, and things began to happen that set in train a series of visits. These visits were not about the honeymoon of land form, colours of country, and Pitjanjatjara people in benevolent teaching mood. They were about a Persephone-like descent into an indigenous contemporary reality, an introduction to ruthless facts about Aboriginal life and death.

The following incidents took place during the course of one year—from April 1990 to April 1991:

- Petchkovsky's snake dream
- Japaljarri's snake dream Response
- Japaljarri's Warna Tjukurrpa (The Snake Dreaming Story)
- The idea of an Alcohol Story—the Parma Tjukurrpa
- Meeting Old Jungarri
- Walking into a site and meeting Nangala's grief.

This cluster, taken together, demonstrates, among other things, two forms of communication at work in an Australian cross-cultural dialogue. First, the arousal and communication of images that, in a symbolic form, reveal an existential issue or problem. Second, the operation of a "tutelary spirit" at work, instructing and/or guarding. These activities can be placed into a category of intuition, the use of the faculty of intuition being perhaps the dominant mode in communication that also involves, of course, the faculties of sensation, thinking, and feeling and a particular method of perception that allows translations to occur between internal perceptions and external or extroverted perception.

Dreams exchanged

April 1990, Easter. We are in Alice Springs. In the office of the Healthy Aboriginal Life Team. Paintings in Central Desert style vibrate from the walls. Most of them are painted by Andrew Spencer Japaljarri and his family. There are images reflecting social disruption and images of the reactions between black and white societies, images of Aboriginal history, family breakdown, the track of AIDS around the country, petrol sniffing among young people, sad boys, bush foods, and alcohol. This is thinking made visible, diagnostic patterns about a society in transition, iconic imagery mirroring the psychopathology of everyday life in central Australia.

Andrew Spencer Japaljarri is sitting at a desk, his left knee restlessly shaking, his large body's frame in repose, his hand sketching a design but attentive to Leon Petchkovsky's discourse. We are talking about dreams and dream interpretation, comparing European and Aboriginal attitudes. Andrew hints to Leon to give him an example, one of his own dreams. Leon hunches himself on the battered couch, taking a characteristic pose of interior reflection. He recounts a most recent dream. It goes like this:

> *I am lying on the ground, on my back, I am sick. I am somewhere in the desert. I can see a wooden structure, a sort of scaffolding made of poles. Ritual poles. A group of Aboriginal people are approaching. Men and women. They are carrying a snake. Oil is dripping, exuding, from the snake. The Aboriginal people rub the oil into my chest.*

Leon comments that he has had heart problems, a dysrhythmia. He has been having a very difficult time over pressing relationship matters. The dream of being ill and on his back is an accurate statement. Leon finishes his account. He is silent. Andrew nods, noncommittally. There is no idle chatter. The conversations come to a close for the day. We agree to meet the next morning. In the morning, the theme is taken up again of dreams and thinking. Andrew is quite present, more so than the previous day. There has been a change in his disposition towards Leon and myself. He says:

> *I had a dream last night. I saw my father. Jungarrai.* My father has passed away but I saw him in my dream. *He came there* (indicating a position on the ground some way off). *He called me to come to him. He put a snake on the ground and sent it along towards me. He said the snake was for you, for the Kardia* [the whitefellers].

We thought about it. Andrew slowly indicated that he took it to mean that he should develop the relationship with the doctor and his friend, myself. He said that the snake was his own dreaming, a dreaming he carries on from his father and grandfather. It belongs in his family line: a very particular dreaming associated with healing practices, a *ngankari* Tjukurrpa. He would think about it and find out what to do about it.

I absorbed all this. The passion was between Leon and Andrew. The coupling happening there, between them. I hadn't yet felt the passage through the membrane to an internal relationship. We started to talk about drunkenness, about bush foods, about native sugars, Parma, the Warlpiri term denoting "sweet edible substance". He showed us the Parma painting, the brushwork carried out by him under instruction from his mother, Nangala, whose dreaming it was. Japaljarri described the way in which bush sugars were collected from various sources, in this case from a kind of flying ant. He contrasted the sparing use of the rare bush sugars with the indulgent and indiscriminate use of alcohol, also a sugar according to the local way of categorizing foods for Aboriginal uses. There was more talk about paintings and a growing sense of intimacy. Japaljarri unrolled a painting of two snakes travelling. He described the story, the Tjukurrpa. I remembered bits of it that night and made notes. I can't write the full story, that is Japaljarri's own affair. This is an outside description of the pattern, as I heard it at the time, in which Japaljarri described a story that recounted the passage and activities of snakes:

Snake story

A male snake who was dispossessed by two serpentine creatures who came travelling from the east and pushed him out of his own place. He went looking for another place and got tangled up with a female who turns out to be his sister. His overtures towards her are rejected. They fight, at a certain place, rearing up. He comes off badly and hurt, keeps travelling.

His travelling is a saga of continual persecution. He was attacked and attacked many times, in different ways by other creatures. He was a mess. Losing everything that gave him his former shape. Things continue to happen, an increasing intensification of pain and dismemberment.

Finally he comes to rest at a certain place. The snake spirit rests in seclusion, then he slides into a water place and a transformation takes place. Somehow the essence of the snake seems to permeate the water.

The remains of the travelling outcast snake becomes the basis for the practice of a traditional healing lineage. The lineage is that of the storyteller's family line. The story in its first version, as told in translation, is never exactly the same. It is not unusual to have a multiplicity of levels and uses of the story line. When a Tjukurrpa is used as communication or as fragment of an instruction, then one must be very cautious in recording and saying: "this is the story". This is why I say that these fragments must be treated with the same respect and same caution as one might treat a reported section of an analytic conversation or "case material". I am not writing anthropology here. Internally, for me, the stark imagery of the story becomes active. I feel myself being caught, a passion emerging, and an exhaustion. Taking in these stories is hard work.

Sugar and alcohol

We have lunch and come back. There is more talk about alcohol and drunkenness and the difficulty that the Healthy Aboriginal Life Team are having getting through to people about alcohol. Japaljarri indicated that the Yappa and Anangu (Aboriginal people) do not think about it in the same way as Europeans do. They seem to miss something that the Europeans know about. In their minds, Yappa don't see it, don't have any power over it.

Japaljarri says this:

This painting is about Parma. A sugar-ant, different to honey ant. It's like a fly.

We have the song for Parma and for strengthening Parma. We haven't got the song (Tjukurrpa song) to send the Whiteman's Parma (grog) away.

We can't get rid of this one. We can only strengthen the good Parma [i.e., the bush sugars found in native plants and insects].

The songs for petrol and alcohol must come from the whiteman, or must dream new ones.

The children can't save the world. You, the white people, have lost your dreaming, maybe you don't know the songs for alcohol

and petrol. You have to learn your songs, your whitefeller Tjukurrpa.

To turn to us . . . for the songs is not right. To expect me to
dream petrol and alcohol songs is too much.

Later Japaljarri asked straight out, "Do whitefellers have Tjukurrpa
for Parma (grog)?" I exchanged glances with Petchkovsky. I said,
"Yes." Japaljarri said, "Well maybe you'd better do and get it. That's
your responsibility." I nodded, "All right, Japaljarri."

We left Alice Springs to go back to work in Sydney. Things dropped
out of mind. The mental ambience of the city is different from that
in the desert. Different priorities. But I keep wondering about the
psychic states of intoxication. Some kind of internal coupling is occurring between the images of a dismembered snake, the sugar-ant
ceremony, and a vaguely emerging image of Dionysus.

A few months later Japaljarri rang Petchkovsky. He told him he'd
thought about the dreams. He reckoned that Petchkovsky and I
should come and visit again. He would take us to visit his other
father. We had to see a few things. We went in October. We held
a workshop on psychological themes for the Alice Springs Jungian
study group, an experimental investigation into the psyche of place.
Andrew picked us up. We drove through the afternoon, on a rough
road, 300 km or so, into country we had never seen before, to visit
Andrew's family and the old man. The country was very dry, simmer-
ing, a few isolated clouds floating in from the northwest.

By now the relationship protocol was being established. Petchkovsky and I had been placed into the Warlpiri kinship as sons of
Japaljarri. This is a complex matter, the meaning and obligations of
a non-Aboriginal placed into the Aboriginal kinship system. For the
purposes of this story, it meant we could be taught about and assume
a certain responsibility for the Tjukurrpa about the unfortunate
snake. The visit to the old Jungarrai—Larry Spencer, Andrew's late
father's brother—was, I think, intended to confirm this responsibility
and give us an opportunity to see if we wanted to handle it.

Milky Way

The meetings themselves seemed to be a very simple yet delicate exchange that mostly centred around Jungarrai drawing and retelling

parts of the snake Tjukurrpa. There were no startling events, simply a long drive through country and two meandering conversations—one deep into the night, mostly with Japaljarri telling stories and describing his vision of things to come; the other in the morning, where Jungarrai carefully drew the snake from the story, described various sites, and spoke quietly about the snake's trials and travels. There were also stories about the Milky Way and how this track of stars figures in the Jungarrai/Japaljarri system.

I remember rusted wrecked vehicles on their backs, golden red in the morning light and in the sunset. I remember dogs and wind whipping plastic bags across desolate dust. I remember an old man's hand gently laid on my elbow and his intense concentration as he drew the travels of that snake and spoke about crossing country, mountains, and the stars—the Milky Way. I remember looking up into the spectacular iridescent Warlpiri night sky and tracking that encircling conflagration of Hera's spattered breast milk. I remember a black billy tea, and flour, and shiny bright eyes of the young girls who came to peer at us, greeting us as new-found family members and resources.

Then a farewell, and Leon and I giving Jungarrai a present of a new cowboy hat, belt, and trousers, and then another long drive to other sites, visiting Andrew's father's grave, an isolated, windswept awesome place overshadowed by a range of hills. Climbing, looking, absorbing, settling down, and then moving towards another place and then suddenly back to Alice Springs, driving into the dark, sitting in the cab with a rifle, alert for kangaroo on the road. This was to be the last and only time we met this distinguished artist and cultural custodian whose paintings are so well known. His spectacular co-work on the Milky Way with Paddy Sims and Paddy Stewart is a masterpiece, now in the National Gallery, Canberra. He died a week after our visit. Quietly, so we are told. His time up.

The reason Japaljarri gave for the unexpected return to the town was to keep ahead of a threatened rainstorm. The dry sky had given way to the rolling darkness of rain.

The world? Who made it?

I wrote about this trip in the script for a one-hour television documentary, *Sugarman Story*, in the section, "Travels of Dionysus". These are extracts from Scene 1, Central Australia. It will give a glimpse and maybe a mood.

"You remember," I said, "there was someone here, singing the morning star."

And I said, "I am going to find him".

Well I did, but he was singing not just one star, but the whole Milky Way. There he was sitting on the ground, wearing an old cowboy hat. There were two sheets of corrugated iron by an over-turned motor car and a black dog in the morning sun.

"Oh," he said, "the stars, the stars, he said, and the snake."

* * *

"Look," I said to the old man, singing the Milky Way. "This world . . . did you find it like this . . . or did you make it?"

"The snake," he said, "the old snake, he made it".

"And you," I said, "who made you?"

"Me," he said. "I'm him," he said, "that's me."

He touched me on the elbow, just like that, the softest touch in the world, just like the morning star or the brush of the Milky Way. An old man's hand which placed me solidly on the solid ground of this continent.

"Thank you," I said. "Here's a new belt and cowboy hat."

* * *

He died a week later, he lay down and died. A Jungarrai man at the end of his Milky Way. They go like that, they go quietly, the grandfathers of the world.

* * *

Down in the creek, down in the apocalypse, the police have arrived.

These things happen. Her face is battered in. She is reading the lips of the dead.

I think the word she is reading is oblivion.

* * *

An old man is singing the milky way.

Someone is remembering to read the lips of the grandfathers of the world.

Some young men are traveling.

They are trying to remember . . . something.[3]

Two more developments

After this October 1990 trip, two things began to happen. I began to take seriously the task of "going to get" a European "dreaming" story related to experiences of intoxication. This, as you may remember, was Japaljarri's suggestive remark in April that year about the absence of a Tjukurrpa for drunkenness. This led to an investigation into the matrix of the Dionysian legends and myths that emanate from and around the Mediterranean basin and the Black Sea. These are the original locations of the wine-making area and the mythology that bubbles along with that most delighting and bitter of intoxicating spirits. Dionysus is presented in vivid theatrical incarnation in Euripides' *Bacchae*. His behaviour and his entire family and life saga can be seen as an elaboration on the varieties of intoxicating experience. Taken together, his life and travels form a powerful structure of story that is akin to the structure and power of Australian dreaming mythology. Maybe some Aboriginal groups have a fermentation process, and a story to go with it, but nothing as visible and powerful as the European's experience. Japaljarri was right: we, the Europeans, have evolved a coded mental structure for the uses and abuses of alcohol and its effects. Nowadays we play with rational alcohol-counselling-speak and an AA mythology, but there is an older mytho-poetic form woven into the oral traditions of our pre-Christian ancestry. The European story is not a secret. Though it may have been a mystery cult at certain times, it can be told. How to tell it and to whom was to be a matter that preoccupied me for the next ten years.

I also began to feel, as a second theme, that the snake story, to which we had been introduced, was taking on a life of its own in my affairs. The details of this effect cannot be recorded here, but the process was some sort of unsolicited identification, whereby enactment in the Tjukurrpa narrative began to occur in my own and Petchkovsky's lives in such a way that it seemed that we were being absorbed into that narrative or being instructed by it. I do not think that identification with a story, as such, is unusual. I have experienced a similar process when working with myth. Nevertheless, it has been an especially uncanny experience to find one's psychological and physical life aligning itself along the spinal column of an indigenous (non-European) mythic saga whose main thrust is to lay an experiential track for the preparation of a traditional healer. This remains a mystery to me, and it has nothing to do with whitefellers in the act of cultural appropriation. Quite the reverse. The indigenous culture is quite capable of appropriating (non-Aboriginal) individuals to itself.

Thinking with Tjukurrpa

The talks with Andrew Spencer Japaljarri on the absence of Tjukurrpa about the creation and handling of intoxication indicated the effort it seemed to be for traditional indigenous people to think about alcohol-abuse and petrol-sniffing prevention and treatment. It was expressed by him as though there was no "place" for thinking about it properly, no location for thought within the Aboriginal culture. His concern also seemed to be that within the whitefellers' health services, the agents and funding bodies seemed most intent on actions and outcomes and fulfilling moralistic or political desires, but not on creating opportunity for sustained thought processes to be established within the Aboriginal milieu.

Andrew's conversations were woven with images, with symbolic thinking, with fragments of Tjukurrpa and dreamlike images—in short, with a kind of thinking language that psychoanalysts are usually fluent in. This is why I keep feeling a kinship between the language of myth and the language of indigenous thinking. I feel there is a resonance between these two orders of symbolic reality, the detailed elements of which are still being made clear, often against formidable cynical dismissal by rationalist associates interested in "no-non-sense". Few professional health people seem prepared to do the hard work of acknowledging just how rich, complex, and un-European the mental life of indigenous Australia actually is.

I have come, so far, to understand Tjukurrpa as being a pre-existing mental condition or cultural template. Its existence in the collective mind of a cultural group enables a particular kind of collective thinking to take place. Without the template—that is, the relevant Tjukurrpa—it is almost impossible to hold a problem, such as catastrophic intoxication, within the collective mind. The non-existence of a Tjukurrpa seems to leave a "black hole" in the constellations of the mind. Tjukurrpa has a linking function between family groups and between different orders of Aboriginal reality, including setting out the authority upon which to enact law. The existence of

Tjukurrpa within the indigenous collective mind provides the template by which a matter can be handled mentally and physically in a lawful manner. If it does not pre-exist the emergence of a threatening problem, then indigenous authorities have to borrow the European law or invent a new one. It could be said that many Aboriginal people have borrowed and reinvented the Christian Tjukurrpa, in some cases in a life-enhancing way. There might be problems, however, with borrowing and with inventing Tjukurrpa.

This idea of Tjukurrpa as a mental template needs more investigation, perhaps by way of the psychoanalytic work developed from Bion, on thought, thought disorder, the absence of thought, and the existence or non-existence of mental containers. Tjukurrpa is, in a sense, a mental container, located both geographically and internally to the thinker/custodian. Thinking has a very particular way of occurring within indigenous circles; it has a quality and mode of its own that is difficult for those trained in British methodologies to appreciate. Bion may or may not help. We might, with caution, say that the British tradition has attained skill at mental colonization, but not much skill at creating a "potential space" between itself and the indigenous Australian psyche.

Walking into a site

The following incident took place in April 1991, a year after the previous April meeting in Alice Springs. I have to leave out some details that might make a more revealing context for the event. I think, however, that this is an instance of intuition at work through "tutelary spirit".

I was going to Alice Springs for the "Healing Our People" Conference. I got onto the plane in Sydney on crutches. For some weeks I had had a most peculiar pain circumambulating through my body, mostly located in the joints. The symptoms were said to be similar to those of a scorpion bite. I had identified the origin of the condition as a psychic attack inflicted by a patient in a psychotic state of "possession". Medical attention to this idea was difficult to get, and the several doctors and osteopaths I consulted were baffled. Finally, an attentive Chinese Australian GP provided me with a course of Chinese herbal medicines normally prescribed for scorpion bite.

They may have had an effect, but the pain and the circumambulating had intensified. When I stepped off the plane in Alice Springs, I found myself walking normally across the tarmac. All pains had gone. Was it the medicine or was it the country?

I came early with the intention of visiting Japaljarri and reporting on the progress of the Alcohol Tjukurrpa project. Following several tragic deaths in the family,[4] he was in "sorry camp" and was not attending the conference.[5] It was still a good idea to visit and offer our condolence to the family. I set off, with two companions, almost immediately on the long drive. Approaching sunset, about halfway and beginning to enter into the feel of the country, we pulled off the road for a rest and made a fire and tea. We were near a collection of hills. One of us—I forgot who now—suggested that we go for a walk and climb up the hill. We did, looking out over the horizons stretching away towards Warlpiri country, the long lines of the running ranges like travelling shapes of snake and lizard. I remember that we lit a little fire in the hollow of a rock, the quiet, clean smoke curving to the northwest, and we, rimmed with silence, paused simultaneously, sinking into a contemplative state, overwhelmed in the presence of the country. A mob of crows was collecting out to the east, their voices breaking the reverie. Ranald (a writer working on a film script) and I drifted together towards a slender valley scattered with large, fallen rocks. The woman who was the third member of the party had followed her own track, sitting near a small cave, observing a hawk flying and collecting delicate parched bones and feathers. She then slowly made her own way back to the vehicle.

Ranald sat there a while, and I picked my way about, looking up at the hawk and the way the valley was constructed. It had a delicate, rather quiet, feel to it. Ranald got up and said, "Why don't you try this seat?" I sat down and began to look at the rock. Quite suddenly it changed appearance, beginning to vibrate and change colour, taking on a greenish-yellow hue with speckles rather like the skin of a lizard. I was rather shaken, of course, and looked up at Ranald, indicating that something was happening with my perception. He had not seen the same thing but sat quietly behind me suggesting I stay there and see what happened. The rock continued to quiver and flicker from red to the yellow-green and I began to feel more and more sensitive, emotional, as though I were going through a drug-induced hallucination. I had taken no drugs.

I stood up, compelled, and, with my companion a little behind doing a sort of guard-dog routine, I began to walk to the left, the eastern side of the rock, circumambulating. I got to a point on the southeast corner of the rock and stepped into a sensation of an invisible stream of feeling. I paused, caught in it, wondering where it was coming from. Had I stepped into it, or was it something inside me? I was overtaken by a feeling of grief. I fell to the ground, shaken by the sensations, unable to hold myself together. I stood up and with Ranald's assistance, retraced my steps back into the "stream". I felt the grief again, beginning to weep now uncontrollably. At the same time, my observation mind was working. I thought, "Shit . . . am I overwrought at arriving and meeting these people again, is this the scorpion bite back again, is this some unresolved childhood grief erupting? Is it in me, or is it something else?"

I kept walking or rather staggering around the rock. I wanted to test something. I had a feeling about the lay of this sensation; it seemed to continue on, to have a direction of its own that was not my invention. At a point at the next corner, the southwest corner, the sensation came again, the same overwhelming grief and the fall of the ground. It was a sensation of imperishable grief. It seemed to emanate directly from the rock, and the rock seemed to have a life of its own. I had a sensation of mothers; the rock sat there quivering, like some great mother. I continued the circumambulating and went back to the stone seat. Gradually the sensations subsided. The weeping and the grievous feelings subsided. The rock ceased to quiver.

Returned to a less altered state, I mumbled to Ranald, grateful for his presence but also alarmed for both of us. We moved out as quickly as my dazed stumbling would allow. Stopped once at a tree—a ghost gum, I think—leaning against it for comfort. It, too, vibrated but with an entirely different sensation, restorative and somehow integrating. I stopped by a fallen rock and lay down upon it to rest the trembling which still accompanied my flight out of the valley. This substantial rock, too, had an accompanying sensation—strengthening, masculine. We kept walking, trying to get out of the valley. It seemed a long way. At a certain point, at the mouth of the valley, we both simultaneously felt released and began to run. We ran hard and fast back to the vehicle near the road. All the sensations left. It was like an ordinary piece of rather nice roadside country, with low mulga and acacia, where you might stop for a cup of tea. The woman wondered why we had taken so long, and she pointed out that the tyre was flat. There was a mulga stake through it. It was nearly dark, and because of the seriously damaged tyre and the lateness we decided, rather reluctantly, to camp and try the repairs in the morning.

That night, half awake, the sensations of the day coursing through me, I began to visualize the construction of the Dionysian epic that would serve as the basis for the intoxication myth, the European alcohol "Tjukurrpa". I had done much of the preliminary research into early Mediterranean-basin myths and had found the Dionysian legends likely to be evocative and useful but also, bewilderingly, in fragments. It was an intellectual effort to gather all the pieces and get a clear sense of the emotional integrity of the various elements of the saga. I wanted to present to Japaljarri the guts of the story without all the classic Greek obscuration and romantic side-business. If you know the way the Dionysus story goes and the complexities of the interconnecting Greek myths in the many versions, then you will appreciate that this is a very difficult task. That night, the whole vision of the structure of the myth fell into place. Over the next days with Andrew, when we had an appropriate moment, I was able to sketch the whole thing out in a simple series of ground designs.

At the "sorry camp" later, Andrew took me to see his mother, Nangala. She was in a state of grief. Unable to drink, unable to get up, all her family thought she would herself pass away in mourning for her son and a family who suffered through such terrible events. Andrew took me aside and spoke quite directly, "We can't fix her. She's your grandmother. You have to help her." I went to sit with her, lying so emptily on the ground under the shade shelter, dogs and silent women all around hidden in the shadows and the heat.

The sensations of the big mother rock came back. I sat down beside Nangala and began to whisper phrases in her ear about grief and lost children and babies not eating and wanting to die and losing their mothers' breast, just as I might to a particularly distressed analytic patient; quiet cadences of intimacy. Maybe after half an hour of this sitting and checking with the sisters and stroking and whispering, I went back to our makeshift camp by the edge of the football field, and, with advice from my two companions, we made a brew of tea with honey and some herbal energy supplement I had been recommended by the Chinese doctor for my own condition. I went back with the tea in a black billy, testing it first with her sisters who were watchfully attending to her, encouraging the continuation of "the treatment".

I dipped my finger in the strong sweet brew and touched it to the old woman's tongue, she tasted then gradually sipped some of the tea. I slowly repeated themes of the lost children and the mother's despair and how hard it is to hold on to life. Stroking and soothing liquid to her lips, she showed some sense of return and gradually through the rest of the day she drank a little more. Her sisters were satisfied; Japaljarri was content. Nangala recovered enough not to pass away. She lived perhaps another two years. It was she who guided the painting of the "Parma Tjukurrpa" that her son, Japaljarri, had been unravelling in our earlier talks about alcohol.

We stayed there maybe one night or two—I can't remember all the details now—sitting in the sorry camp, painting with the children as a diversion, working some more on the Snake Tjukurrpa, and doing the ground designs for the Dionysus story, then back to Alice Springs for the conference.

The whole ambience of the conference was charged. I have never attended a conference like it since. It was very intense, much happened, and I was in a volatile state. Wanting to get some perspective on what had happened in the valley and looking for some guidance, I described a little bit about my experience to someone local—Japananka Williams, an Aboriginal man working for Correctional Services. He pointed out an older man sitting over near the swimming pool, Jangala Egan. "He will know," said Japananka. Egan is a man well known for his charm, his knowledge, and his tracking ability.

I introduced myself, laying out my family connections as identification and my given kin name, which has a specific brother-in-law relationship to the Jangala kin group. That helped. Then I asked him if he knew the place where we had stopped, describing it carefully. "Oh yes," Jangala said, smiling in his characteristic, wily way. "That's my dreaming along there . . . my country. Jangala country. You can go there, too, Jungarrai, don't worry. That's where all the lost children go. There's a big mother there crying out for her children. When all the kids get lost, that's where they go, into that place. . . . You walked in there . . . where the lost children go. Poor things. You walked in there".

I remember still, ten years later, the rock in the valley. A site of perennial grief. I have not been back into the valley, but when I drive on that road and pass it, a feeling of quiet and anxiety always catches me. I think now that the experience was an eruption of unresolved childhood feelings—but not only an individualistic loss, it is also a location of a loss in which I participated: a shared connection point to an unrelieved and unresolved spring of loss that permeates our existence here in this country. It is objective, somehow, and independent, an irrefutable source of sorrow, a custodian point in the country. There is something precious about that place, but it is not something to be precious about. There is something ruthless about that site. I have been to other sites that are sources of awe, of violence, of imperishable sweetness. There is a plurality of experience embedded somehow in the rocks of the country. This plurality I can accept, even if I do not understand how sites can be alive to human feeling.

The main point

The sequence of incidents just presented have to do with psychic pain and have something to do with developing the therapeutic capacity to meet with cultural conditions that trouble many of us. In presenting these incidents, I am trying to approach something about what happens in the mental space between indigenous Australians and more recent settlers. Between the Tjukurrpa and the European dream there is a region of psychic pain. The professional challenge is in feeling, finding, and clarifying the details. I am thinking now of these incidents as generated by the activation of intercultural transference processes. I wish I understood better how this kind of process works. They are condensed images; some are communications, some have a premonitory seminal quality, for they gave a direction and a shape to the relationship and the business that was to grow up over the next ten years. I feel that what happened in the exchange of snake images from the Tjukurrpa and the penumbra of incidents surrounding it had a binding function. We did help Japaljarri and family, and they did help us.

The snake story held two subtexts. The *first* is simple, even conventional—that is, a coded statement, in symbolic traditional form, on the rites of passage of a traditional *ngankari*. This is indigenous business, but we were being shown something about it because of a professional affinity. And there is much on this theme that could be developed for mutual benefit to therapeutic practitioners in intercultural health. The *second* subtext has a twist to it: the story of the trials of the westward-travelling snake is a coded statement by Andrew Spencer Japaljarri on the condition of his own people as the interlopers (the serpentine creatures from the east, figured in the story as brown snakes) moved into his black-snake territory and began a dispossession saga. Brown snakes are known to eat black snakes; the brown snakes move into black-snake territory and eat—they cannibalize or dispossess. In the story, sexual trouble ensues, another set of creatures enters the tale, and the black snake undergoes successive dismemberment. Now, if you were an analyst and were being told a tale like this in your consulting room, what would you make of it? If you were a white man being told a tale by a black man in the black man's country, what would you make of it?

The Central Australian Aboriginal experience of the relationship with the incoming "brown snakes" is, after all, mainly a tale of displacement, seduction, family fighting, breakdown of kinship protocols, sexuality turned to aggressive ends (incestuous rape in various forms), further injury, revenge attacks, dismemberment, loss of skin, blood, and organs, loss of capacities, senses, and functions, leading to dispersal across the country in all directions. All this has happened to the people in Andrew's family system. The Tjukurrpa, retold in terms of today's actuality is, in effect, a diagnostic account of the prevailing sociocultural condition; the pain of it is made plain, yet with an implicit hopefulness for a healing transformation.

The main point is this: the Tjukurrpa is timeless. It exists in the present. It describes exactly what is happening in the country, not only once upon a time but now. The snake Tjukurrpa happens to have been communicated from one culturally active man with an intense therapeutic sensibility to two other men who are attuned to symbolic communications with therapeutic content. Japaljarri, at his father Jungarrai's behest, tells us precisely what is happening and will be happening in his country.

In the final section of Japaljarri's dreaming story, there is a kind of apotheosis where the now bodiless spirit recovers vitality, after seclusion. Somehow this beleaguered being is transformed into a curative force, which becomes available to potential healers to use in their work. Japaljarri took the trouble to take both of us at different times to the specific sites of many of the events. He was not acting as a tour guide. He was making a point. I think I see the point, but what I do not see is whether the transformation and the healing process will be attained and activated in the present. Will this transformation happen? Will the healing spirit seize the time? I have an awful, sickening feeling that the Tjukurrpa has failed or has been let down.

How is it possible for Japaljarri's family group to come through these contemporary trials and manage to get some purchase on healing the problems he has so accurately diagnosed in his paintings and his story? Who are the potential healers in his kin group who, having undergone the twentieth-century dismemberment of body and spirit, will be able to turn back upon the deintegrative process and transform it? I know his brothers, his sisters, his wives, his children, his cousins, and the circumstances of their lives and the impossible demands when diabetes and alcohol and petrol's derangement have the upper hand. What support do they need to carry out the task— or, rather, is that support likely to be manifested? And by whom?

I suspect that uncertainty about having enough resources and reinforcements from within the family and the government system has led Japaljarri to attempt to recruit these resources from outside, from the "whitefeller" domain, swallowed and set to work with therapeutic purpose.

Conclusion

Aboriginal Tjukurrpa, although transmitted in a veiled way and guarded according to the conventions of a mystery, is nevertheless an active psychic force. It is not simply a metaphor for the country. Nor is it a poetic way of coding environmental knowledge. Listened to carefully and taken into use in contemporary situations, Tjukurrpa has a very powerful psychological function. The European tradition, too, has a semblance of the Tjukurrpa. It has its own access to a similar or cousin-like state, which the great archetypal myths contain and reveal. Knowing this does help us be more humane and perhaps better, culturally alert practitioners. An appreciation of both the indigenous and the European psyche is necessary for those of us who suffer under the contemporary Australian disorder. This consists of an emptiness created by the absence of authentic interaction between the indigenous presence and the European presence.

The stories and dreams exchanged, as well as the lost-children incident, presented here indicate in a condensed form a presentation of a collective cultural condition in which both black and white people participate. The white doctors need curative attention from the black, and the black need curative attention from the white doctors. Both may have to undergo a re-training. People and doctors, both black and white, need to attend to the reality and dynamics of the Tjukurrpa realm itself. It does seem to be psychically alive and, properly credited, may provide a common meeting ground, a true "potential space" (Winnicott, 1971a).

Note

1. The Tjukurrpa fragments and the personal dreams should be treated with the same caution and ethics as confidential case material.

2. A historic 1991 decision re Eddie Mabo's land claim over the Murray Islands (*Mabo vs Queensland*), the High Court definitively recognized prior indigenous possession. In essence the finding made a legal but also psychological point demonstrating to Australians that the pre-existing notion of Australia as "terra nullius" (i.e., vacant possession) was a Colonial fiction (e.g., see Reynolds, 1999).

3. This extract is from the performance text of "The Sugar Man Song Cycle", a retelling by C. San Roque of mythological events pertinent to intoxication and to the legends of Dionysus, reset in a central Australian indigenous context. The performance project, a venture in cultural psychology, was the subject of a 1996 Australian Film Commission documentary video, *Sugarman Story*, directed by David Roberts, Antipode Productions, Sydney.

4. Eleven or twelve aboriginal people, including children and an infant, were stranded without water in a remote area following a vehicle accident. Several people perished, including members of the Spencer family. This occurred just before the incidents recounted.

5. In desert aboriginal society it is customary for close family to remain in a seclusion camp set aside from normal habitations during the ceremonial mourning period. This is referred to as "sorry camp".

6

Creating mental space:
assimilating recovered Maori self-representations

Stuart W. Twemlow & Nicholas A. Twemlow

The task of this chapter is a complex one, being written by a father and son about a matter of great importance to both of us. We wish to note at the outset that the format of this paper is somewhat unorthodox. The paper employs three "voices": that of a unified third person, as well as interwoven first-person commentary written by both of us. Paradoxically, one of us, the father, comes from a scientific tradition, and the other, the son, from a tradition embedded in the arts and humanities. We see many things differently, so this chapter is in part a dialogue and possibly an argument, between the two of us, and presents our thoughts about our shared origins and dramatic emotional experiences that both of us have had in recent months.

Psychoanalysis was once defined as the search for the truth about oneself; whether that truth is palatable or not, yet it should be known. Platonic as that ideal is it encourages a mindset in the practitioner of ongoing self-exploration, self-awareness, that both hermeneutic/introspectionist and scientific approaches would undoubtedly agree is helpful. The matters addressed in this chapter were not prominent in my [S.W.T.] training analysis. They did emerge for my son as part of an exploration of his heritage that was part of his successful completion of a Fulbright scholarship in New Zealand.

Nicholas has known about his multicultural background since birth, but in recent years he and I have been preoccupied with the social context of psychopathology and experience, which he has captured in his poetry (N. Twemlow, 2006a, 2006b). It is now quite clear that social context is a major determiner of psychopathology (Akhtar, 1988, 1995, 1999a; Twemlow & Wilkinson, 2004; Twemlow, Fonagy, & Sacco, 2004, 2005).

We concluded that an in-depth experience and understanding of one's various cultural self-representations is an important part of the development of a collective identity in Erikson's (1950,1959) sense or true self in Winnicott's (1960a) terms—true in the sense of the self that one is, with the counterpointed false self being false in the sense of the self that one has adapted to cover and adapt to circumstances that interpersonal experience reveals. Winnicott also suggested that the false self is not to be cast off as being all patho-logical. It has a protective function, like the holding mother, or any defence for that matter. This elaboration suggests that timing for the emergence of the true self requires a complex set of factors, one of which is an ongoing, never finished discovery of the true self, per-haps, we hypothesize, aided by uncovered and assimilated cultural self-representations. The idea is, then, that knowing who you are and the detail of the various mixes of your culture allows you to tran-scend a great number of prejudices, created by a false sense of being "pure bred", including ones connected with race. DNA studies of a number of well-known people of various races (Adelman, 2003) im-ply that most if not all of us are of mixed bloodlines. Hamer (2007) suggests that in racism, there is a false dichotomy where white is the gold standard thus defining black as less. Being a mixed-breed can be hidden as something to be ashamed of or can lead to the ultimate realization that the differences between people are more apparent than real and that issues that create a sense of separateness (e.g., unique customs, social rituals, physical differences, etc.) do not alter the fundamental similarity between all human beings.

Stuart, on New Zealand's cultural background

An old Maori proverb, *Haere Mai Ra, E Te Manuhiri Tuarange* [Wel-come to the guest from afar] embodies the Maoris' time-honoured friendliness, interest in others, and anticipation of lively debate, discussion, and even fun fighting, which lasts in the culture to this day. I knew from childhood that my mother was part Maori, but I was raised in a Pakeha[1] atmosphere. In her nuclear family, my mother was prohibited from discussing her Maori origins and was discouraged from participating in any Maori rituals or using the language. Right up until her death, at age 91, her attitude was awkward about her heritage. When I asked about our people, she said "Why would you want to know about that anyway?" as if it were irrelevant to the understanding of my origins as a New Zealander, perhaps even to be hidden.

In the past several years, New Zealanders have been engaged in vigorous discourse about the effect of colonialization on the image of the Maori people, with discussion about what a New Zealander really is. There is a move afoot to change the name of New Zealand to its Maori name *Aotearoa* [land of the long white cloud or clear burning light]. Maori can now be a first language and is part of doctoral-level academic studies. Recently land disputes have been successfully settled for large amounts of money against the New Zealand government.

A New Zealander filmmaker, Jane Campion, provides a contemporary view of Maori/Pakeha relations in the movie *The Piano* (Campion, 1993). Ironically, Campion spent most of her adult life outside New Zealand, returning at 31 to satisfy a lifelong desire to make this very local film. Campion, a Pakeha, noted that the main stimulus for writing the movie was to support the Maori culture. She says: "I wish to protect the Maoris in the film and I was sure that I showed their right spirits" (quoted in S. Twemlow, 2001a, p. 83). Seeing this movie will make this essay more understandable, since it makes a beginning attempt to integrate a multicultural image of a people of vastly mixed heritage and blood lines.

Leome Pihama, a lecturer in the Department of Education, University of Auckland, New Zealand, has written several articles on the image of the Maori in *The Piano*. In one called "Are Films Dangerous? A Maori Woman's Perspective on *The Piano*" (Pihama, 1994), she concludes that films that are constructed and controlled by the colonial days are dangerous and stereotype images. She reacts strongly, but in a scholarly way, to the image of the Maori as a happy-go-lucky native, with the sexualization of the Maori woman, available at all times to service Pakeha men. The idea conveyed by the movie was that the Maori were naïve, simple-minded, lacked reason, acted impulsively, and spoke only in terms of sexual innuendo, with a particular obsession with male genitalia. She points out (correctly, I believe) that the Maori characters "are the background against which images of white are positioned" (p. 2). Almost any thinking person, Maori or Pakeha, looking at *The Piano* for the first time can empathize with Pihama's viewpoint. These roles, however, are clearly caricatures, and one realizes quickly that many caricatures also apply to several devastating depictions of Pakeha: stupidity, crudeness, insensitivity, incapacity to see the obvious, and driven by greed and envy of the Maori carefree attitude.

A snippet of New Zealand history might help place this social conflict in perspective, since there are parallels with the plight of African Americans and Native Americans in the United States. With the rediscovery of New Zealand by Captain Cook in 1769, gradual colonization occurred by settlers from Scotland, Ireland, and England, mostly farmers, together with a small enclave of enthusiastic Wesleyan and Baptist missionaries. The Maori people welcomed these "guests from afar". Over a period of some sixty to seventy years, small pockets of colonists began peaceful coexistence with the Maori people by farming and largely friendly interaction. With the rather awkward Christianization of the Maori, and the cultivation of a written form of the Maori language, there was a slow assimilation of the Maori people into the colonial culture, culminating in the Treaty of Waitangi willingly signed in 1840 by Maori chiefs and white, colonial representatives of Queen Victoria. Then the trouble began. Little by little the Maori were exploited. Their land ownership was jettisoned, and they were not reimbursed fairly. They also began to contract diseases imported by the whites and to have disagreements with other Maoris who sold land for quick money. Mounting unrest and a series of bloody wars lasting through the 1860s led to the loss of large numbers of white and Maori lives. In spite of parliamentary representation for the Maori and no formal slavery, a dark colonial shadow was cast over the Maori people as they emerged into the twentieth century.

This contrasts starkly with the pre-colonial Maori culture. Pihama (1994) says that Maori people maintained specific forms of identification and interaction dependent primarily on *whakapapa* [genealogical connections]. Relationships with people were crucial to the daily existence of the Maori. She goes on to note that Maori society used a range of oral, rather than written, methods for transmission of knowledge and information. The "literacy" of the Maori existed not for written work but through carving and weaving; stories were expressed and knowledge was transmitted in this way. The imagery of carving and the architecture of weaving were the "books" of indigenous cultural lore.

This victim/victimizer theme is represented sociologically in the history of many extant cultures, we hypothesize, in part created by the false dichotomy of the illusion of racial purity. The victimized are seen as an unconscious threat to this imagining. We explore this idea as a possible aetiological factor in racial and other prejudices (Twemlow & Sacco, 2007), with the full realization and acceptance of one's mixedness being a major factor in the amelioration of prejudices, as we elaborate later.

In Stuart's voice, again

As my son and I were discussing the idea of being—as a Maori elder described, to Nicholas, those who were of mixed race—a "half-breed", we were struck by how clearly white we look (I have pale skin, and he certainly has no obvious physical features that would identify him with the Maori ethnic group). He mentioned to me the experience of a friend of his who played the role of a physician in a television soap opera and was socially considered by others to have medical knowledge, and how awkward he felt about being treated as if he were a physician when he was not. The question then becomes: How am I not a white person? Or, more specifically, "What is white about me" has a difficult time answering the question "What is not white about me?"

The modern young New Zealander has a rather blasé attitude towards notions of Maori or Pakeha self-identification. In contrast with US immigration policy, the Maori culture is not defined by bloodlines, but by family membership. So a Pakeha child adopted into a Maori family is Maori without question. There are many features of Maori culture that I have experienced as part of myself without being aware, until now, of the origins of these aspects, since they were in contrast with my adoptive home, which did not emphasize family values but, instead, emphasized intellectual achievement, successful competition with others, a mindset that sees the world as unfriendly, and one in which the individual fights to survive. Maoris live in a

Table 6.1.   Community philosophies

Pakeha Philosophy: Universe is unfriendly	Maori Philosophy of the Universe is friendly, or at least benignly indifferent
Individual focus (closed)	Group/family focus (open)
Competitive	Collaborative
Independence	Interdependence
Quantity of possessions	Quality of possessions
Reason emphasis	Intuition emphasis
Logic & causality	Beauty & feeling
Technological	Spiritual/Personal

culture that is a vastly different, more friendly, and benignly indifferent universe. Table 6.1 summarizes these differences.

In another context (S. Twemlow, 2001b), I used this table to illustrate differences between violent and non-violent community philosophies. During the wars with the British, the Maori showed themselves as very capable fighters who outfoxed the British, who were unfamiliar with guerrilla warfare and had to import Australian Bushrangers to teach them Maori fighting techniques. When there was no necessity to fight to protect the family and tribe, the Maori culture, as I experienced it through contacts with my mother, was not warlike but, instead, very family-oriented and altruistic, as Table 6.1 suggests. My "Maori" identity as a child was formed by a mother who had been taught to eschew her Maori heritage, yet who embodied it in the way she taught me. I had had an onslaught of Pakeha women influence my upbringing, who emphasized the individualistic competitive philosophy of the affluent white British culture. Visits to my Maori mother, from whom I had been separated at the age of 4 years, were very precious because they made me feel part of a family and safe. As a child, I yearned to live with her. My son's research unearthed a Maori lineage that identified our family as warrior-protectors of families and tribes.[2] All of my children and I have a personality trait that protects. We protect the "weak"—those who cannot protect themselves through physical and mental disability, and those who are persecuted and bullied through lack of mental and physical skills or knowledge. We patrol boundaries to ensure safety of the group and are of a personality structure such that we rarely lose our presence of mind—that is, are still standing "when the dust settles", indeed, part of the Maori heritage.

The Pakeha philosophy emphasizing the importance of the individual fighting all others to emerge as successful materially was, for my whole life, a particularly aversive idea, since such attitudes create elitist groups and do not encourage altruism and protection of the poor and weak. Until my recent enlightenment about my Maori culture, whose values are similar to mine, I did not fully understand that my interest in the role of the social context and the fact that people are more the same than different, and the importance of service to others, with altruism as a fundamental principle governing all one's actions, were influenced by these early unconscious and preconscious experiences with my mother.

Nicholas interjects: a note on cultural ambivalence

When I was assembling my application for a Fulbright fellowship to New Zealand, roughly three years ago, I knew that the foremost part of the application was a two-page description of my intended project. The more specific the project, logically, the better, but there was also the central question: Why do I, the applicant, need to go to the host country (New Zealand) to do my research? And here was the rub. As my father has noted above, I grew up with some awareness of my mixed cultural heritage; the word "Maori" was bandied about our household, and what it signified—at least for me, the only sibling of four born in the United States—was an otherness. But this otherness was limited to my sense of growing up in a household where I was decidedly not a New Zealander. In a strange way, the terms Maori and New Zealander had been conflated for me. They interchangeably represented the thing that I was not: I was American. This idea extended beyond family conversation to the playground, high school, and even into graduate school. I learned the familiar tropes of cultural stereotype, assimilated the surfaces of my Maori heritage, and succeeded in completely misunderstanding them.

So, when I applied for a Fulbright, I proposed a two-pronged project. The first part would require me to write a monograph on the life and works of my great-aunt, Joyce West, my father's last legal guardian and my biological grandmother's adopted sister. West

[1908–1985] had been a prominent writer in her day, and she remains well known for her cycle of children's novels, especially *Drover's Road* (1963). She was the daughter of the two schoolteachers who set up an English-language school in Makomako, which my biological grandmother attended. She was later adopted by them.

The second prong invoked my Maori past, wherein I proposed that I would write a collection of poems about my family's immigration from New Zealand to the United States and about the muddy waters of our Maori background. I noted in my proposal that, as far as I knew, I was "1/8th Maori". I acknowledged that my understanding of what this bloodline might mean was unclear (not only to me, but to my entire family) and that I would embark on a quest to uncover as much as possible about my grandmother's Maori past, which had been veiled in an awkward secrecy for nearly seventy-five years.

This chapter is not the proper forum in which to detail my literary work while a Fulbright fellow, but some observations on my interactions with Maori and Pakeha, when the discussion at hand concerned my own Maori heritage, as well as my research into my grandmother's, and thus my family's, Maori lineage, will serve to clarify the issues at hand.

An aside: on my first day in Wellington, where I spent my year in New Zealand as a guest and student at the International Institute for Modern Letters at Victoria University, I woke from an eight-hour, middle-of-the-day nap to wander down to the hotel bar. It was 2 a.m. My sense of my environs was pretty much limited, at this point, to a car drive through downtown Wellington and my hotel room. The bar was closed, so I stepped outside onto a patio, to get some fresh air. Several people were seated at a table on the patio, carousing a bit, a few drinks past sensible. One called out to me, asked me over, and I accepted his blousy invitation. Soon after opening my mouth to introduce myself, I was accosted, in a reasonably non-threatening way, about my American accent. Before I could say another word, one of the men at the table, the three of whom were in town for a week-long labour job, presented a litany of questions that went something like this: "Are you one of Bush's boys? Why are all Americans fat? Why are you wearing such a gay powder-blue jacket", and so forth. Each question was becoming more specific in its fingering of me as foreign, each question borrowing the gloss of stereotype. The one woman among them, who was on the last leg of a six-week vacation with her two sons from Britain, intervened, asking my interrogator to calm down, to which he replied, "I don't mean it personally. I just never met an American bloke." Suffice it to say, I didn't get the opportunity to answer even one of his questions. I was already in a laconic way, jet lag creeping its way into my system, and now this litany. I chatted him onto other subjects, careful to avoid further investigation of my American-ness, if you will, and was successful. The night ended with me apologetically declining their invitation to visit a strip club just around the corner. Apparently, my alignment with Bush, with fat Americans, and with my outré clothing had been forgotten. But if I had any pretensions that I was one of them, a Kiwi, I was reminded, quite jarringly, that I was not, at all. I was an American. And this fact—whether indicated by my passport, my flat accent shaded in by my Midwestern upbringing, my American clothes, my American sensibility, whatever the external signs might have been—informed every interaction I was to have during the next ten or so months in New Zealand.

The central issue I had thought I was going to investigate took the form of a line of poetry I wrote some years ago, in graduate school, a scrapped jotting I recently rediscovered in an old journal, a jotting that my father mentions above, with a slight modification, and which helped us formalize the central question of this paper: "'What is white about me' has trouble answering the question, 'What is non-white about me?'" Several years later, now in New Zealand, I seemed to be asking that question over and over. My mentor, the poet Bill Manhire,[3] a Pakeha, noted quite early on during one of our discussions that I occupied a rather unique position: I was an American in New Zealand searching for his Maori past, but by dint of being born and raised in America, at a far remove from any Maori influence, I was, in effect, less Maori (my term) than he was. Manhire wasn't suggesting that he was Maori, just that his lifelong exposure, research, reading, and so forth—in effect, his status as a Kiwi—put him, culturally at the least, in touch with the Maori culture. What I took from this was that no matter my blood connection, I didn't have the slightest clue what it meant to be Maori.

But my meeting with the two Maori lecturers surprised me. You are, they both said, Maori. No question. The fact that I was in New Zealand, researching my grandmother's connection to Makomako, made me a Maori. But that did not mean, they continued, that I should stop at my research. My first visit to meet my grandmother, Marion, was one steeped in the formalities of seeing a relative one hasn't seen in years—in my case, since I was 7 years old. She warmly received us, and her illness, which we would later realize was in fact leukaemia, had left her in a mode of repetition. I barely knew her, but I wanted to ask her about her Maori background. The facts I had at hand, I was coming to realize, were flimsy. We had some knowledge of our whakapapa (our family line), the central piece of knowledge to establish one's Maori connection, but did not know, for example, the names of her mother and father. But when I asked her about them, and her time growing up in Makomako, she was evasive. Not in a pernicious way; she seemed stressed, and it was clear that my visit was overwhelming to her.

A couple of months later, when my father travelled from Brazil to be with Marion as she was hospitalized, and dying, she was somewhat more forthcoming, which my father has commented on. I had some new information about our Maori family: Maori land records indicated that, at some point, Marion was deeded land by a person who was probably her brother. Though it was still not clear who her parents were, I managed to ascertain the names of a few of her relatives and to locate the region where she had been born and raised. After her death, I travelled to Makomako, a small country village, little more than two crossroads, just a few miles inland from the western seaboard of the North Island, where I met several people who had known her when she was a child. They confirmed the identities of her parents: her father had been a local Pakeha landowner; her mother, a Maori woman who lived and died in the seaside area of Aotea Harbour, which is near Makomako. My time in Kawhia, the region that encompasses Makomako, put me in contact with several incredibly generous people, who are still at work trying to trace me and my family back to the Tainui waka, which is the canoe our people travelled to New Zealand on.

Stuart notes the impact of the discovery

It has always been difficult for both of us to identify with the ruling majorities' values, precepts, and priorities. We have both felt not at home in ourselves. My experience was that of a fatherless child adopted as a 4-year-old by a single woman who died when I was 10 years old. Having moved over twenty-six times during my childhood and adolescent years, I evolved a concept of home that is different from the usual, stable, and singular one. I became quite good at setting up temporary home environments (even in a hotel room) and making necessary adjustments to whatever space I happened to be in at a given time. The idea of using a concept of identity based on home, a particular town or city or ethnic group, had no meaning or reality to me. I remember wistfully humming Maori lullabies and enjoying visits with my biological mother, who was depicted to me as an errant aunt who had been too immature to bring me up. A photograph of this mother, pregnant with me, seems starkly unreal. I felt white and only academically interested in the Maori piece of my origins.

Although I had early memories of being breastfed till 3 or 4 years of age, a tradition in Maori families, these snapshots of experiences were never integrated into any sort of identity. When I came to leave New Zealand permanently at age 29 in 1970 to emigrate to the United States for psychiatric training, for reasons that were not clear at the time, a Maori chieftainess and her Pakeha husband, who was a carver of Maori totems, had a send-off ritual with me in which she sang some songs that cautioned me against the dangers of being in America. A carving of the Maori myth of Narcissus was ceremonially presented to me, since it was considered too easy to lose your humility in America. The carving is of a *tuatara*, an ancient reptile unique to New Zealand, perhaps the most ancient of all living animals. The story sung to me in a variety of beautiful phrases was the myth of a young Maori maiden who fell in love with her reflection in the water and spent all day combing her hair rather than doing her chores. One day she fell into the river and turned into a tuatara so she could never get back to her village, because she was already partially non-human. She began to cry at her plight of never being able to return home. Her tears formed a river, and she floated out to sea to live on an island, which to this day is a primary respite for the *tuatara*.[4] The reminder was that being a member of a community and family, doing one's chores, and realizing humility is more important than anything else.

The realization of my connection with the Maori race became quite acute during the July 2005 Congress of the International Psychoanalytical Association in Rio De Janeiro. During the meeting, I was informed that my mother was terminally ill with leukaemia. I had some quite strenuous and complex presentations to make, which I did, but when the pressure was off I collapsed emotionally. In my hotel room, I descended into a deep and childlike regression to a form of neediness, with dreams of breastfeeding and of feeling and being helpless. I did not know what to do with myself, isolated I as was in a foreign country. I had not experienced a depth of regression like this even within the analytic process. I was aware that I had mixed feelings about what I should do about her imminent death, and I contacted female members of my family for assistance. I received a wide range of advice, like "make a tape saying goodbye to her" and "you need to go see her". The latter recommendation was the right thing to do, I felt on deep reflection, and it became of great urgency to me. I was able to enlist the help of several people, including my oldest daughter, Lee, and unusually sympathetic airline personnel, to get a trip organized at very short notice.

Arriving in New Zealand, I spent a week with my mother before her death, revisiting many childhood memories of her presence, and singing Maori lullabies that I had sung to soothe my children during their early years. One of my daughters was also present, and we moved together in and out of reminiscences and tearful regressions. Insofar as I was with my mother and daughter, an oedipal triangle was created through several generations—an uncanny recreation of a lost childhood, perhaps. My mother had lived her whole life as a companion to white people and had been taken care of by them. She had never had a job, except briefly when I was a small child, and did not ever learn to drive a car. Her accommodating and gentle manner attracted people to her. She appeared to have not a single person who ever disliked her in the whole world. Covertly, this was seen as "the Maori" in her.

Although she had been adopted into an affluent white family, possibly to care for or to be a companion for that family's children, she felt socially isolated in New Zealand farm life. Whether or not this kind of racism—exemplified in the American South as well—was part of the early New Zealand culture remains quite controversial. What is clear is that Marion managed to remain part of the Pakeha culture, based on her extraordinarily gentle and empathic manner. She was always more interested in what you were doing and feeling than anything else, and she delighted in feeding all-comers with her delicious cuisine. This endeared her to generations of children and adults of all ethnic groups.

Nicholas interjects

That is all background for the issues under discussion here. I should curtail the discussion in order to highlight a few concerns I came away from New Zealand with regarding Pakeha/Maori relations. As my year there progressed, and as the details of my Maori heritage became somewhat clearer, I continued my discussions of what I thought of as race issues with Maori and Pakeha. In general, I found little common ground. Those who self-identified as Maori were extraordinarily accommodating of my own misgivings about my reasons for even investigating my Maori lineage. While I often felt like a fraud, I was told, at every turn, that I was on the right path, so to speak. But the responses I received from some Pakeha—and I wish to stress that the majority of Pakeha were very supportive of my research—were somewhat distressing. Several people I spoke with expressed disbelief after I explained what I as doing in New Zealand and also how embracing the Maoris I had met had been, that the Maoris had in fact been so embracing. These Pakeha viewed me with suspicion. As one noted, I didn't look Maori, I didn't act Maori, I knew nothing of the Maori. Why, they continued, would the Maori take me in?

A good question, and one that I think I can have some beginnings of an answer in how my grandmother must have navigated her own Maori identity after she left Makomako and the Ngate Tewehi, her hapu (family). My father has hypothesized that my grandmother's adoption into the Pakeha family that had come to her area to teach in the school may have been the result of a family looking for a child to act as a caretaker around the house. He and I have discussed at some length this idea of a sort of Maori indentured servitude. In personal discussion with one of the Maori lecturers I mentioned above, I floated this idea to her. She did not seem to recall that the idea had been posited before, but had her suspicions, if only because things were never quite that clear. This chapter is not the place for a considered analysis of Maori–Pakeha relations in the twentieth century, but to say that they were strained and complicated would be fair and perhaps appeasing to the often brutal realities. Still, the analogies to the Civil Rights movement here in the United States at roughly the same time period, while interesting, are perhaps not very helpful.

The facts of my grandmother's life after leaving Makomako are hard to piece together; as I've noted above, she wasn't forthcoming about her life before meeting her adoptive family. In all of our conversations about her past, her stories started with that meeting and moved forward in time. But it seems her own sense of being a Pakeha, the identity she would have claimed if anyone had asked, is possibly a useful way to look at her own sense of being Maori. She married a Pakeha man, a man several other members of the family remarked was quite racist. He had little tolerance for the blunders and laziness, as he might have put it, of the Maori. Though this isn't quite true—he married a Maori woman. It is likely that my grandmother's own sense of her Maori identity was buried as a simple response to a set of societal pressures.

Stuart replies

Explorations of the tribal roots of our family by Nicholas found that our tribe originated in Kawhia. My mother was a "half-breed"—not used as a term of abuse, but merely as a statement of fact. She had a white father and was one of three children, all with different fathers, of an indigent Maori mother and was adopted, quite late in her life, into the Pakeha family.

Her parting gesture to me remains an important and highly emotional experience: as a child when I would visit her, she always gave me some chocolate fish, as a snack. These were fish-shaped marshmallow candies, covered with chocolate, and this is what she gave me as I departed from her to return to the United States. It took me some considerable time to finish my last supply of chocolate fish from my mother.[5] And so the play goes on. A side issue that evolved from this explication of our cultural heritage was the discovery that my father had never become a New Zealand citizen—he was Irish, and had a brother who lived in County Antrim in Northern Ireland, but that is another story and another integration!

Dynamic and structural vicissitudes

One stanza from a poem by Nicholas, "Unspecified Threat", captures the task of this section to describe the psychology of the process that occurred and to place it, including its importance in the psychic economy and life of both authors. The stanza says:

Certainty
is all I ask of my fork, that it

perform well when called upon, that I may
customize

A widower's grief to fit my walk
down First Avenue to meet Kevin or Andy . . .

Unfortunately the security of one's relationship in the external world is dependent on the stability of internal objects. A fork, however structurally stable it is, will perform no useful function unless the internal object world of the user of the fork knows how to use it appropriately.

Our hypothesis is that the total self of an individual depends on many complex factors. If an individual's life is very limited in terms of demands and interpersonal relationships, imagination, intelligence, and skills, then a very limited life can be led quite happily with what would be, under other conditions, a highly deficient or pathological internal-object world. We see this often in the individuals who cannot adapt to change, but otherwise lead quite restricted but happy lives. Thus a child's ethnic group, when diminished in the family, as was the case for the senior author's mother, nonetheless provided for her a stable life in which she thought of herself largely as white. This choice served her well. How can one make a case, then, for digging into these deeply buried identities, or is it unnecessarily disturbing and possibly even harmful? I think not for my mother.

What are the vicissitudes of the unconscious determinants of culture? Winnicott (1971a) suggested a useful bridging concept from his studies of the mother–infant relationship, that of potential space, which becomes real when necessary and unreal when unneeded. Winnicott felt that at times this may be necessary from a developmental perspective, including the transitional-object phase, when a child is trying to determine his or her capacity to separate from the maternal object. Winnicott also referred to potential space as part of the development of cultural experience and creativity. It is on the area of cultural experience that we want to focus our attention here in this section.

Ogden (1986), has suggested that the dialectical process (p. 204) is a useful explanatory mechanism for the time when individuals create mental space from potential space. The implication is that distinguishing between co-created roles—the "me and not-me", for example—enables a period for exploration uncontaminated by reality or other demands, so that the various aspects of the "me" and "not-me" relationship can be explored. Culture fits well within this model. The issue that has preoccupied my son and me is "who am I?" Not in the sense of "I" as an intentional being similar to all other intentional beings in some particular culture, but in the broader sense—that is, where is my home and how am I not white?

Winnicott (1967) calls this potential space the "hypothetical area that exists (but cannot exist) between the baby and the object (mother or part of mother) during the phase of repudiation of the object as not-me, that is at the end of being merged in with the object" (p. 99). Thus Winnicott feels that his potential space and the activities in it are a critical part of object differentiation leading to the capacity to establish self and other boundaries, with cultural differentiation being an important aspect of this transitioning to the establishment of boundaries between "me" and "not-me". Fonagy, Gergely, Jurist, and Target (2002) developed the construct of psychic equivalence, when a thought and thing are considered real and needing to be transitioned out of, otherwise the individual becomes developmentally fixated in a pretend world. There evolves a devastating effect on internal objects, which are unable to integrate reality into their object field and, of course, interpersonal relationships.

Ogden (1986) has suggested a mechanism by which this occurs, using the concept of dialectics. Our own work (Twemlow, Fonagy, & Sacco, 2004) with the victim–victimizer and bystander relationship supports this idea. Whereas Ogden (1986) and Winnicott (1967) regard such roles as deeper aspects of the unconscious mind, we feel instead that they are constantly re-enacted in all social experience every day, in all relationships, consciously and preconsciously. That is, the definition of self involves an endless reworking of the "me" and "not-me", victim–victimizer and bystander, dialectic that enables people to differentiate from or fuse with objects they are relating to—that is, to know them as both me and not-me. Our feeling is that the capacity to fuse in a non-defensive way depends largely on the existing capacity to differentiate from such objects, so that one can adopt a passive role only when one is comfortable with an activity—that is, it is only when one is aware of one's capacity to victimize that one becomes a self-agent. The bystander aspect of this refers to the way in which one is both an audience to and facilitates, by participation or abdication, in endlessly and continuously redefining the dialectically determined co-created victim–victimizer roles. This victim–victimizer–bystander *trialectic* never really differentiates the individual into clear fixed patterns unless serious psychopathology exists (Twemlow, Fonagy, & Sacco, 2002); instead, by virtue of the dynamic fluidity of the dialectic, the process of creating or being created and creating new aspects by each interaction keeps a dynamic tension that allows the individual to feel alive and not trapped in the artificial choice to be one or the other of several choices. In other words, aliveness is in part created by the tension between paradoxical opposites of this nature. Elements of this reasoning are derived from the existential philosophy of Martin Heidegger (1962), who proposed that being- alive-in-the-world (*Dasein*), and knowing you are alive, is only truly realized at death, when one can feel life leaving. In a more developmentally focused adaptation of this idea, the dialectical tension is captured in the cultural paradox that Nicholas and I faced from the outset: "How am I not a white person?"

Thus, from our point of view, the capacity to move in and out of these meditations in potential space becomes a critical aspect of health, not only in childhood but throughout adult life. This is possibly what the individual is doing when he or she takes time out from the worries of the day, which control and drive behaviour, to take an inventory of him/herself (playing in potential space).

The illusion and symbols created in transitional space by cultural elements is part of the separating out of the world of objects from the self, a necessary developmental achievement for the infant from Winnicott's point of view. The developmental qualities of Winnicott's (1971a) idea of potential space and its expansion by Ogden (1986) suggest that the dialectic is always "standing in a dynamic ever changing relationship with the other . . . and leads towards integration, but integration is never complete, since each integration creates a new dialectical opposition and a new dynamic tension" (Ogden, 1986, p. 208). Thus this realization of the role of culture does not produce complacency, but adds a new level of aliveness to the totality of the individual, as both of us experienced with the discovery of the aspects of our life that had been clearly influenced by the Maori culture.

As Erikson (1950) elaborated, deep existential questions about one's identity become urgent at different stages of growth. Cultural explorations can easily be seen as an essential part of all of Erikson's eight stages of man, from the cultural issues around child rearing through identity, midlife, and even in the stages of later life where issues of legacy, stagnation, and generativity become prominent.

Man's cultural-object representations ultimately help deepen his core self-representation. Psychotherapeutically working with them is therefore beneficial on many counts: (1) They consolidate a broader sense of identity. (2) They help the individual to create a sense of wholeness and being at home in oneself. (3) They open up options to be spontaneous and free—that is, to play with the various aspects of one's self (e.g., as a white person, as a Maori, as an Irishman). (4) They assist the creation of a richer sense of self, to establish a more reflective mentalizing attitude to self and others (Fonagy, 2001; Fonagy et al., 2002). (5) They enable the establishment of a flexible, rich, mentalizing, and playful identity, which allows the adoption of an active self-agent posture (Munich, Allen, & Rogan, submitted), enhancing interpersonal effectiveness, and accentuating one's re-sponsibility for oneself. (6) They facilitate the capacity to mentalize in this way, which allows one to realize a self-transcendent perspec-tive as being part of a larger whole. Helen Keller (1940), seemed born with this capacity :

> Security is mostly a superstition.
> It does not exist in nature,
> nor do the children of men as a whole experience it.
> Avoiding danger is no safer in the long run than outright
>   exposure.
> Life is either a daring adventure, or nothing.
> To keep our faces toward change and
>   behave like free spirits in the presence of fate is strength
>   undefeatable.

Put in more concrete terms, the realization that we are all "half-breeds"—that is, all of mixed racial descent—can help us feel a closer connection with others who appear to be culturally and physi-cally different. The human race can then become a whole, "not two", as the classic Zen conundrum notes. Striving to show that mind and body are separate in the natural-science sense has proved a fruitless search. We are defined by the way we think, and our sense of security in that fluid distinction can be depicted verbally as a relaxing faith in the universe (both one and two), or pictorially as in Figure 6.1—that is, as a freedom created by the realization that such a question is both unanswerable and stupid.

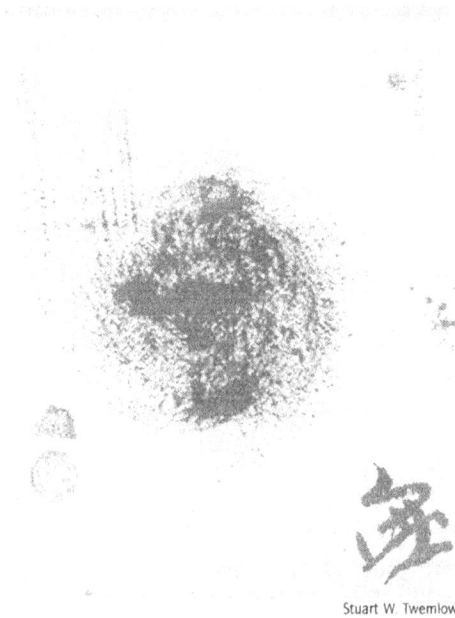

Stuart W. Twemlow

Figure 6.1.   Solid Impermanence.

Concluding remarks

We have proposed that the multicultural identity of the individual, patient, or analyst—as: "I am not just a Jew, I am not just a New Yorker, I am not just an African American, nor only my parents' child. I am more than the pieces patched together"—is critical to a full development of mental health. Such an expansion of the self creates a sense of agency and intention and also the risk of hypomanic exaltation, often evident in the poetry of Walt Whitman (1982). The defensive use of this happiness is indeed tempting and itself needs to be mourned. The actualization of the process of discovery as part of an analytic process requires one to see the importance of playing with these ideas of social context and identity in a dialectical way, as part of the overall capacity to differentiate self from not-self, an extension of Winnicott's (1971a) and Ogden's (1986) idea of potential analytic space. Such work encourages mentalization—that is, the capacity to reflect, regulate affect, empathize with self and others, and establish boundaries, all functions of a healthy and happy mind.

We use our personal epiphanies about our cultural background to illustrate the point, as in this poem that Nicholas wrote while in New Zealand (N. Twemlow, 2006b).

Te Po-tahuri-atu[6]

There's my father's biological mother,
scrubbing the dark from her arms,
the dark pooling in the corners of the room, the dark that
turns
dark as the darkening day brings home
her husband, who screams at the dark
TV, the dark refrigerator, the dark spot
on his lung. "What dark woman art thou?"
"It is gone. I've scrubbed it clean."
"There is darkness everywhere I look." "You haven't
looked at me." "You're all I see." "I've scrubbed
it clean, just for thee." "Mark this down.
Not this dark day, not this dark night, not
this dark life, nor this dark semblance
of an afterlife. Not you dark, not you not dark."
When the lights came on,
the refrigerator shuddered into its steady hum,
the TV snapped on.
When the lights came on, she sat in her chair
by the kitchen, watching him sit down to his dinner,
watching him watch his rugby, his gimp leg
tender from standing all day. Later,
when he fucked her in the dark, he whispered
in her ear he was going to fuck
the Maori clean out of her.
Te Po-nui (the great night)
Te Po-roa (the long night)
Te Po-uriuri (the deep night)
Te Po-kerekere (the intense night)
Te Po-tiwhatiwha (the dark night)
Te Po-te-kitea (the night in which nothing is seen)
Te Po-tangotango (the intensely dark night)
Te Po-whawha (the night of feeling)
Te Po-namunamu-ki-taiao (the night of seeking the passage to
the world)
Te Po-tahuri-atu (the night of restless turning)

This is a poem in which Nicholas first employed Maori language, a language he knows only in the most rudimentary sense. The poem is an attempt, one that quite possibly fails, to illustrate much of what this essay has been exploring. The main figure is a composite of several abstract and concrete representations of Maoris who might have grown up and lived in circumstances similar to his grandmother's. The Maori language at the poem's end are pulled directly from a Maori incantation that describes how night came to be. That incantation ends with a blessing of sorts, of the dawning of the new day. The poem, however, does not. It simply contains the pain and the wonder accompanying it.

Notes

1. Pakeha has been defined variously over the years, but we are using it in a very general sense to mean any New Zealander who is not Maori. Refer to Ranford's (2004) "'Pakeha': Its Origin and Meaning" for a substantial consideration of the matter.

2. Maori heritage very generally breaks down to tracing one's family bloodline (*whakapapa*) back to one of the original seven canoes (*waka*) that brought the original Maori settlers to New Zealand/Aotearoa. Our *waka* is *Tainui*. From there, one identifies an *iwi*, which is roughly equivalent to a tribe. Ours is *Maniapoto*. Next is the *hapu*, or sub-tribe, a sort of extended family. Ours is *Ngati Patupo*, who were highly skilled in warfare and were King Tawhiao's bodyguards.

3. Bill Manhire [1946–] is one of New Zealand's most visible writers and certainly its best-known poet. The country's inaugural poet laureate, Manhire is the author of more than ten books of poems, including *Lifted* (2005a) released by his long-time New Zealand publisher, Victoria University Press. Throughout his career, which spans over four decades, he has also managed to find time to write a children's book, a collection of short stories, several non-fiction titles, and several anthologies, the most recent among the last mentioned category being *121 New Zealand Poems* (2005b), published by Random House New Zealand. His day job, as Director of the International Institute of Modern Letters at Victoria University in Wellington, New Zealand, may be what brings Manhire into international focus.

4. The actual site to which this fable is attributed is called Mayor Island, which is located in the Bay of Plenty, thirty-five kilometres north of Tauranga, New Zealand.

5. These candies could be seen to embody my hybrid identity: brown on the outside and white on the inside, the dilemma of our lives in reverse, and strangely available for me to internalize.

6. Maori for "The night of restless turning".

III

Dislocation

7

The trauma of geographical dislocation: leaving, arriving, mourning, and becoming

Salman Akhtar

Moving from where one has lived for a long time to a new place of residence can have destabilizing effects upon the mind. How traumatic the situation will become depends on the age at which the move occurs, the depth of attachment to the original abode, the degree of choice in leaving it, the extent of anticipatory planning for such a change, the intrapsychic capacity to tolerate separations, and the magnitude of difference between the two places of residence (Akhtar, 1999a; Grinberg & Grinberg, 1989). While leaving home to attend college, "moving out" in the course of divorce, and even travel for vacations offer glimpses into its nature, the *trauma of dislocation* is most starkly evident in the setting of immigration and exile.

In sorting out the nuances of this disturbance, psychoanalytic literature has paid due attention to the accompanying disruptions in language fluency, work-related efficacy, and patterns of interpersonal relations. After all, what is a geophysical move without such internal fractures? Indeed, every major move alters both the human and the non-human components in our environment, which are densely intertwined. When we leave a place, we lose ties not only with friends and relatives but also with a familiar, non-human environment. The same applies to arriving at a new place: we not only meet different sorts of people, but encounter unfamiliar landscape, climate, and architecture as well. Changes in human and non-human environment always coexist when it comes to immigration and exile. Nonetheless it seems that the impact of the altered non-human surround has received less than optimal attention within the psychoanalytic literature. To be sure, there are exceptions in this regard. Denford (1981) is especially outstanding in declaring that

> Going away leads to different consequences for a man's human and non-human experience. He can reproduce the old life with people in the new place, because people do not differ greatly from one to the other. He eventually finds new friends. But places can differ so profoundly that it is no longer possible to have certain sorts of experiences of place at all. Such deprivations and losses inevitably increase awareness of the non-human world, both in the old and the new. [p. 325]

Grinberg and Grinberg's (1989) description of *disorienting anxieties* faced by recent immigrants, and my own inclusion of an unmistakably spatial metaphor—*from close and far to optimal distance*—among the four tracks along which post-migration identity change takes place (Akhtar, 1995, 1999a),[1] are among other evidences that the emotional impact of altered physical surround has not gone entirely unnoticed in the psychoanalytic literature.

Yet something is missing. The role of changed "non-human environment" in the trauma of dislocation lacks finer explication. The analytic literature has brought us to the theatre but not lifted the curtain from the stage. We cannot see what really is going on. We cannot decide, for instance, what all is to be included in "non-human environment". How does the changed physical surround actually affect the mind? What are the specific manifestations of the ruptured inanimate background and of the *self-righting tendency* (Lichtenberg, 1989) to redress them? And, how do such matters make their appearance in the clinical situation?

Striving to answer these questions forms the impetus for this chapter. It is my contention that the "environmental releasers" that Hartmann (1939, p. 35) deemed to be important in actualizing psychic potentials are not limited to relational scenarios involving human beings but also include cues from the inanimate physical surround. I further believe that *reality constancy*, which evolves out of "a concatenation of environmental experiences, memories, perceptions, ideas, etc. deriving from cathectic relationships with the human *and* non-human environment" (Frosch, 1966, p. 350, italics added), is not achieved once and for all; indeed, stability of internal representations of external reality requires continued input from outside. Also to be considered here is the *waking screen* (Pacella, 1980), which "plays an active role in scanning, integrating, reject- ing, or modifying all the newer percepts of object representations throughout life" (p. 130). Like the *dream screen* (Lewin, 1946), this blank background is seen to arise from the visual and tactile scan- ning of the mother by the infant during the first year of life. Mother's skin colour, facial characteristics, smell, height, and so on, all play in the evolution of this primal sensual meld, and the child (and, subsequently, the adult) tries to fit all new objects into this familiar configuration. It is my sense that non-human elements of the child's environment (e.g., toys, crib, blanket, home, trees, local animals, the street on which the family lives, regional landscape, and even sounds and climate that are typical of the early environment) also contribute to the texture of the waking screen, although they are not explicitly noted in the structure's original description.

In this contribution, I attempt to demonstrate how a major envi- ronmental change lacerates the above-mentioned structures, threat- ens the *safety feeling* (Sandler, 1960) that all human beings need, and therefore becomes traumatic. I go over the individual components of this change and attempt to show that, acting in unison, they can give rise to considerable perceptual and emotional imbalance. Following this, I describe the mind's restitutive efforts to undo the noxious impact of such trauma and conclude with some observations regarding the analytic treatment of individuals who have suffered from the *trauma of dislocation*, either as children or as adults.

The traumatic ingredients of environmental change

"Familiar and constant things in the child's environment carry a special affective value for the child in that they are more easily perceived—colloquially we say that they are known, recognizable, or familiar to the child. The constant presence of familiar things makes it easier for the child to maintain its minimum level of safety feeling."

Sandler (1960), p. 361

> "By remaining within a familiar environment an animal, or a
> human, knows at once where food and water are to be found,
> not only at different seasons of the ordinary year but also
> during those exceptionally bad years that occur from time to
> time; he knows too, where shelter from the weather can be got,
> where there are trees or cliffs or caves that provide safety, what
> are the common dangers and from what quarters they are likely
> to come."
>
> Bowlby (1973), p. 178

While separation from loved ones also constitutes an "environmental change", for the purposes of this contribution the expression is taken in its literal sense—that is, leaving one geophysical locale and going to another. Even with this restriction, matters remain far from simple. Significant environmental change, especially that associated with immigration and exile, involves losses of many kinds and destabilizations of many varieties. Prominent among them are (1) separation from a familiar ecological surround; (2) loss of valued personal possessions; (3) alteration in man–animal relationship; and (4) encounter with new utensils of living.

Separation from a familiar ecological surround

Leaving a country for another, or even one particular region for another region in the same country, involves a disturbing loss of familiar topography. Mountains can dissipate into low-lying flatlands and expansive views of blue sky brutally interrupted by skyscrapers. One can hardly ski in the tropics, and a town without a river feels strangely dry when compared to the one that has the grace of water. The task of adjusting to such changes takes a toll on the ego. Changes in the modal architecture, typical vegetation, and prevalent climate can also be distressing. The "mental pain" (Akhtar, 2000; Freud, 1926d [1925]) caused by the concomitant ruptures in ego-continuity is often at the forefront of the immigrant's mind. Counterphobically and a bit like the rapprochement-phase toddler (Mahler, Pine, & Bergman, 1975), the immigrant might libidinize the newness and feel excited by it for a little while. More often the tragedy of having exceeded the usual symbiotic orbit that one had established with one's environment hits home, so to speak. Pain, regret, and feelings of unbelonging (of oneself to the external world, and of the external world to oneself) emerge and cause great distress. One just does not feel "at home".

This state of alienation is dramatically unmasked when one comes across topography, climate, or vegetation that formed a part of one's formative environment. I have seen an analyst colleague born and raised in Botswana burst into delirious joy upon seeing bougainvilleas as we were driving from the airport to our hotel in Hawaii. I have heard the boyish thrill in the voice of another colleague, born and raised in South Africa, while he was describing his encounter with the Australian prairie. And I myself have experienced near "oceanic" (Rolland, quoted in Freud, 1930a) waves of happiness upon visiting Mexico and parts of the southeastern United States whose geophysical texture reminds me of the region in India where I grew up. Such pleasurable moments paradoxically give testimony to what otherwise is lacking. A glass of water appears irresistible only to one who is thirsty.

Loss of valued personal possessions

Leaving home inevitably involves leaving certain physical objects behind. In situations where the separation from home is volitional, development-facilitating, and time-limited (e.g., an adolescent going away to college, an out-of-town business trip), parting from one's cherished possessions remains tolerable. However, in the setting of divorce, immigration, and especially exile—where one's break with home is involuntary and psychologically violent—the loss of personal possessions can have a devastating impact. The loss of a house, automobile, grand piano, furniture, and similar "big" things is readily understood as being hurtful. But the loss of "small" things can be equally distressing. A misplaced stamp album can cause lifelong suffering. A toolbox given by one's father that is now lost to the fiasco of exile can be the source of sleepless nights for years. The loss of such objects threatens to wreck the intrapsychic relational bridges that are constituted by them. With each lost possession, the memories of a specific self–object relation becomes internally dim. In contrast, the loss of things that are largely "self-directed" causes narcissistic incoherence. The mundane paraphernalia of identity like clothes, wallet, shoes, and glasses connects us to reality and society in an unassuming but deep manner. Upon losing it, we feel existentially naked and robbed of subjective continuity.

Alteration in man–animal relationship

Yet another aspect of non-human environment affected by migration is man's relationship to animals. This is especially true of migration from predominately agrarian societies to industrialized nations, but it is also valid for migrations from rural areas to large cities within the same country. In rurally based societies, animals of all varieties—cows, buffaloes, horses, donkeys, cats, dogs, camels, monkeys, snakes, spiders, and even elephants, bears, and tigers—can form a part of people's everyday existence. They become receptacles of mythic projections, containers of unexpressed emotions, carriers of phallic exhibitionism, providers of maternal soothing, targets of dark eroticism, and brotherly companions in the journey of life (Akhtar & Brown, 2005; Akhtar & Volkan, 2005a, 2005b). When an individual thus raised moves to a country where contact with animals is limited to the possession of pets or visits to the local zoo, something subtle but of paramount importance is lost from his or her subjective experience. The different ways in which a particular animal is viewed in the immigrant's two different cultures shifts the nature of projections contained by the animal. The linguistic ploys of curses and endearments involving that animal therefore suffer the fate of confusion, contradiction, and atrophy. The resulting discontinuity taxes the ego, but the pain, unknown to the natives of the adoptive country, goes unnoticed. The frequent use of animal metaphors by immigrant poets from the so-called third-world countries (Akhtar, 1999a, pp. 37–38) testifies to the subterranean existence of such pain.

Encounter with new utensils of living

As one moves away from a known physical environment, one comes across new objects, literally speaking. The ego, already inwardly destabilized, owing to new id freedoms and changed superego dictates, turns to external reality in desperation. External reality, populated with unfamiliar accoutrements of life, in turn, fails to provide the needed coverage. The result is greater anxiety.

Matters do not end here. Unlike the previous mastery of life's tools and instruments, which was acquired gradually and with the loving help of parents, the immigrant's encounter with new physical objects is sudden in timing and excessive in amount. It is a matter of "too much", "too quickly". Moreover, learning in this context often involves seemingly elementary matters and therefore becomes shame-laden. This propels an inordinately autodidactic attitude,[2] which increases a sense of aloneness.

Their deleterious impact on the human mind

"Out of his usual habitat, the newcomer no longer has the necessary corroborative environmental feedback for his ego identity. . . . The more serious the break with the newcomer's continuity of his identity, the greater his yearning for those lost love objects (abandoned culture) which in the past provided a comfortable sense of continuity. On the other hand, the greater his longing for those lost love objects, the more afflictive are the threats to his identity."

Garza-Guerrero (1974), pp. 418–419

"Depression is a many-sided phenomenon comprising those painful and complex manifestations triggered off by the meaning or the 'meaninglessness' that each individual ascribes to the experience of loss. Every loss, be it of an object, external or internal, or of parts of the self, may arouse the feeling that the fulfilment of the wish to recover the loss is impossible."

Grinberg (1978), p. 275

Working in unison, the four factors outlined above (separation from familiar topography, loss of personal possessions, alteration of man–animal relationship, and encounter with new physical objects) mobilize the anxiety of adjustment and the ache of mourning (Freud, 1917e [1915]) but also lead to subtle perceptual disturbances of the ego. Prominent among these are alterations of the figure–ground relationship and an excessive tendency towards sensory compartmentalization. The former manifests in heightened awareness of one's actions and even one's whereabouts. Living for the first twenty-six years of my life in India, I, for instance, never registered that I was "living in India". I was just "living". Now residing in the United States for over thirty years, I am off and on conscious of "living in the United States"; this awareness was ever-present when I arrived and has diminished over time. I am "living in the United States". In contrast, my friends who are born and raised here do not feel that they are "living in the United States"; they are simply "living". The two experiences are hardly the same. The experience of "living" implies a seamless fusion with one's inanimate surround, as well as a painless demarcation from it. The experience of "living in someplace" belies a rough-edged union and narcissistically taxing demarcation from the environment. Let me reiterate: *living* and *living in some place* are poles apart. The difference between them is that between the subjectivities of the soup and the dumpling.

Such figure–ground incoherence also involves daily actions, especially those requiring newly acquired skills. Constantly speaking in a new language,[3] operating unfamiliar household machines, and participating in new social customs increases self-awareness to levels that cause a disjunction between action and its context.

Another phenomenon that results from the above-mentioned disturbances and, in a dialectical fashion, causes them is that the dislocated person finds insufficient opportunity to cross and re-cross without challenge "the transitional area between synaesthesia and sensory compartmentalization" (Kafka, 1989, p. 47). Now, from a developmental perspective, we are aware that synaesthesia is more characteristic of early experiences and that sensory compartmentalization is more characteristic of later experiences (Schachtel, 1947). Moreover, the freedom to fuse and separate different modalities remains available in healthy development. Enjoyment of metaphor especially depends on this perceptual liberty in imagination. The fresh immigrant, however, lacks opportunities to move freely between the self-abandonment of rapture and alertness of task-orientation, between perceiving the figure and ground separately sometimes and together at other times, and between the dreamy conflation of sensory modalities and a hyper-realistic separation of them. Poetry of communication escapes him. Literalness is his prison.

Another type of disturbance is also evident, especially in the case of those who migrate from less industrialized to more industrialized societies. They come from a culture where contact with nature—in the form of rain, thunder, wind, wood, big and small animals, trees, plants, and rivers—is of daily occurrence, and such intimate relationship with the non-human environment produces a sort of respect for, and even personal kinship with, the elements of nature (Searles, 1960). When such individuals arrive in a society where the average individual lives with an abundance of physical objects with relative ignorance of their natural origins, a disturbing shift takes place in his or her inner self. Pressured to assimilate, the individual undergoes a subtle transformation into one who can no longer experience the non-human environment as something meaningful. Hence he or she can feel "neither a sense of profound kinship with that environment, nor a sense of profound difference from it" (Searles, 1960, p. 396). The dislocated person might thus become over-, and under-, differentiated from his or her inanimate surround at the same time. In either case, the end result is far from his previous *going-on-being* (Winnicott, 1960b).

This brings up the subjective experience of time. Note that such experience is governed by forces of the culture at large, and hence it is not easily transportable across national and cultural boundaries. Pande (1968) has eloquently summarized the difference between East and West in the time experience; the same, by and large, applies to most less-industrialized, third-world countries. For the East, relatively speaking, past, present, and future merge into one another; for the West, they are discrete entities. For the East, experience in time is like water collected in a pool (stagnant, perhaps); for the West, time is more like water flowing in a stream, and one is acutely aware that what flows away, flows away forever (pp. 428–429).

I have elsewhere attempted to trace the roots of this difference by noting the fact that, in industrialized nations, time was gradually rendered into a commodity, whereas in non-industrialized nations it was not. In the former,

> passing moments were captured, named, measured, and sold. Like water, time was put into a tray and frozen into ice cubes of designated length. Each cube has its price, depending upon the size. Hiring of labor, operation of production lines, rental of property, all became time-dependent and tied to capital generation. Efficiency and punctuality became nearly synonymous. Thus was born what I call the *time of the mind* or the *time of money*. In contrast, the non-industrialized nations, where planes, trains, phones, faxes, and e-mail did not create rapid access to others and where the manufacture of commodities did not take over

the community, the beginning and ending of various social get-togethers continued to depend upon the arrival of loved ones (often by treacherously unreliable means) and the permissive winks of gods and seasons. Action began only when the libido–aggression balance in the social matrix shifted in favor of the former. This is what I call the *time of the heart* or the *time of love.* [Akhtar, 1999a, p. 117]

When someone from a third-world country emigrates to an industrialized country, he or she carries within him/herself the *time of the heart* but has to adapt to the *time of the mind.* What appears as a lack of punctuality in such circumstances might be an obedience to a different internal clock. Similarly, when someone from an industrialized nation emigrates to a third-world country, he or she carries within him/herself the *time of the mind* but has to adapt to the *time of the heart.* What then appears as an inordinate and rigid reliance on punctuality is merely a matter of loyalty to a different inner sense of time. There is, in the end, it seems, a *bicultural punctuality* that needs to be empathized with while dealing with all immigrant individuals.

Defensive and restituitive efforts

"All infants like to venture and stay just a bit of distance away from the enveloping arms of the mother; and, as soon as they are motorically able to, they like to slide down from the mother's lap. But they tend to remain or crawl back as near as possible to play at the mother's feet."

Mahler (1974), p. 155

"To this day, immigrants to the United States gravitate towards certain towns and to neighborhoods that become the enclave of their culture of origin, recreated in their adoptive country. Here they feel at home; here they belong. From this mooring, they can safely venture forth to explore the unknown culture beyond the borders of the neighborhood."

Kahn (1997), p. 277

In an attempt to diminish his anxiety, pain, and perceptual instability, the dislocated person resorts to a number of measures. These involve operations in the inner world, interpersonal realm, and external reality. An admixture of regressive and progressive trends is evident in all such mechanisms. In itself, their presence does not belie psychopathology. It is only when they become literal, tenacious, grossly unrealistic, and ego-depleting that the threshold to illness is crossed. Otherwise, they are stop-gap, *transitional phenomena* (Winnicott, 1953) that facilitate self-holding in perceptually uncertain and affectively turbulent times. Five such measures are: repudiation; return; replication; reunion; and reparation.

Repudiation

While trying to adjust to new external realities, many immigrants continue to deny the change at the deeper level. Such repudiation can extend to their perception of the environment around them, their feelings about it, and their interactions with it. Thus they are involved in a process of denial on many levels.

> In sensory denial, the physical location is experientially denied: "I am not here; I am there." In psychological denial, the immigrant status is denied: "I don't have to mourn; I am going back." In social denial, the immigrant rejects the local community and disassociates from it: "I am not one of them." [Knafo & Yaari, 1997, pp. 230–231]

The last-mentioned mechanism can also act in the opposite direction and cause *counterphobic assimilation* (Teja & Akhtar, 1981). By rapidly and fully taking on the dictates of the adopted country, the immigrant seems to be declaring that no discontinuity exists between his or her prior and current norms of thinking, language, food, attire, and behaviour. Denial thus extends to internal as well as external reality.

Such *manic defence* (Klein, 1935) might help one survive for a while, or, if it is focal, for a long time, in situations of major environmental change. More often the traumatic impact of the disruption makes itself felt. A common manifestation of this occurs via the *ocnophilic bent* (Balint, 1959) to hoard things, cling rigidly to one's personal possessions, and get upset if physical objects in one's environment are moved.[4] The tendency to take too many things while on a trip, and phobic avoidances of travel, also emanate from such trauma. To wit, the founder of psychoanalysis—twice an immigrant (at ages 3 and 4) and once an exile (at age 82)—himself displayed symptoms of this sort. The journey from his birthplace Freiberg to Leipzig, at age 3, was especially traumatic for him.

> On the way to Leipzig the train passed through Breslau, where Freud saw gas jets for the first time; they made him think of souls burning in hell! From this journey also dated the beginning of a "phobia" of traveling by train, from which he suffered a good deal for about a dozen years (1887–1899), before he was able to dispel it by analysis. It turned out to be connected with the fear of losing his home (and ultimately his mother's breast)—a panic of starvation which must have been in its turn a reaction to some infantile greed. Traces of it remained in later life in the form of slightly undue anxiety about catching trains. [Jones, 1953, p. 13]

Such neurotic symptoms might coexist with persistent denial or might be the first evidence that underlying distress can no longer be repudiated, that something needs to be done about.

Return

Once "repudiation" is given up (and, sometimes, even in its split-off presence), the returning to the original homeland develops. Understandably, it is more marked among immigrants than among exiles who have been forced out of their homes. It is psychologically interesting that the date of return is always placed in the distant future; it is not next month or even next year. Structurally and dynamically speaking, the *fantasy of return* is essentially a *someday fantasy* (Akhtar, 1996) which rests upon denial of discordant sectors of reality, splitting-off of self- and object-representations that mobilize aggression, defensively motivated inauthenticity in the perceptual rind of the ego, and a temporal displacement (from past to future) of an idealized state of man–environment symbiosis. In other words, the immigrant comes to believe that he or she came from an "all-good" world and one day will return to it.

The defensive nature of such fantasy is evident in two ways. First, the ambivalence underlying it shows. In myriad rationalized ways, acting upon it is postponed. Conditions (e.g., saving money, earning a diploma, children growing up) are set for fulfilling the fantasy, but in reality this never happens. Few immigrants return to their original homes. They remain on an existential treadmill. A second evidence of the hollowness of the return fantasy is presented by what happens when immigrants do go back to their homeland. They experience what the Spanish journalist Maruja Torres has called *the wound of return* (cited by Grinberg & Grinberg, 1989). The immigrants find that they have changed and that the country they had left behind is also no longer the same. The encounter is not a smooth resumption of life; it feels like another immigration. To their surprise and shame, the immigrants now find themselves missing their country of adoption.

A variant of the fantasy of return is the *fantasy of burial* in one's homeland. The echo of "emotional refuelling" (Mahler, Pine, & Bergman, 1975) through return to early infant–mother symbiosis is unmistakably present here. However, such genetic reductionism and the associated compulsion to view all relationships with the inanimate world as "displacements" must be resisted. Adult development, while often reworking childhood conflicts, is not the same as early development. The "fantasy of burial" might give expression to symbiotic longings that were either characterologically unresolved or are resurrected by old age *and* also contain direct yearnings for the texture of one's land.[5] Madow (1997) observes that as we grow old, "we become more and more dependent, increasingly helpless, and, to conclude metaphorically, end up with an I.V. drip as an umbilical cord and ultimately are reunited with Mother Earth" (p. 166). I agree with him but feel inclined to break his expression "Mother Earth" into "Mother *and* Earth".[6] Wish for merger with *both* might lie at the deepest core of human psyche, even if one may at times stand for the other. And it is the combination of these two "pull" factors (working in unison with the "push" factor of chronic unbelonging to the country of adoption) that gives the burial fantasy its allure and strength. No wonder many immigrants arrange for their bodies or their cremated remains to be sent back to their countries for burial.[7]

Replication

Less concrete than the immigrant's wish to return is his or her wish to replicate what he or she has lost. Here the longing for the original homeland emerges as an attempt to re-create that home in the country of adoption. The immigrant adorns his or her residence with ethnic artefacts, often to the extent that the home acquires a shrine-like quality (Akhtar, 1995, 1999a; Grinberg & Grinberg, 1989; Teja & Akhtar, 1981). Dislocated individuals of this type also tend to eat only their ethnic food, listen to their own music, and associate only exclusively with homoethnic groups. It is as if they have never left their lands of origin. A wish-fulfilling dream is thus transposed on to day-to-day reality. This relieves pain but also causes a perceptual inversion that impedes ego growth.

A compromise between "return" and "replication" is evident in the immigrant's desire to find an area in his or country of adoption whose topography, climate, and vegetation resembles what he or she had left behind. Indeed, the immigrant might get involved in a lifelong attempt at such symbolic restitution. A cardiologist friend of mine, who grew up in Kenya and now lives in Boston, feels a persistent desire to relocate to Southern California, Arizona, or New Mexico, which remind him of his childhood environment. And, to be sure, there are numerous such individuals among us.

Reunion

Subject to *Seelenschmerz* (Freud, 1926d [1925], p. 169) of separation from a familiar topography, the immigrant often resorts to its hypercathexis. This mechanism whereby a lost object tends to be idealized was first pointed out by Freud (1917e [1915]) in his seminal paper, "Mourning and Melancholia". In the immigrant's case, this results in an exaggerated love for the houses, cafés, street corners, hills, and the countryside of his or her land. The strongest affects are reserved for moments when he or she recalls them or talks about an old grandfather clock, a crockery set, a gramophone, or sewing machine. At such times, the wish to recapture an idealized past stirs up a "bittersweet pleasure" (Kleiner, 1970, p. 11) of pain and joy. Pain is caused by the awareness of separation from the now-idealized object and joy by a fantasied reunion with it through reminiscences. "It is the subtlety, iridescence, and ambivalence of these feelings that gives nostalgia its inimitable coloration" (Werman, 1977, p. 393). (For an elucidation of the more personal ontogenetic roots of nostalgia, see Sterba, 1934; Fenichel, 1945; Fodor, 1950.)

Through repeatedly dipping into the Ganges of nostalgia, the immigrant expresses his or her core dilemma: he or she can neither give up the attachment to the internal representation of primary environment by mourning nor ever re-create it in external reality to his or her ego's satisfaction. Instead, he or she retains the memory of the original land in a psychic limbo by a stubborn *nostalgic relationship* (Geahchan, 1968) with it. "This leads to an indefinite and indefinable quest—and if an object should appear that seems to correspond to the nostalgic desire, it is promptly rejected, it becomes demytholo-gized; it is not what it promised to be. The subject can thus only enjoy the search and never the possession" (Werman, 1977, p. 391).

This element of search in nostalgia gives a clue to its psychody-namic kinship with the *someday fantasies* described above. Often *if only* and *someday fantasies* coexist, with nostalgia stirring up the hope of return, and inability to return fuelling the need for nostalgic regression.

Reparation

Besides its externalized versions of going back to build actual struc-tures (e.g., a house, a clinic) in the country of origin, the wish for reparation—arising out of the inner awareness that in leaving home one has, in a way, attacked it—also propels sublimation and creativ-ity. The laceration of the *waking screen* (Pacella, 1980) is, after all, self-caused and is a source not only of anguish but of unconscious guilt. Creativity helps manage both these emotions. The former is di-minished by the manic triumph of giving "birth" to an artistic prod-uct, and the latter is reduced by the reparative value of that product. The combined force of pain and remorse therefore can give rise to remarkable creative output. One's mind becomes the fertile *mother-land of ideas* in a reparative identification with the idealized artistic productivity of the lost country. The orphaned inner child can thus reclaim, inch by inch, the psychic territory lost.

Conspicuous examples of such creative achievement are the Ital-ian landscapes made by the artist Giorgio de Chirico. Born of recent-ly migrated Italian parents in Greece, de Chirico grew up knowing dislocation. His parents frequently moved from one home to an-other during his childhood, and his mother returned to Italy after her husband's death when de Chirico was 18 years old. As an adult, he led a peripatetic life, frequently moving between Greece, Ger-many, Italy, and France, until he finally settled in Italy. Throughout these sojourns, de Chirico seemed to be searching for an environment that would be congenial and soothing (Krystal, 1966). Not surprisingly, his paintings are replete with allusions to travel and migration—horses, trains, and railroad stations—as well as to architectural nuances of his true motherland, Italy.[8] Most immigrants are not so talented, yet many do write memoirs, poems, and fiction involving their motherland, even though these never get published. Still others enjoy the creativity of migration vicariously and let an established homoethnic poet assume the role of their "community's daydreamer" (Arlow, 1986, p. 58).

* * *

Together these five measures (*repudiation*, *return*, *replication*, *reunion*, and *reparation*) help the immigrant manage the trauma of his or her dislocation. The pain nonetheless remains and colours both the neurotic as well as the day-to-day suffering that the immigrant, like anyone else, is vulnerable to in the course of his or her existence.

Technical implications

"Spatial partitions clearly divide more than just space. The lines that mark off supposedly insular chunks of space often represent the invisible lines that separate purely mental entities such as nations or ethnic groups from one another, and crossing them serves to articulate passage through such mental partitions."

Zerubavel (1991), p. 7).

"There can be no interpretation without competent management and no useful management without interpretation. When linked to the shared task of understanding, the two methods—understood psychoanalytically—provide tools for examining the boundary between the patient's inner and outer worlds."

Shapiro (1997), p. 12

In dealing with individuals suffering from the *trauma of dislocation*, the analyst might benefit by keeping the following five guidelines in mind. It should not be overlooked, though, that these guidelines are not designed to replace the customary work of transference interpretation, reconstruction, and countertransference vigilance. Nor are they meant to interfere with the classical "trio of guideposts" (Pine, 1997, p. 13) of abstinence, neutrality, and anonymity that is central to our work. They are neither rigid rules of technique nor irrelevant garnish of good manners. They simply constitute the background[9] for the "evenly suspended attention" (Freud, 1912e, p. 111) needed for conducting psychoanalysis.

Allowing the patient a greater amount of physical settling in the office

Based on clinical work with immigrant, exiled, and recently divorced patients and those with a history of multiple moves of residence during their first few years of life, I have arrived at a sense that such patients require a greater than usual latitude in physically settling in the analyst's office. They look around the office more intently, let their hands linger for just a moment longer on the door handle as they enter and leave the office, and rub their hands on the couch with ever so slightly marked desperation. They play with the corners of the analytic napkin, touch the wall next to the couch, gently adjust a crooked picture in the waiting room, glance at a lamp or rug solemnly, and occasionally even sit up not only to see the analyst but to see the office itself. They develop special fondness for one or the other physical item in the analyst's office and, incredible though it may sound, might even have chosen the analyst for that reason in the first place.

This concern leads some analysts to have rather spartan offices, though certainly bare walls can evoke as much projection as a shelf overflowing with books. Pertinent in this context is Kurtz's (1988) observation that Freud had filled up every conceivable space in his office with things of beauty and value to compensate for the loneliness he felt in sitting behind the patient.

I, too, have wondered about the profusion of books, painting, and sculptures in analysts' offices and have concluded that four factors are responsible for this. First, most analysts are cultured individuals, knowledgeable in humanities and aesthetically inclined; the cultural artefacts represent their authentic existence. Second, most analysts identify with Freud and thus carry some attributes of his office to theirs. Third, spending long hours behind closed doors listening to conflict and pain mobilizes the necessity (both as a healthy adaptation and manic defence) to surround oneself with objets d'art. Finally, the presence of such things in the office betrays an unconscious power in the course of treatment. In this way, the analyst's physical possessions come to acquire *totemic* (Freud, 1912–13) and *shamanic* (Kakar, 1997) attributes.

Patients who are deeply concerned about the analyst's office also tend to give gifts to the analyst more frequently and often bring things (e.g., photographs, letters) to show him or her for enlivening their narratives. Conversely, they also tend to take little things from the analyst's office and, at times, save all their bills as a token of their connection to the analyst and as a tangible glue to their internally destabilized perceptual world.

Clinical Vignette: 1

Lisa was 2 years and 3 months when her beloved nursemaid abruptly left, taking with her all the familiar possessions that the little girl treasured—clothes that were used for "dressing-up", a special pillow that Lisa slept on in the nursemaid's room, a menagerie of tiny china animals, a collection of children's books they read together at bedtime. The family soon moved to a new country, and all trace of the room shared with the nursemaid was gone. Thirty years later, Lisa's analysis began not with her lying on the couch, but perched on it, legs tucked under her, and her arms hugging the pillow. From time to time, she would startle me by taking one of my books from the shelf, opening it, and starting to pore through its pages, talking to herself as she went from page to page. Two years later, she confessed that she frequently swiped magazines from the waiting room: "Just to have for keeps in case something happened to you." For vacations, she took more, "enough for bedtime reading till you get back". I took all this to be a basic *environmental provision* (Winnicott, 1956) and a particular form of holding that she needed and indeed took for herself. It was not to be questioned or interpreted until, years later, she began to wonder about it herself. As interpretative work about her attachment to my things began, she exclaimed one day, "I am glad you didn't say anything about all this in the beginning. It would have made me too self-conscious, and then I couldn't have taken your stuff home with me. But I wouldn't have been able to survive without them either."

The proper technical stance with such patients, I believe, is to allow such "micro-enactments" to continue for a very long time, if not interminably. The analytic greed for interpretation must be restrained, and the broad, stabilizing purposes of their attitude towards the inanimate aspect of the clinical situation should be respected over and above the potential deconstruction of such attitude.

Validating the feelings of dislocation

The analyst must offer empathic resonance to a patient's sense of geographical dislocation. He or she must convey to the patient that he or she values the human need for relatedness with the inanimate surround and understands how a disruption of such relatedness can be disorienting. The analyst must also demonstrate to the patient that he or she can bear the latter's occasional (and, sometimes chronic) unrelatedness to the land where he or she lives and where they are conducting the analytic work. In a lecture titled "Nothing at Centre", delivered on 19 June 1959, Winnicott addresses this matter, even though he was talking of seemingly different clinical issues:

> In this particular patient, it was vitally important that I must recognize that at the centre there is nothing . . . he not only has no belief that there is anything there which could be called he; rather he knows that at the centre there is nothing and it is only this that he can tolerate. If I were to provide any hope that there is something there, he would have to destroy me. [1959, p. 51]

In other words, the analyst needs to avoid manic attempts at reassurance and overzealous discernment of symbolism in a dislocated person's alienation. The analyst simply has to bear the analysand's agony of dislocation and communicate, in one form or the other, that he or she knows and respects the malady. The following clinical interaction related by Searles (1960) illustrates this point.

Clinical Vignette: 2

The poignant moment of all came near the end of the hour when, after having talked in this vein [excitedly about her home city, Boston], she laughed in an embarrassed way and said "Oh, I know what is so funny: I thought Boston was right around here! Isn't that funny?" The "right around here" had the connotation of "right outside the window". The emotional tone of her words unconcealed by her embarrassed laughter was one of tremendous nostalgia. I replied, deeply moved, "I guess you must miss Boston an awful lot, Doris." [p. 333]

Note that the analyst avoids the temptation of pointing out that the comment about Boston being "right around here" occurred just when the patient was about to leave; it seemed to be mobilized by the anxiety of separation. Bringing this to the patient's attention might have been a clever (and, not entirely inaccurate) intervention but one that would most likely be ill-timed and misattuned.

Affirmatively as well as interpretatively dealing with nostalgia

The analyst needs to respect the immigrant's lapses into nostalgia and must provide ample space for its elaboration. At times a clear *affirmative intervention* (Killingmo, 1989) confirming the "validity" of the patient's yearning might be necessary before (or even in lieu of) handling the material interpretatively. However, in the long run, the analyst does have to consider the fact that nostalgic yearning can be used as an ointment against frustration and rage in the external reality and as well as in the transference.

Clinical Vignette: 3

Dina, a Peruvian woman in analysis, began talking about her beloved grandmother's funeral some years ago, almost immediately after I had told her of my unavailability for a few days. The connection was obvious. I waited. Gradually, intricate details of Peruvian funeral rites began to occupy her associations. Dina's momentary sadness upon my telling her that I would not be available for three days was now replaced by the vigour of story-telling. I found myself raptly absorbed in the material, feeling enriched by learning the cultural details. Returning to a self-observing stance a few minutes later, I noted that she not only had defensively warded off her pain but also had given me a parting gift, as it were. Interpretative interventions along this line deepened the material and facilitated the analysis of her disappointment at my being away and the subsequent anger about it.

Expressing warm feelings about things "back home" can also be a shy deflection of acknowledging comfort in the analyst's office. Awareness of this and other varied *screen functions* of nostalgia (Freedman, 1956; Sohn, 1983; Werman, 1977) would prepare the analyst for its interpretative handling in the later phases of the analyses of immigrant patients.

Work with refugees and exiles requires a different approach (Akhtar, 1999b). Here the analyst's task, for a long time, is to silently note the absence of associations to the homeland or empathize with how bad, and not how good, was the original homeland. As this work proceeds, the patient might unwittingly reveal the existence of some pleasant memories of the homeland as well. The analyst, however, must not bring these to the patient's attention too quickly; that would only lead to a defensive recoil. After a sufficient length of time and with the security that his complaints are regarded as legitimate—as they often are—the patient might be prepared to bring into his full consciousness the opposite constellation of his attitude. To undo such psychic compartmentalization necessitates that the analyst retain the patient's contradictory emotional attitudes in mind and make "bridging interventions" (Akhtar, 1998; Kernberg, 1975, p. 96) that gently demonstrate the existence of ambivalence to the patient. The analyst must also analyse the defences against the emergence of nostalgia. He or she must demonstrate to the patient that the catastrophe that forced him out of his homeland is precisely what renders him unable to recall anything positive about that nation. The effects of the ethnopolitical trauma have spread backwards to spoil the memory of earlier good times.

Conducting developmental work
in regards to the changed physical reality

The analyst of a dislocated person must bear in mind the relatively greater role he or she plays as a new object for his or her patient. The overlaps between the developmental process and the analyst process (Fleming, 1972; Loewald, 1960; Settlage, 1992) are more marked in such treatments. Here the analyst must cultivate a *developmental stance* (Settlage, 1992) or generative attitude. Besides helping the patient resolve his psychopathology, the analyst must seek to release developmental potential by silently but decidedly expecting their blossoming and by explicitly acknowledging the patient's ego growth when it occurs. Such *developmental work* (Pine, 1997) should also involve helping the patient find words for new external and internal experiences, maintaining hope over long periods of time, correcting culturally emanating misunderstandings of social reality, and genuinely believing that development is a lifelong process and that ego-mastery does not halt with one or the other developmental epoch. A judicious use of educative measures, especially if the patient is a fresh immigrant, can also facilitate (rather than impede) the analysis of deeper, more personal conflicts.

Clinical Vignette: 4

Fred was a long-haired and gaunt second-year psychiatric resident who had arrived in the United States from South Korea only fifteen months earlier and had entered psychoanalysis with an American-born, Jewish analyst. He felt inhibited in a number of social realms. One situation that was especially difficult for him involved placing his order when he and his American classmates went for lunch at restaurants near the hospital. They seemed to know exactly what to order whereas he became tongue-tied. He did not know how to order things, what certain things were, what food items went together, and so on. As a result, he would lie and avoid going for lunch, but then he was left alone and hungry.

In his analysis, the anxiety of eating was found to have deeper roots. When he was 6 years old, his mother died of scleroderma, having become quite emaciated and restricted due to contractures. He had memories of taking home-cooked food to his mother during her last days in a hospital. She would often give him portions of food from her plate. Eating and asking for food thus became highly charged with emotional conflicts. In the transference, too, he showed little entitlement, little desire to receive love or attention from the analyst. Instead, he felt compelled to be on time, pay promptly, and produce rich associations (food!) for the analyst, who he believed was depressed (his suffering from scleroderma!). As interpretative work proceeded, Fred's inhibition in eating began to diminish, but the fear of ordering food in restaurants remained. Shame over not knowing what to order was intense and pervasive in his associations.

During one such session, the analyst (who had recently learned that Fred had no inhibition in ordering food in Korean restaurants!) decided to put aside his usual exploratory and reconstructive approach. He said: "Look, this is the United States. It is a country of immigrants. Lots of people here go to restaurants and don't know what this or that particular dish is. So, they ask. They say to the waiter 'Excuse me, what exactly is such and such?' The same applies to you. Nobody will care if you ask. In fact, it is the waiter's job to tell you what this or that food is." Fred responded with a profound sense of relief and gratitude. Even though it took him some time to put this fully in practice, he reported feeling immensely helped by this intervention.

Maintaining receptivity to non-human transferences and countertransferences

The analyst working with traumatically dislocated individuals must be prepared to "receive" non-human, largely environmental transferences despite their subtle and, at times, uncanny qualities. It cannot be overemphasized that

> the non-human environment of the infant and the young child, through its being in general more simple and stable and manipulable than the human environment, provides him with a kind of practice-ground in which he can develop capacities which will be useful to him in his interpersonal relationships. [Searles, 1960, p. 85]

Indeed, this early "dialogue" with the inanimate surround is often reactivated during analytic regression. The subsequent feelings may get attached to specific things in the analyst's office or at times to the analyst's person him/herself. Such transferences, if they can be called that, emanate from the patient's need to re-create the inner representation of his earlier ecologic surround and then mend its rupture in proxy. A common manifestation is the patient's "loving" a chair or rug or painting in the analyst's office or sometimes passing by the analyst him/herself without noticing him or her, as if the analyst were a tree in the backyard of the patient's childhood home. Or, the patient might want a particular kind of relatedness with the analyst that he originally experienced with a childhood pet.

Clinical Vignette: 5

Four years before starting analysis, Stacy, a 30-year-old child welfare worker, had moved from Israel to the United States. More significant were her two childhood immigrations at ages 2 and 4. Even in Israel (where her family had arrived when she was 6 years old), she was subject to frequent changes of residence. Raised by a depressed mother and an extremely busy father, she found solace in her relationship with a puppy that her father bought her. It became her inseparable companion and often slept in her bed. She would snuggle against the dog, gently kiss his wet nose, and breathe in the moist air that came out of his nostrils. Wishes reflective of similar relatedness with me came out during her analysis. She wanted to play with me, hold me tightly, go running with me, and look intently in my "big, brown eyes". The reconstruction of such wishes had to include not only what was missing in her childhood but also the soothing companionship provided by her contact with the dog.

At other times, such phenomena are evident in the countertransference experience only.

Clinical Vignette: 6

To Logan, an immigrant analysand who was profoundly upset about my upcoming vacation, I once said: "It seems to me that sometimes I am like an ocean to you, in which you swim freely like a fish; at other times, I am like a jar and you the water nicely contained in it. In either case, my leaving feels profoundly threatening to you, since it is like an ocean drying up for a fish or a jar breaking for the water in it." The patient sobbed but indicated feeling understood.

A significant thing to note about this interpretation is that it referred to her transference to me as an environment rather than as a person and, in doing so, relied heavily on Winnicott's (1963a) concept of the *holding environment*. An extension of such thinking is that the analyst's moving things (e.g., a bookshelf, a rug, a lamp) in and out of his or her office might re-create, for the dislocated patient, the trauma of territorial instability. Piaget's (1937) concept of *object permanence* acquires an enlarged connotation here, insofar as the analyst has to be mindful of his or her patient's need for environmental stability, though not at the risk of overlooking the specific meanings of the changes in the office to the patient.

Concluding remarks

"It appeared then, that Freiberg was an encapsulated ideal in the past, and that England was an ideal 'other place' in the future. Freud's journey to England, therefore, may also have been a return to some idyllic fantasy of childhood."

Ward (1993), p. 38

"There are some cultures in which to be a separate differentiated self, as we know it, would be anathema. There are other cultures where the deep inner self, upon maturity, does not separate but finally merges with the cosmos. While this is a deeply spiritual concept, which is foreign to us in the West, we have only to analytically treat a patient from an Eastern culture to be struck by the fact that our metapsychological concept of the self in the Anglo-American West is by no means universal; it is highly ethnocentric and circumscribed to our own unique view of humanity."

Perez-Foster, Moskowitz, & Javier (1996), p. 7).

In this contribution, I have offered a conceptual survey that highlights the role of the non-human environment in the growth and sustenance of the human psychic structure. I have also delineated how a major spatial dislocation impacts upon the mind and what psychosocial measures are taken by individuals to rectify the resulting destabilization. I have then offered some guidelines for conducting analytic work with dislocated individuals.[10]

Through all this, I have attempted to show that a laceration of *reality constancy* (Frosch, 1966) and the inanimate constituents of the *waking screen* (Pacella, 1980) occurs in situations of major geophysical dislocation. Life continues, but something about its truth becomes shaken up. It is as if a movie is being shown and someone has caused a gash in the screen with a knife. The drama goes on, but its seeing (and emotional experiencing) is disturbed. It is my impression that empathy with such a perceptually fractured and emotionally frustrating situation and its repair through judicious and dignified environmental provision is necessary glue for mending the associated ruptures of the ego. Only then can analysis—in its traditional sense—begin, proceed, and be meaningful.

Notes

Presented at the 44th Congress of the International Psychoanalytical Association, Rio de Janeiro, Brazil, 28 July 2005. The author wishes to thank Jennifer Bonovitz, Seymour Rabinowitz, and William Singletary for providing a clinical vignette.

1. These four tracks are: from love or hate to ambivalence, from near or far to optimal distance, from yesterday or tomorrow or today, and from yours or mine to ours (Akhtar, 1995, 1999a). Respectively, they attempt to address the dimensions of affect, space, time, and mutuality in the realm of identity transformation following immigration.

2. In an unfortunate reversal of generational functions, children of immigrants often get saddled with teaching social skills to their parents. This burdens their egos and also makes it difficult for parents to let go of them (Akhtar & Choi, 2004).

3. The impact of immigration on language and its representational attributes constitutes a vast topic, which is beyond the scope of this chapter. While I have myself addressed this matter elsewhere (Akhtar, 1999a), for a truly comprehensive explication of it I refer the reader to Amati-Mehler, Argentieri, and Canestri's (1993) outstanding monograph, *The Babel of The Unconscious*.

4. The syndrome of compulsive furniture-moving constitutes a libidinized and counterphobic defence against an underlying dread of sudden environmental change.

5. To be sure, it can be argued that this land itself contains the remains of previously buried ancestors and therefore is an external representation of the multi-layered internal world of objects. Striking in this light is the proclamation of the valorous American Indian chief, Crazy Horse [1845–1877], who declared: "My lands are where my dead lie buried!" (quoted in DeWall, 1984, p. 26).

6. A counterpart to Winnicott's (1963a) notion of "mother as environment" is my implication here of "environment as mother".

7. Among psychoanalysts, Margaret Mahler is a prominent example of having done so. Some eight years before her death, she arranged to have her ashes transported to Sopron, Hungary, and interred in the Jewish cemetery next to her father's grave (Stepansky, 1988).

8. The titles of de Chirico's painting tell a similar story: *The Departure of a Poet*, *The Anguish of Departure*, and *The Melancholy of Departure*. The latter is an especially powerful depiction of his desperate and lifelong homesickness.

9. According the eminent British photographer Lord Snowdon, "A background has to be just this side of being something and just the other side of being nothing" (quoted in Lacayo, 1984, p. 55).

10. My focus in this chapter has been on immigrant patients. Elsewhere (Akhtar, 2006), I have elucidated the technical challenges faced by immigrant analysts.

8

The clinical discovery of time and place

James Telfer

It is possible to be with someone who does not feel him/herself to be in a place. Such a person can be with you, as far as you are concerned, but cannot determine whether he or she is awake or dreaming and would not know if he or she had invented you in a dream.

This is not dementia or delirium: this person can tell you the time of day and the address, but these facts have no psychic reality. One such patient, a young librarian whom I shall call "K", often had dreams within which she could not tell if she was awake or not. She would often wake up believing for a minute or two that she was in Brazil or at a former home, or else somewhere eerily familiar but not recognizable.

With her boyfriend "Q" she had often felt that she was with someone else. She had sensed momentarily that she was with a former boyfriend, or with someone she didn't know, because she had forgotten him. In sexual intercourse she vividly felt held by a former lover or by someone she didn't know but should remember as someone from a forgotten past. Q became increasingly impotent with her and started to accuse her of making him so. He returned to his native Brazil, asking K to visit him there. She had been noncommittal.

Since he left her, K had experiences of "jamais-vu": feeling familiar places and people to become suddenly momentarily strange, as if she had never seen them before. In her dreams she was in unfamiliar places and had a recurring image of drab brown-toned streets that had a "1930s look". The tonality and atmosphere of this dream superimposed itself on the scenes of her everyday life, giving the obverse experience to "jamais-vu", of "déjà-vu": she had already been there in a dream. People assumed this quality, too, and she felt increasingly alienated from old friends and disconcerted by meeting new people, although superficially gregarious. She said these experiences of estrangement were why she sought an analysis.

Her mother lived in the same block of apartments. K could spend much of her time with her as usual, but she found the closeness increasingly "suffocating". And her mother, too, seemed to grow unfamiliar—there was a "grim and dreadful depressed secret in her", hitherto unknown to K, who came to believe that it had "always been there". After Q went to Brazil, the relationship was continued by e-mail. He said he had found himself in a new relationship, with "R", that he was potent with her but could not make love without thinking it was with K. He wanted to have "e-mail sex" with K.

Shortly before coming to see me she travelled to Brazil, to stay with him, to see if there was any future for her with him. She found that the new girlfriend had just moved in. Q tried to have an affair in the house with K behind R's back. K soon returned to Australia feeling demeaned and confused. He kept sending e-mails saying that she was his only love and would always be so. K worked with a man who had almost the same name as Q; they had an on-and-off affair, but in his company she felt that she was still physically with Q, could not free herself from that. So she was unable to respond sexually or emotionally to her new lover. When I first met her, she appeared to instantly trust the relationship. She said an earlier experience of therapy made it easy for her to understand the usual arrangements for fees, session times, breaks, and so on.

She seemed to be "at home" with me. But I was having my own "déjà-vu": I felt I had seen her before or at least someone "just like her", but this was not the case. I had never met anyone like her. However, there were some uncanny points of similarity to several other patients I had seen elsewhere, in terms of superficial biography, family history, and physical illness.

She wanted to work out her continuing vacillations and preoccupations with Q, still transacted by e-mail. She said: "I think of doing extreme things, something that would show him he doesn't know me at all—I could get tattoos! Something that doesn't fit with his idea of me, it's the only way I can stop him from forcing me into his idea of me. I can't stand that." She hated to feel so unfree, but she was virtually addicted to her e-mail attachment to Q. This had clearly substituted for her earlier attachment to her mother. This addicted, constricted feeling made her connection with Q intolerable, but it was even stronger with her mother: "suffocating". Once she used to tell her mother "everything" "five times a day" but even after she had decided not to, still felt fitted into her mother's stereotype of her, and that was unalterable and changeless. She felt everything she did to be an expectation of mother: her vocation, her style of speech, her body—even in coming to see me she had followed her mother, who had recently found a therapist for herself and had "always known" that K would have an analysis.

K had an unusual illness, which had damaged her liver. In an acute episode at its onset five years before, she had become desperately ill when travelling alone in South America. She had met Q then. In hospital, he was the only other English speaker, and he had cared for her like a nurse. She still saw a physician for treatment of the illness; it appeared to be quiescent now but required close monitoring.

She had been frankly psychotic for a month and had then a delusion that she was not in a hospital, that the personnel were impostors, and that she had literally lost her mind. She said that Q had "re-orientated" and "re-educated" her. When she came home, she saw a therapist who helped her "come to terms with the illness" in weekly sessions, with preset termination after twelve sessions. K described the treatment as "making an inventory of dysfunctional cognitions and managing them according to a protocol". She described a recurring dream of her illness: There was some "*organ inside which was coated with a kind of thick slime*". This was her illness, an auto-immune disease. She dreamt that *if only she could pour clear alcohol over the viscous surface it would clean it, if only she could get enough clean spirits*. It occurred to me that this illness seemed the one thing in her mind or body that didn't fit the images that she sensed mother and Q to have of her. Every attempt to separate was just what she thought they would expect and suggest; only this sickness was not to do with them. But as our work continued it became clear to me that it was also partly an introject from her mother's mind: the object in the dream was what K called her mother's "grim depression". This was the part of her mother's mind that K did not know. I doubt if the mother herself was aware of it. Its imagery may only have appeared in the daughter's body, then this dream. Now it was the "Other" within K, intolerable to her system, and a cause of shame. K's latent illness was an understandable cause of great grief to her mother, who worried about the possibility of recurrence, fussing over details of health maintenance.

The strangeness of our predicament became a strong atmosphere. I was bewildered each time we met, because she felt so at home with me. She suffered from nostalgia, for the good times with Q, childhood games with the family, for a sort of timeless golden age dimly remembered before she had gone to preschool. "We had all been together and my parents were young, my grandparents were alive, and it seemed to have always been like that." There were many indications that I was part of that time too and therefore she felt completely accepted by me. Nothing I could say was new or unfamiliar for her. She had what she termed "an ongoing virtual conversation" with me in her head between sessions and did not much feel breaks.

At her many schools she had been bullied and teased—on account of her big ears, awkward ways, shyness, and academic success. She had felt a misfit ever since, until meeting Q, who convinced her when she was desperately ill in Brazil that he had always known her. A "mesmerizing" feeling in her voice as she related this led me to infer and interpret to the effect that I was now experienced as the original agency that had derealized her, and maintained her in a seamless harmony with no separations and no reality to place or time. K felt an increased empathy in response to my interpretations. I had not presented them as part of a theory, and had not attributed the ideas to anyone else. The interpretations were responses to her references to timelessness in the sessions. But K seemed aware that her predicament had been accommodated by me into a schema made for and by other people in other times and places, and she reacted as if understood and reassured. Although this gave her a sense of harmony, it had a cost: she felt more disembodied and would not find a new beginning in this state of attunement.

The feeling that we had always empathically known each other recurred in the sessions. I noticed it was always matched by K reporting intensified feelings of dislocation and a hopeless feeling of estrangement, of not being in real time in an actual place, of there being no future.

She could feel transiently that she was actually in the consulting room with the analyst, and these moments in ordinary time were repeated and marked by us often and reliably enough over many months, enabling her to develop another precarious vantage point. From this point she observed how she could be in a daydream, "miles away" from the here-and-now. She suffered both within and outside the sessions because she was not accepted as "other", but, rather, as the stereotype perceived by her mother, by Q, by her employer and colleagues, by this analyst. I worked with this by observing how she would speak. For example, she would rephrase most of what I said to her: "you mean to say that . . . in other words". This kept our shared words within her preconceived patterns. She became concerned for a while that I would condemn her for various acts of infidelity to Q, that I would be hurt or incapacitated (impotent) if she did not go on asking what she thought I expected of her. She became depressed, ashamed, feeling herself to be disloyal and in "bad faith". I did not reassure her on this issue. These were attempts to control me, to have me as she had imagined. Within the sessions, feelings of betrayal and "bad faith" were part of a sequence and the consequences of her striving to invalidate me as having a mind of my own. I was able to observe how she strove to position me when she would say such things as "I know just what you are going to say" or "I felt you really understood how I felt" and also in various subtle ways of using language and voice tones to create an impression of timelessness in the sessions. When she found that what she did was observable, she was uniquely surprised. She felt less helpless. Her shame and victimhood transposed into a concern for her own actions. But still I was with someone who often did not know who was with her, where she was, how long she had been there, or, indeed, whether she was in a dream or not. She could barely experience anything new, just recurrences and reunions, more of the same.

While she was in this state of mind, I would discover myself more than usually noticing the particularity of the room, the specific way natural light patterned it, the unrepeatable quality of certain distant sounds. I found that I could use such perceptions of the place as imagery in interpretations of the transference and that K would feel less disembodied as a result.

Narrative of a dislocated family

K was the inheritor of generations of displaced people and of that process represented within the mind. Through working with K, I became aware of the importance of place in clinical work. This led me to a kind of meditation that started in the sessions and has continued elsewhere: that dislocation in place is the context for our collective pain. We may assume dislocation as given, or as fate. Australia is a country of exiles, of the disinherited—perhaps most of all for the indigenous people of our land. K inspired me to focus on dislocation, represented in the mind, as a clinical issue.

A disjunction between where, when, and who did not begin with K; it was her inheritance. Reconstruction, in instalments, of a transgenerational family history helped K to place herself in the here-and-now. The family history told to me by K was one of extended dislocation. The father's family, of old Australian stock, appeared to have obliterated their genealogy. Her mother's refugee grand-parents arrived in Australia dispossessed and destitute on the eve of World War 2. They gladly made a lifelong sacrifice for the education of their children. K's parents, both technicians in scientific fields, moved around Australia frequently during her childhood. They had a jovial, dismissive attitude to separations, treating all places as interchangeable. Her father had a saying, "wherever I hang my hat is home, wherever I sit is the head of the table". Her mother had a particularly disembodied lifestyle, neglecting her own appearance and physical health, giving up her career to preoccupy herself with the children, of whom K was the last to leave home. Despite an outward display of optimism and political progressiveness, K's mother carried an inherited nostalgia for Europe before the 1930s in a concrete unmentalized archive everywhere, in old photographs of former neighbours and neighbourhoods that no one could name now. K recalled these mementos as the only constants in her nomadic childhood. They were not discussed. The father remained in the background, a gentle, dreamy man. There was a vague kind of mythology of a golden age of elegant fashionable maternal ancestors in the great cities of central Europe, of something called "culture" over there. "Everyone" knew it to be absent in Australia and now virtually extinct in Europe. This mythology included some distant relatives several generations back who were supposed to have had an analyst. As K reconstructed her family past, she felt less hopeless as she developed a more real sense of the passage of time and, accordingly, of a future.

Displacement and the psychology of place

Displacement is a *double entendre*. In one sense, for psychoanalysis, it is the transvaluation of psychic values: abstract ideas or feelings can be transposed to an equivalent that lends itself to visualization; in this way psychic interest is transferred into sensory vividness. This is a familiar process in dreams. Displacement functions as a defence commonplace in clinical analysis; in a phobia, for example, displacement onto the phobic object permits the objectification, localization, and containment of anxiety. It subserves avoidance in this context. In this sense, displacement is a metonym in which association is based on contiguity, in contrast to symbolization in which association is based on similarity (Laplanche & Pontalis, 1985).

In metonymy, juxtaposition equates one element with another. For example: "Moscow criticizes Washington" equates capital cities with nations: a part may stand for the whole. Metonyms include puns and rhymes. By contrast, metaphors link elements by shared meaning, not by juxtaposition. (For example: "the fire of lust", "sweet words"). In metaphor, one element is not a component or extension of the other. In clinical work, the shared meaning between the elements of the metaphor is the quality of emotion. These linguistic terms can describe states of mind and also the nature of the link between analyst and patient, which is both emotional (metaphoric) and a function of proximity (metonymic).

Because of the inevitability of separation in both physical and psychic reality, we experience an unconscious that is structured by constant displacement, metonyms. Lacan (1970) contrasts this to metaphor, which he assimilates to Freud's concept of condensation. He considers the nature of desire as metonymic.

A second meaning of displacement is spatial dislocation. This sense of the word begs a question: what do we mean, in psychological terms, by place? Place connotes a geographic centre. Place also refers to a psychosocial moment. Psychoanalytic theory deals with "space" but rarely with "place". But clinical practice depends on a place: a meeting in historic time in a real place, the consulting room, the couch, the session. This setting cannot be entirely defined in psychological terms. Interdisciplinary studies can be helpful in finding a concept of place (as distinct from "space") relevant to psychoanalysis.

The geographer Anssi Paasi (1991) suggests that places represent the nodes of a life biography, which is a unique web of situated life episodes. In this sense, person–place interactions include the perspective of an individual's whole lifetime, which comprises memory, transgenerational patterns, and historically remote events.

The American Community researcher M. T. Fullilove (1996) describes displacement as disrupting three psychological processes: familiarity, attachment, and identity. The ensuing disorientation, nostalgia, and alienation may undermine the sense of belonging and mental health. Sudden loss of an exterior world that validates our spatial routines is felt as a loss of self. It is a psychosomatic trauma. "Geographic orientation is embedded in the whole body."

A sense of alienation may become a transgenerational legacy, as in the case of K's family. This is the social and political aspect of the psychology of displacement, which we in Australia witness in Aboriginal land rights determinations (Butt & Eagleson, 1996; Hiley, 1997). The concept of alienation, first developed by Hegel, is that the world (nature, things, others, and ourselves) has become estranged from the human. Erich Fromm (1961, 1962) developed this concept of alienation to explain the incapacitating effect of an idealizing transference. Only by submitting to this object of projection can the alienated patient feel in touch with self. For dislocated K, this meant feeling especially secure, at home, and understood when with the analyst. Passivity in the presence of an idealized object may be based on the fact of the individual's alienation. Fromm considered it to be the central dynamic of transference, that which gives transference its strength and intensity.

Nostalgia

Attachment theory describes how attachment to place—originally union with mother's body, our first place and primal source of imagery— is elaborated in separations and reunions from earliest infancy. Insecure attachment status in infancy appears as a precursor to later psychopathology, including depression (Schore, 1994): severe disorganization is a predictor of dislocations throughout life and, in the extreme, of suicide (Adam, Sheldon-Keller, & West, 1995). But the awareness of desire as a "bittersweet nostalgic feeling" may be a signal that the capacity for new attachment remains viable (Fullilove, 1996).

The agency of the patient in generating alienation

The analysis of K disclosed the damaging effects of displacement, nostalgia, disorientation, and alienation. These could be attributed to an environment deficient in secure place attachment, familiarity, and identity. The environment included projective activity from her parents. Much of the nostalgia had been unmentalized, itself displaced, externalized. The work of analysis was largely to develop a reflective capacity, as described by Fonagy, Steele, Moran, and Higgitt (1991,) to make that feeling thinkable and bearable.

This formulation of displacement as caused entirely by a traumatic environmental dislocation was misleadingly plausible. K's illness was not simply post-traumatic or environmental deficiency. Therapeutic results depended on K's discovery of her own agency in the displacement and of becoming aware of when, why, and how she used this process as a defence against awareness. An alternative to a simple environmental formulation was presented by a coincidence.

There is a wonderful sad postmodern song about alienation and nostalgia from one of the world's most alienating cities, São Paolo. I had heard it once in another place. It was a coincidence that K had the tune in her mind and the poignancy of it, but only a fragment of the words. She hummed the tune and tried to remember the words. By another coincidence, as I wrote this chapter I came across them, a song in Portuguese by Caetano Veloso: *Sampa*. The writer is clearly an exile in his own land. The nostalgia is in all in the music, composed by another man. In a very condensed form the words explain K's act of perception that generated her alienation and lost identity:

> *Quando eu te encarei frente a frente não vu o meu rosto*
> *Chamei de mau gosto o que vi, de mau gosto o mau gosto*
> *É que Narciso acha feio o que não é espelho*
> *É a mente apavora o que ainda não é mesmo velho*

When I stared ahead I didn't see my face
I called what I saw bad taste, bad taste, bad taste
Does Narcissus find ugly what's not a mirror
And the mind scares off what's not really old

It was difficult for me to put words to K's emotional music. There were sessions where anything new that came to mind to express the atmosphere in the room was instantly "recognized" by K—that is, codified and filed into a predetermined "library" scheme of things. Nothing new was allowed to be; nothing was unknown. It was all banal, "bad taste" until it was sorted. She was an obsessive system-maker, fastidious with detail like de Sade, Fourier, and Loyola in Roland Barthes's (1996) account of them. Like them she isolated herself emotionally and dwelt in schemata, a secondary language to which everything could be referred, like a library catalogue. "That's just like. . . . That's another one of those . . . just the same as. I really should have known that already. Oh, you mean to say that. . . ." Terminology from her reading of cognitive-behavioural psychology readily lent itself to such systematizings: she would often say: "the same old tapes, again and again" . . . "That was another sociotropic dysfunctional assumption." So she did away with the ordinary here-and-now. There was a tidy, satisfied feel to her familiarizing word-rituals. Narcissus found ugly what was not a mirror.

Places in the countertransference

For me it felt like travelling interminably through a monotonous-featured depopulated landscape; occasionally there would appear an odd-looking rock formation, or a discontinuity on the horizon, or a clump of strangely configured trees. Our all-knowing guide said each of these belonged to another story in another time, not our time, but that of an ever-present recycling myth, already finalized and fixed. Each irregularity marked an old story that was in the beginning, is now, and ever shall be. I found ways to talk to K about this "guide" who converted the New, the Other, into the Primordial and ever-known. The use of metaphor catalysed K to associations that gave me an understanding of the landscapes of my reverie. The desert scenery represented the mind of the father who had not be able to sustain a sense of inhabitable space for K and her mother in the face of the seductive derealizing "guide".

K felt these metaphoric interpretations linking the past to the present as "astringent, cleaning", a relief from a "gluggy, slimy state". She was then able to disclose a transference to me as the vague father. Later sessions had a fresh feel; she felt woken from a trance.

New experiences as incomprehensible

It is sometimes useful to consider the individual mind as a group, and observation of group processes as images of a person's inner world. I will take a liberty in applying a recent study of group processes in this way. Claudio Neri (1998), in his recent work on groups, describes the reaction to the entry of new members of the group: "A phantasy appears that the new members are 'the returning dead.'"

The expression "returning dead" refers to a few members of the original group who had abandoned it for various reasons, leaving a sense of negative feelings.

Because K could not bear to know anything as "Other", any new emotional contact was, for her, a meeting with the living dead. That is, with the bits of her self that had been dislocated by projective identification to preserve a narcissistic order.

This phantasy, that the newcomer is a revenant, occurred in early encounters between indigenous cultures and modern Europeans. In Mexico the Spanish invaders were at first thought to be "long lost rulers, or even gods, returning" (Thomas, 1993, pp. 181–187); in Melanesia and Australia first meetings with European expeditions were believed to be with ancestral spirits or the dead returned (Blainey, 1980, pp. 64–67; Souter, 1963, p. 182). The inability to see the "Other" was mutual and had tragic consequences, a notorious instance of which was the legal fiction that Australia was "terra nullius" (Butt & Eagleson, 1996). K treated the space between us as she did her inner life, as if it were a "terra nullius" that could not possibly contain any mind not already known. But it was also a "terror" of absence. She had filled the absence where she could not see the Other with her derealizing system, the already known. Mircea Eliade (1954) has drawn from ancient traditions of Aboriginal Australia to describe a state of mind called "the myth of the Eternal Return". It was this fantasy—that there are only recurrences—that maintained K's disorientation in the face of innovation. Her mind "scared off" anything that was not "really old" and part of her "same old story".

The fear of time and place

The State of Mind described by Eliade (1954) is a longing for a universe without anything new in it, "a ceaseless repetition of gestures". There is "no act which has not . . . been given by someone else", and ultimately, "by some other being not human". The condition where there would be no "Other" is a powerful opposition to the discovery of time and place. This discovery involves what Eliade called "the terror of history". Because of K's illness, the beginning of "another" within her, a pregnancy—real or metaphoric—could prove her death warrant. For K it would be hard to bear the knowledge of irretrievable loss and a future beyond prophecy.

The quality of the "Other" necessary for consciousness had been relegated by K to the system of "the one story that will prove worth your telling". When a fresh encounter began, as it might at the start of every session, the otherness could still be unbearable to her, an incomprehensible, monstrous absence, and she would "scare off" the newness of it with some rehearsed anecdote or formula from "cognitive science". But an increasing trust in metaphor, arising from visuospatial imagery, like that of the "guide", came to supplant the endless cycle of metonyms (displacements).

Implications for technique: frame and metaphor

These reflections on place point to a question. How can we help an alienated patient recognize the "Other" as distinct from the work of their own mind, projection, preconception, dream, hallucination? Maybe this is the fundamental task of psychoanalysis. Language is stretched by this question: Is this a place that has dreamt us up? Or by which we are slept? (This may not be a mystical question—it is Darwinian evolutionary theory in brief.) If this place and ourselves are "Other" to each, how would we know?

Ronald Baker's work on the discovery of the analyst as a new object addresses this problem. Baker (1993) describes how the survival of the analyst in the frame is itself an implicit transference interpretation. Above all, safety, like survival, can mean that the patient is not in the original traumatic (dislocating, disorientating) transference situation. The analyst may be the first survivor in the patient's life; Baker considers that this is what is therapeutic. This establishes the conditions for the patient to find the analyst as a new object. This was vital for K, who tended to make any new object relationship into an old one. Explicit transference interpretation could feed into her "more-of-the-same-from-the-past" resistance to a new beginning. It was against the analyst as a new object that she was most defended. Furthermore, Baker suggests that an implicit, as distinct from verbalized, transference interpretation can also be potentially mutative. But explicit transference interpretations were necessary for K, who was not simply traumatized but now actively perpetuated her alienation. This impasse was negotiated by a particular application of the frame to make interpretations of displacement processes.

Psychoanalysis developed historically among people who had been, or were soon to become, displaced, and they understood that displacement like all defences against awareness leaves symptoms behind it. The invention of the analytic frame (Langs, 1981) addressed dislocation. It defined the analyst's psychic activity on behalf of another in an objective form, in a geographic space located in unidirectional linear time. This is also an ethical space, a container of moral values. In that context I was able to use my consulting room to observe the spatial aspects of transference and countertransference. K was often virtually disembodied. An analysis by e-mail—"virtual" sessions (the way of the future?)—would have made matters worse. Analysis needs a physical body as does a person. There is no real person without their place, just as there is no such thing as a baby without their mother. Unlike many other patients, K made no reference to the place she was in. This work fell to the analyst. Metaphoric reference to the implicit therapeutic properties of the frame–place itself could be made in verbal interpretations. By attaching a transference meaning to real aspects of the immediate physical setting, we were able to see projective activity that negated space and time against the relative constancy of the frame.

Genius loci: the spirit of the place

Claudio Neri adds a new intuitive dimension from group work and classical mythology to the analyst's maintenance of the frame. He describes how a condition for group thought is "the presence of a 'genius loci'". He means that a point of reference is needed, so that all members realize that they are not only referring to one another but also to another common point. This common point is cared for by the genius loci, the spirit of the place. The function of the genius loci is to find ways of staying together, and to know a group spirit. The genius loci is not necessarily within the analyst, not an object of interpretation. It is something that comes from nature and the environment and includes thought (Neri, 1998). Each real place has a genius loci. The "feel" of a place is discovered by intuition and represented by this tutelary spirit.

I propose that Neri's concept be developed to understand the individual analytic situation as *a place that can be known intuitively*. In the clinical context the genius loci presents the analyst with the "feel" of the session, which from time to time may be represented by the particular sensory properties of the room and coincidental physical phenomena. These provide imagery for metaphor. To make our place new and real for a group, whether intrapsychic or social, we need to invoke the genius loci, the spirit of the place, and, like a good architect, to ask what should be made here, whom we can be with here, and what we share. We may not always agree. The genius loci may also ask us not to visit some places. We should not climb to the top of Uluru or Mt Kailas just because it is there. Some places in the mind, as in the natural world, need to be left alone.

Links between theory and practice

There cannot be such a thing as an idiographic analysis with its entirely unique clinical theory. There is implicit theory in each interpretation. Theories of any sort, clinical or general, applied by the analyst with K could be an acting out in the countertransference to perpetuate mutual estrangement from each other. The experience of dislocation was so central for K that I felt strongly invited to make interpretations informed by attachment theory. But K was hypervigilant to theory, and when she sensed it at work she became less embodied in time and place. Rosenfeld (1987) found an impasse caused by interpretation of separation reactions based on general theory rather than clinical evidence. K had an unconscious envy for the emplaced, including the analyst and the frame, as it became more real to her. Rosenfeld's later view was that interpretations to address the pain of envy would be more effective than a direct interpretation. This seemed to apply to K.

Clinical experience showed that a particular use of metaphor could help K discover herself in place and time, a process that would mean an encounter with the Unknown Other. By attaching transference meaning to uncontrived coincidental place-defining events—like the sound of wind, of rain, of traffic, the cry of birds, the fall of light in the room—she became placed in time. Such events were not distractions, and certainly not omens. With this imagery we could articulate meaning. The inevitable theoretical dimension of interpretation was thus linked to immediate emotional experience in real time and place.

Antal Borbely (1998) describes how, in traumatized patients, "networks of meaning which may have been metaphorically related to each other" come to form "rigid dialogical, unchanging relationships". "Freud's repetition compulsion described the analysand's inability to remain responsive, i.e., to relate metaphorically (with imaginative rationality) to present-day circumstances." Borbely considers that whatever the school of psychoanalysis influencing the analyst, an effective interpretation "aims, in principle, at kindling metaphor". This is done by linking emotionally charged images of the past and present to each other.

K had been traumatized by the external and internal processes of dislocation and displacement. With the loss of her place, she had lost her potential for metaphor—that is, for symbolic thought—and was living in a state of recycling metonyms. To Borbely's psychoanalytic concept of metaphor, I would add that the actual content of imagery chosen by the analyst used in interpretations was important in relocating her in time and place.

Guy Da Silva's paper describing "Borborygmi as Markers of Psychic Work" (1990) is a rare example of the intentional metaphoric use of immediate physical events (bowel sounds) in analytic interpretations. It illustrates a matter-of-fact approach (which, of course, involves humour) to including the somatic physical event in the psychological.

Conclusion

Analysis of a patient for whom place had no psychic reality disclosed difficulties in thinking metaphorically. These prevented the communication of symbols as words and caused an impasse in analysis. An explanation for this predicament is that metaphor-making requires imagery ultimately derived from an actual place. Thus, dislocating processes working against the discovery of place compromise symbolic thought.

Dislocation in time and place was demonstrated in the personal and transgenerational history of the patient and paralleled in transference and countertransference experience. An internal process of displacement perpetuated alienation and disorientation.

In this state of mind the patient was unable to emotionally distinguish self from other and consequently unable to recognize new experience. The concept of place developed here considers it to be "other" from the subject, not adequately described as a mental construct and not explicable in exclusively psychological terms. The participation of the analytic experience in a real place at a unique time kindles metaphor. Imagery provided by the place can make interpretations mutative. New images for emotion made from the immediate physical properties of the setting and uncontrived coincidental events are symbolic connections made by intuition. They are discoveries that link us to an area beyond the psychic domain. They define time and place.

Epilogue

Maria Teresa Savio Hooke

What does it all mean?

The geography of meaning has taken us on a journey from thinking about internal space, to the space in which we live; to space conquered, colonized, and ensuing brutalities; to the meaning of space as land; to space as a place where culture and history develops; to the consulting room, where these losses are relived and processed.

The journey has involved the gathering of works from different psychoanalytic cultures. We can borrow Twemlow's concept of multicultural identity and speak of the multicultural identity of the book, of a mix of cultures attempting to begin a dialogue with each other.

Although the essays come from diverse points of view and experiences, some touchstone concepts are so often employed as to become part of a collective way of thinking. Among these are Freud's concept of repetition compulsion, working through, and the work of mourning; Winnicott's transitional space; and Bion's idea of container–contained and of transformations. These concepts are used in this book by the psychoanalysts and the historian and are intuitively "known" by the novelist. In particular, Freud's concepts applied both to social phenomena and to the understanding of history feel extremely relevant to contemporary issues.

Another common ground is the extension and exploration of the concept of place. This has the effect of sensitizing the reader to her or his physical surroundings in an unusual way. The book highlights something that has not been perceived before with the same clarity and which is now shining a spotlight on and bringing sharply into focus something previously known but only hazily. We become more aware of how rooted in landscape our lives are and of the importance of our physical context. By the end of the book, the significance of losing one's home, land, country, culture, and of being displaced and dispossessed becomes for the reader a much more poignant and distressing reality. In the same vein, the relevance of the ordinary and the familiar is highlighted. The detailed description of scenarios of everyday life and domesticity and the significance of everyday objects—what Akhtar calls the utensils of living—details the concept of loss and gives it a more familiar and approachable tone.

Similar words like rupture, fracture, and laceration are used by some of the authors to describe dislocation and separation. Such words evoke a visual image that brings to mind the architecture of Daniel Libeskind's Jewish Museum in Berlin, where the historical wounds are symbolically represented in the building, allowing the visitor a perspective from which history can be observed and reflected upon (Cobbers, 2001).

As I mentioned, two of Freud's most significant papers, "Remembering Repeating and Working Through" (1914g) and "Mourning and Melancholia" (1917e [1915]), reverberate through the book, in some chapters openly acknowledged, in others implied. In "Remembering Repeating and Working Through", Freud wrote that what is forgotten had always been known, but just not thought about. He also says: "It is a triumph for the treatment if he (the analyst) can bring it about that something that the patient wishes to discharge in action is disposed of, through the work of remembering" (p. 153), "[as] we may say that the patient does not remember anything of what he has forgotten and repressed, but acts it out" (p. 150).

These passages seem particularly significant as we look at the defences set up against remembering both in the silence of nations about their traumatic past and in the avoidance about confronting it, as well as in personal stories where secrets, silence, inner blindness, ambiguities, manic attitudes, and projection into the other are used against experiences of loss and pain which cannot be tolerated.

With silence, secrecy, and lack of awareness, there will be both repetition and the passing on of depriving experiences and brutalities from one generation to another. Some of the chapters provide tragic testimony to this, but they also propose ways to move forward. Such ways—the psychological work needed for the processing of psychic pain—are formulated differently by different authors.

This book's introduction to the geography of meaning—to the importance of place and its effect on the mind, to the trauma of displacement and dislocation, to the consequences of silence and denial both for individuals and nations—represents the beginning of a discourse that could open up in many different directions.

REFERENCES AND BIBLIOGRAPHY

ABC (1996). *4 Corners: Telling His Story* [TV documentary]. Australian Broadcasting Corporation, 15 July.

Adam, K. S., Sheldon-Keller, A., & West, M. (1995). Attachment organisation and history of suicidal behaviour in clinical adolescents. *Journal of Consulting and Clinical Psychology, 64*: 264–272.

Adelman, L. (2003). *Race: The Power of an Illusion.* PBS Mini-Series. Produced by California Newsreel.

Akhtar, S. (1988). Four culture bound psychiatric syndromes in India. *International Journal of Social Psychiatry, 34*: 70–74.

Akhtar, S. (1992). Tethers, orbits, and invisible fences: Clinical, developmental, sociocultural, and technical aspects of optimal distance. In: S. Kramer & S. Akhtar (Eds.), *When the Body Speaks: Psychological Meanings in Kinetic Clues* (pp. 21–57). Northvale, NJ: Jason Aronson.

Akhtar, S. (1995). A third individuation: Immigration, identity, and the psychoanalytic process. *Journal of the American Psychoanalytic Association, 43*: 1051–1084.

Akhtar, S. (1996). "Someday . . ." and "If only . . ." fantasies: Pathological optimism and inordinate nostalgia as related forms of idealization. *Journal of the American Psychoanalytic Association, 44*: 723–753.

Akhtar, S. (1998). From simplicity through contradiction to paradox: The evolving psychic reality of the borderline patient in treatment. *International Journal of Psychoanalysis, 79*: 241–252.

Akhtar, S. (1999a). *Immigration and Identity: Turmoil, Treatment, and Transformation.* Northvale, NJ: Jason Aronson.

Akhtar, S. (1999b). The immigrant, exile, and the experience of nostalgia. *Journal of Applied Psychoanalytic Studies, 1*: 123–130.

Akhtar, S. (2000). Mental pain and the cultural ointment of poetry. *International Journal of Psychoanalysis, 81*: 229–243.

Akhtar, S. (2001). Things are us: A friendly rejoinder to Marianne Spitzform's paper "The ecological self: metaphor and developmental experience". *Journal of Applied Psychoanalytic Studies, 3*: 205–210.

Akhtar, S. (2003). *New Clinical Realms: Pushing the Envelope of Theory and Technique.* Northvale, NJ: Jason Aronson.

Akhtar, S. (2006). Technical challenges faced by the immigrant analyst. *Psychoanalytic Quarterly, 75*: 21–43.

Akhtar, S. (2007). From unmentalized xenophobia to messianic sadism: Some reflections on the phenomenology of prejudice. In: H. Parens, A. Mahfouz, S. W. Twemlow, & D. E. Scharff (Eds.), *The Future of Prejudice: Psychoanalysis and the Prevention of Prejudice* (pp. 7–19). Lanham, MD: Jason Aronson.

Akhtar, S., & Brown, J. (2005). Animals in psychiatric symptomatology. In: S. Akhtar & V. D. Volkan (Eds.), *Mental Zoo: Animals in the Human Mind and Its Pathology.* Madison, CT: International Universities Press.

Akhtar, S., & Choi, L. (2004). When evening falls: The immigrant's encounter with middle and old age. *American Journal of Psychoanalysis, 64*: 183–191.

Akhtar, S., & Volkan, V. D. (2005a). *Mental Zoo: Animals in the Human Mind and Its Pathology.* Madison, CT: International Universities Press.

Akhtar, S., & Volkan, V. D. (2005b). *Cultural Zoo: Animals in the Human Mind and Its Sublimations.* Madison, CT: International Universities Press.

Amati-Mehler, J., Argentieri, S., & Canestri, J. (1993). *The Babel of the Unconscious: Mother Tongue and Foreign Languages in the Psychoanalytic Dimension,* trans. J. Whitelaw-Cucco. Madison, CT: International Universities Press.

Arlow, J. A. (1986). The poet as prophet: A psychoanalytic perspective. *Psychoanalytic Quarterly, 55*: 53–68.

Armstrong, K. (1993). *Through a Narrow Gate.* London: HarperCollins.

Atkinson, A. (2002). *The Commonwealth of Speech: An Argument About Australia's Past, Present and Future.* Melbourne: Australian Scholarly Publishing.

Attwood, B. (2001). "Learning about the truth": The stolen generations narrative. In: B. Attwood & F. Magowan (Eds.), *Telling Stories: Indigenous History and Memory in Australia and New Zealand* (pp. 183–212). Sydney: Allen & Unwin/Bridget Williams Books.

Attwood, B. (2005). *Telling the Truth about Aboriginal History.* Sydney: Allen & Unwin.

Baker, R. (1993). The patient's discovery of the psychoanalyst as a new object. *International Journal of Psychoanalysis, 74*: 1223.

Balint, M. (1959). *Thrills and Regression.* London: Hogarth Press.

Balint, M. (1968). *The Basic Fault: Therapeutic Aspects of Regression.* New York: Brunner/Mazel.

Balint, M. (1969). *Thrills and Regressions.* London: Hogarth Press.

Barthes, R. (1989). To Write: An intransitive verb? In: *The Rustle of Language,* trans. R. Howard. Berkeley, CA: University of California Press.

Barthes, R. (1996). *Sade, Fourier, Loyola,* trans. R. Miller. Baltimore, MD/London: Johns Hopkins University Press.

Batty, J. (1963). *Namatjira, Wanderer between Two Worlds.* Adelaide: Rigby.

Berndt, C. H., & Berndt, R. M. (1988). *The Speaking Land.* Sydney: Penguin.

Bion, W. R. (1962). *Elements of Psychoanalysis.* London: Karnac.

Bion, W. R. (1977a). *The Grid and Caesura.* Rio de Janeiro: Imago Editora; London: Karnac, 1989.

Bion, W. R. (1977b). *Seven Servants: Four Works by Wilfred R. Bion.* New York: Jason Aronson.

Bion, W. R. (1978). *Four Discussions with W. R. Bion.* Strath Tay: Clunie Press.

Bird, C. (Ed.) (1998). *The Stolen Children: Their Stories.* London: Virago; Sydney: Random House Australia.

Blainey, G. (1980). *A Land Half Won.* Adelaide: Griffin Press.

Bleger, J. (1967). Psychoanalysis of the psychoanalytic frame. *International Journal of Psychoanalysis, 48:* 511–519.

Bloch, M. (1954). *The Historian's Craft,* trans. P. Putnam. Manchester: Manchester University Press, 1992.

Borbely, A. F. (1998). A psychoanalytic concept of metaphor. *International Journal of Psychoanalysis, 79:* 923–936.

Boswell, J. (1990). *The Kindness of Strangers: The Abandonment of Children in Western Europe from Late Antiquity to the Renaissance.* New York: Vintage.

Bowlby, J. (1951). *Maternal Care and Mental Health* [A report prepared on behalf of the World Health Organisation as a contribution to the United Nations Programme for the Welfare of Homeless Children]. Geneva: WHO.

Bowlby, J. (1953). *Child Care and the Growth of Love.* London: Penguin.

Bowlby, J. (1969). *Attachment and Loss, Vol. 1: Attachment.* London: Hogarth Press & The Institute of Psychoanalysis.

Bowlby, J. (1973). *Attachment and Loss, Vol. 2: Separation, Anxiety and Anger.* London: Hogarth Press & The Institute of Psychoanalysis.

Bowlby, J. (1979). On knowing what you are not supposed to know and feeling what you are not supposed to feel. *Canadian Journal of Psychiatry, 24:* 403–408.

Bowlby, J. (1980). *Attachment and Loss, Vol. 3: Sadness and Depression.* London: Hogarth Press & The Institute of Psychoanalysis.

Brenner, I. (2005). *Psychic Trauma: Dynamics, Symptoms, and Treatment.* Lanham, MD: Jason Aronson.

Briggs, F. (Ed.) (1995). *From Victim to Offender.* Sydney: Allen & Unwin.

Butt, P., & Eagleson, R. (1996). *Mabo: What the High Court Said and What the Government Did* (2nd edition). Sydney: The Federation Press.

Campion, J. (1993). *The Piano.* Produced by Australian Film Commission, CiBy 2000, and New South Wales Film & Television Office.

Casebier, A. (1976). *Film Appreciation*. New York: Harcourt, Brace Jovanovich.

Cawte, J. (1993). *Healers of Arnhemland*. Sydney: UNSW Press.

Chasseguet-Smirgel, J. (1985). *Creativity and Perversion*. London: Free Association Books.

Cobbers, A. (2001). *Daniel Libeskind*. Berlin: Jaron Verlag.

Crawford, E. (1993). *Over My Tracks: A Remarkable Life*. Melbourne: Penguin.

Da Silva, G. (1990). Borborygmi as markers of psychic work. *International Journal of Psychoanalysis, 71*: 641–659.

de Certeau, M. (1986). *Heterologies: Discourse on the Other*, trans. B. Massumi. Manchester: Manchester University Press.

Denford, S. (1981). Going away. *International Review of Psychoanalysis, 59*: 325–332.

DeWall, R. (1984). *Korczak: Storyteller in Stone*. Crazy Horse, SD: Korczak's Heritage.

Drewe, R. (1976). *Savage Crows*. Sydney: Picador.

Drysdale, I., & Durack, M. (1974). *The End of Dreaming*. Adelaide: Rigby.

Durack, M. (1967). *Kings in Grass Castles*. London: Corgi.

Earnshaw, A. (1998). *Time Bombs in Families and How to Survive Them*. Sydney: Spencer.

Eliade, M. (1954). *The Myth of the Eternal Return*. Princeton, NJ: Princeton University Press.

Ellenberger, H. F. (1970). *The Discovery of the Unconscious*. London: Allen Lane.

Erikson, E. (1950). *Childhood and Society*. New York: W. W. Norton.

Erikson, E. (1959). *Identity and the Life Cycle*. New York: International Universities Press.

Evans, D. (1996). *An Introductory Dictionary of Lacanian Psychoanalysis*. London/New York: Routledge.

Falk, A. (1974). Border symbolism. *Psychoanalytic Quarterly, 43*: 650–660.

Faye, E. (2003). Impossible memories and the history of trauma. In: J. Bennett & R. Kennedy (Eds.), *World Memory: Personal Trajectories in Global Time*. New York: Palgrave.

Felman, S. (1995). Education and crisis, or the vicissitudes of teaching. In: C. Caruth (Ed.), *Trauma: Explorations in Memory*. Baltimore, MD: Johns Hopkins University Press.

Fenichel, O. (1945). *The Psychoanalytic Theory of Neurosis*. New York: W. W. Norton.

Fink, B. (1997). *A Clinical Introduction to Lacanian Psychoanalysis: Theory and Technique*. Cambridge, MA: Harvard University Press.

Fleming, J. (1972). Early object deprivation and transference phenomena. *Psychoanalytic Quarterly, 21*: 23–49.

Flood, J. (1983). *Archeology of the Dreamtime*. Sydney: Collins.

Fodor, N. (1950). Varieties of nostalgia. *Psychoanalytic Review, 37*: 25–38.

Fonagy, P. (2001). *Attachment Theory and Psychoanalysis*. New York: Other Press.

Fonagy, P., Gergely, G., Jurist, E., & Target, M. (2002). *Affect Regulation, Mentalization, and the Development of Self*. New York: Other Press.

Fonagy, P., Steele, M., Moran, G., & Higgitt, A. C. (1991). The capacity for understanding mental states: The reflective self in parent and child and its significance for the security of attachment. *Infant Mental Health Journal, 13*: 200–216.

Freedman, A. (1956). The feeling of nostalgia and its relationship to phobia. *Bulletin of the Philadelphia Association for Psychoanalysis, 6*: 84–92.

Freire, P. (1973). *Education for Critical Consciousness*. New York: Seaburg Press.

Freud, S. (1900a). *The Interpretation of Dreams. Standard Edition, 5*: 583.

Freud, S. (1909b). Analysis of a phobia in a five-year-old boy. *Standard Edition, 10*: 3–150.

Freud, S. (1909d). Notes upon a case of obsessional neurosis. *Standard Edition, 10*: 192.

Freud, S. (1911b). Formulations on the two principles of mental functioning. *Standard Edition, 12*: 218–226.

Freud, S. (1912e). Recommendations to physicians practising psychoanalysis. *Standard Edition, 12*: 111–120.

Freud, S. (1912–13). *Totem and Taboo. Standard Edition, 13*: 1–61.

Freud, S. (1914g). Remembering, repeating and working-through. *Standard Edition, 12*: 147.

Freud, S. (1915d). Repression. *Standard Edition, 14*: 141–158.

Freud, S. (1917e [1915]). Mourning and melancholia. *Standard Edition, 14*: 237–258.

Freud, S. (1920g). *Beyond the Pleasure Principle. Standard Edition, 18*: 63.

Freud, S. (1923b). *The Ego and the Id. Standard Edition, 19*: 24.

Freud, S. (1926d [1925]). *Inhibitions, Symptoms, and Anxiety. Standard Edition, 20*: 77–175.

Freud, S. (1930a). *Civilization and Its Discontents. Standard Edition, 21*: 57–145.

Freud, S. (1933a). *New Introductory Lectures on Psycho-Analysis. Standard Edition, 22*: 78.

Fromm, E. (1961). *Marx's Concept of Man*. New York: Frederick Ungar.

Fromm, E. (1962). *Beyond the Chains of Illusion: My Encounter with Marx and Freud*. New York: Trident Press.

Frosch, J. (1966). A note on reality constancy. In: R. M. Loewenstein, L. M. Newman, M. Schur, & A. J. Solnit (Eds.), *Psychoanalysis: A General Psychology. Essays in Honor of Heinz Hartmann* (pp. 349–376). New York: International Universities Press.

Fullerton, P. (2001). Stories in the making. In: H. Formaini (Ed.), *Landmarks: Papers by Jungian Analysts*. Manuka: Australian & New Zealand Jungian Analysts.

Fullilove, M. T. (1996). Psychiatric implications of displacement: Contributions from the psychology of place. *American Journal of Psychiatry, 12*: 1516–1524.

Garcia-Marquez, G. (1985). *Love in the Time of Cholera*. London: Penguin.

Garza-Guerreo, C. (1974). Culture shock: Its mourning and vicissitudes of identity. *Journal of the American Psychoanalytic Association, 22*: 408–429.

Geahchan, D. (1968). Deuil et nostalgie. *Revue Française de Psychanalyse, 32*: 39–65.

Gill, A. (1998). *Orphans of the Empire* (revised edition). Sydney: Random House.

Ginsburg, C. (1999). *The Judge and the Historian: Marginal Notes on a Late-Twentieth-Century Miscarriage of Justice*, trans. A. Shugar. London: Verso.

Goding, A. (1990). *This Bold Venture: The Story of Lake Tyers House, Place and People*. Bairnsdale, Victoria: E-Gee Printers.

Gooder, H., & Jacobs, J. (2000). "On the border of the unsayable": The apology in postcolonising Australia. *Interventions, 2* (2): 229–247.

Goswell, J. (1990). *The Kindness of Strangers*. New York: Vintage Books.

Greenson, R. (1967). *The Technique and Practice of Psychoanalysis, Vol. 1*. New York: International Universities Press.

Grenville, K. (2005). *The Secret River*. Melbourne: Text Publishing.

Grenville, K. (2006)."Unsettling the Settlers: History, Culture, Race and the Australian Self." Paper presented at the Open Day of the Australian Psychoanalytical Society (available on podcast at www.psychoanalysis.asn.au).

Grinberg, L. (1978). The "razor's edge" in depression and mourning. *International Journal of Psychoanalysis, 59*: 245–254.

Grinberg, L., & Grinberg, R. (1984). A psychoanalytic study of migration: Its normal and pathological aspects. *Journal of the American Psychoanalytic Association, 32*: 13–38.

Grinberg, L., & Grinberg, R. (1989). *Psychoanalytic Perspectives on Migration and Exile*, trans. N. Festinger. New Haven, CT: Yale University Press.

Grotstein, J. (1978). Inner space: Its dimensions and its coordinates. *International Journal of Psychoanalysis, 59*: 55–61.

Hamer, F. (2007). Anti-Black racism and the conception of whiteness. In: H. Parens, A. Mafhouz, S. Twemlow, & D. Scharff (Eds.), *The Future of Prejudice: Applications of Psychoanalytic Understanding towards Its Prevention*. Latham, MD: Rowman & Littlefield.

Hamilton, P. (2003). Sale of the century? Memory and historical consciousness in Australia. In: K. Hodgkin & S. Radstone (Eds.), *Contested Pasts: The Politics of Memory*. London: Routledge.

Hartmann, H. (1939). *Ego and the Problem of Adaptation*. New York: International Universities Press, 1960.

Heidegger, M. (1962). *Being and Time*, trans. J. Macquarie & E. Robinson. New York: Harper & Row.

Henson, B. (1992). *A Straight-out-Man: F. W. Albrecht and Central Australian Aborigines*. Melbourne: Melbourne University Press.

Herbert, X. (1938). *Capricornia*. Sydney: HarperCollins, 1996.

Herbert, X. (1975). *Poor Fellow My Country*. Sydney: Collins.

Hiley, G. (Ed.) (1997). *The Wik Case: Issues and Implications*. Sydney: Butterworth.

Hooke, M. T. (1997). *Freud's Papers on Technique* [Audiotape]. Public Lecture Series 1997. Sydney: Sydney Institute for Psychoanalysis.

Hooke, M. T. (2000). Is psychoanalysis still relevant? *Psychotherapy in Australia, 7* (1): 42–46.

HREOC (1997). *Bringing Them Home: Report of the National Inquiry into the Separation of Aboriginal and Torres Strait Islander Children from Their Families*. Sydney: Human Rights and Equal Opportunity Commission.

Humphreys, M. (1995). *Empty Cradles*. London: Corgi.

Isaacs, J. (1995). *Marika Wandjuk: Life Story*. Brisbane: University of Queensland Press.

Jacobs, J. (1993). *The Death and Life of Great American Cities*. New York: Modern Library.

Jones, E. (1953). *The Life and Work of Sigmund Freud*. New York: Basic Books. 1981.

Jung, C. G. (1964). Psychological types. In: *Collected Works of Carl Jung, Vol. 6*. Princeton, NJ: Princeton University Press.

Jung, C. G. (1966). The practice of psychotherapy. In: *Collected Works of Carl Jung, Vol. 16*. Princeton, NJ: Princeton University Press.

Kafka, J. (1989). *Multiple Realities in Clinical Practice*. New Haven, CT: Yale University Press.

Kahn, C. (1997). Conclusion. In: P. H. Elovitz & C. Kahn (Eds.), *Immigrant Experiences: Personal Narrative and Psychological Analysis*. Cranbury, NJ: Associated University Presses.

Kakar, S. (1997). *Shamans, Mystics, and Doctors: A Psychological Inquiry into India and Its Healing Traditions*. London: Oxford University Press.

Keenan, B. (1993). *Evil Cradling*. London: Random House.

Keller, H. (1940). *Let Us Have Faith*. New York: Doubleday & Doran.

Kennedy, R. (2001). Stolen generation testimony: Trauma, historiography and the question of "truth". *Aboriginal History, 25*: 116–131.

Kernberg, O. F. (1975). *Borderline Conditions and Pathological Narcissism*. New York: Jason Aronson.

Kernberg, O. F. (1992). *Love Relations: Normality and Pathology*. New Haven, CT: Yale University Press.

Kertzer, D. (1998). *The Kidnapping of Edgardo Mortara*. New York: Random House.

Kestenberg, J. (1980). Psychoanalyses of children of Holocaust survivors. *Journal of the American Psychoanalytic Association, 28*: 775–804.

Kestenberg, J. (1989). Transposition revisited: Clinical, therapeutic, and developmental considerations. In: P. Marcus & A. Rosenberg (Ed.), *Healing

Their Wounds: Psychotherapy with Holocaust Survivors and Their Families (pp. 67–82). New York: Praeger.

Kestenberg, J., & Brenner, I. (1996). *The Last Witness: The Child Survivor of the Holocaust.* Washington, DC: American Psychiatric Press.

Khan, M. M. R. (1983). *Hidden Selves: Between Theory and Practice in Psychoanalysis.* New York: International Universities Press.

Kidd, R. (1997). *The Way We Civilise.* Brisbane: University of Queensland Press.

Killingmo, B. (1989). Conflict and deficient: Implications for technique. *International Journal of Psychoanalysis, 70:* 65–79.

Klein, M. (1935). Contribution to the psychogenesis of manic depressive states. In: *Love, Guilt, and Reparation and Other Work, 1921–1945* (pp. 262–289). New York: Free Press, 1992.

Kleiner, H. (1970). On nostalgia. *Bulletin of the Philadelphia Association for Psychoanalysis, 20:* 11–30.

Knafo, D., & Yaari, A. (1997). Leaving the promised land: Israeli immigrants in the United States. In: P. H. Elovitz & C. Kahn (Eds.), *Immigrant Experiences: Personal Narrative and Psychological Analysis* (pp. 221–240). Cranbury, NJ: Associated Universities Press.

Kogan, I. (1995). *The Cry of Mute Children.* London: Free Association Books.

Krystal, H. (1966). Giorgio de Chirico: Ego states and artistic production. *American Imago, 23:* 210–226.

Kurtz, S. A. (1988). The psychoanalysis of time. *Journal of the American Psychoanalytic Association, 36:* 985–1094.

Lacan, J. (1970). The insistence of the letter. In: J. Ehrmann (Ed.), *Structuralism.* New York: Doubleday Anchor.

LaCapra, D. (1989). *Soundings in Critical Theory.* Ithaca, NY: Cornell University Press.

LaCapra, D. (1998). *History and Memory after Auschwitz.* Ithaca, NY: Cornell University Press.

LaCapra, D. (2001). *Writing History, Writing Trauma.* Baltimore, MD: Johns Hopkins University Press.

LaCapra, D. (2004). *History in Transit: Experience, Identity, Critical Theory.* Ithaca, NY: Cornell University Press.

Lacayo, R. (1984). Meeting of two masters: Sir David Lean and Lord Snowdon take aim at *A Passage to India. Time,* 27 August, pp. 54–55.

Langs, R. (Ed.) (1981). The therapeutic relationship and deviations in technique. In: R. Langs (Ed.), *Classics of Psychoanalytic Technique* (pp. 469–487). New York: Jason Aronson.

Laplanche, J., & Pontalis, J.-B. (1985). *The Language of Psychoanalysis.* London: Hogarth Press.

Latz, P. (1995). *Bushfires and Bushtucker.* Alice Springs: IAD Press.

Lear, J. (2007). Working through the end of civilization. *International Journal of Psychoanalysis, 88:* 291–308.

Lewin, B. D. (1946). Sleep, the mouth, and the dream screen. *Psychoanalytic Quarterly, 15*: 419–434.

Lewis Herman, J. (1992). *Trauma and Recovery*. London: Pandora–Harper Collins.

Lichtenberg, J. D. (1989). *Psychoanalysis and Motivation*. Hillsdale, NJ: Analytic Press.

Lockwood, D. (1962). *I, the Aboriginal*. Adelaide: Rigby.

Lockwood, D. (1964). *The Lizard Eaters*, Adelaide: Rigby.

Loewald, H. W. (1960). On the therapeutic action of psychoanalysis. *International Journal of Psychoanalysis, 41*: 16–33.

Lovelock, J. (1987). *A New Look at Life on Earth*. Oxford: Oxford University Press.

Lovelock, J. (1988). *The Ages of Gaia: A Biography of Our Living Earth*. Oxford: Oxford University Press.

Lowe, P., & Pike, J. (1994). *Jilji: Life in the Great Sandy Desert*. Broome: Magabala Books.

MacDonald, R. (1995). *Between Two Worlds*. Alice Springs: Australian Archives, IAD Press.

Madow, L. (1997). On the way to a second symbiosis. In: S. Akhtar & S. Kramer (Eds.), *The Seasons of Life: Separation–Individuation Perspectives* (pp. 157–170). Northvale, NJ: Jason Aronson.

Mahler, M. S. (1974). Symbiosis and individuation: The psychological birth of the human infant. In: *The Selected Papers of Margaret S. Mahler, Vol. 2* (pp. 149–165). New York: Jason Aronson.

Mahler, M. S., Pine, F., & Bergman, A. (1975). *The Psychological Birth of the Human Infant: Symbiosis and Individuation*. New York: Basic Books.

Malouf, D. (1994). *Remembering Babylon*. London: Penguin.

Malouf, D. (1998). *Boyer Lectures. Lecture 1: The Island. Lecture 2: A Complex Fate. Lecture 3: Landscapes. Lecture 4: Monuments to Time. Lecture 5: The Orphan in the Pacific. Lecture 6: A Spirit of Play*. Sydney: ABC Radio National Publications.

Malouf, D. (2000). *The 2000 National Trust Heritage Lecture*. Website of the NSW National Trust (www.nsw.nationaltrust.org.au).

Malouf, D. (2003). Made in England: Australia's British inheritance. *Quarterly Essay, 12*: 1–67.

Manhire, B. (2005a). *Lifted*. Wellington: Victoria University Press.

Manhire, B. (Ed.) (2005b). *121 New Zealand Poems*. Auckland: Random House New Zealand.

Manne, R. (1998). The stolen generations. In: P. Craven (Ed.), *The Best Australian Essays 1998*. Melbourne: Bookman Press.

Manne, R. (2001). In denial: The stolen generations and the right. *Quarterly Essay, 1*: 1–113.

Masson, J. M. (Ed.) (1985). *The Complete Letters of Sigmund Freud to Wilhelm Fliess, 1887–1904*. Cambridge, MA: Harvard University Press.

Meltzer, D. (1973). *Sexual States of Mind.* Strath Tay: Clunie Press.

Miller, A. (1985). *Thou Shalt Not Be Aware.* London: Pluto Press.

Miller, A. (1987). *For Your Own Good.* London: Virago.

Miller, A. (1991). *Banished Knowledge.* London: Virago.

Modell, A. (1992). The private self and private space. *Annual of Psychoanalysis, 20:* 1–24.

Morgan, J. (1852). *The Life and Adventures of William Buckley* [Hobart: Archibald Mcdougal]. Melbourne: Text Publishing, 1996.

Morgan, S. (1987). *My Place.* Fremantle: Fremantle Arts Centre Press.

Morgan, S. (1989). *Wanamurraganya: The Story of Jack McPhee,* Fremantle: Fremantle Arts Centre Press.

Mowaljarlai, D., & Malnic, J. (1993). *Yorro Yorro, Everything Standing up Alive: Spirit of the Kimberley.* Broome: Magabala Books.

Muecke, S. (1997). *No Road (Bitumen All the Way).* Fremantle: Fremantle Arts Centre Press.

Munich, R., Allen, J., & Rogan, A. (submitted). Agency in illness and recovery. *Bulletin of the Menninger Clinic.*

Myers, F. (1986). *Pintupi Country, Pintupi Self.* Berkeley, CA: University of California Press.

Neri, C. (1998). *Group.* International Library of Group Analysis. London: Jessica Kingsley.

Novick, P. (1988). *That Noble Dream: The "Objectivity Question" and the American Historical Profession.* New York: Cambridge University Press.

Ogden, T. (1986). *The Matrix of the Mind: Object Relations and the Psychoanalytic Dialogue.* Northvale, NJ: Jason Aronson.

Paasi, A. (1991). Deconstructing regions: Notes on the scale of spatial life. *Environment and Planning, 23:* 239–256.

Pacella, B. L. (1980). The primal matrix configuration. In: R. Lax, S. Bach, & J. A. Burland (Eds.), *Rapprochement: The Critical Subphase of Separation–Individuation.* New York: Jason Aronson.

Pande, S. K. (1968). The mystique of "Western psychotherapy": An Eastern interpretation. *Journal of Nervous and Mental Disease, 146:* 425–432.

Perez-Foster, R., Moskowitz, M., & Javier, R. A. (Eds.) (1996). *Reaching Across Boundaries of Culture and Class.* Northvale, NJ: Jason Aronson.

Perkins, H. & Fink, H. (Eds.) (2000). *Papunya Tula: Genesis and genius* [Catalogue to the Papunya Tula collection]. Sydney: Art Gallery of NSW.

Phillips, A. (2004). Close-ups. *History Workshop Journal, 57:* 142–149.

Phillips, M. S. (2004). Distance and historical representation. *History Workshop Journal, 57:* 123–141.

Piaget, J. (1937). *Origins of Intelligence in Children.* New York: International Universities Press, 1952.

Pihama, L. (1994). Are films dangerous? A Maori woman's perspective on "The Piano". In: *Hecate: Special Aotea/New Zealand Issue,* ed. C. Ferrier. Brisbane: Hecate Press.

Pine, F. (1997). *Diversity and Direction in Psychoanalytic Technique.* New Haven, CT: Yale University Press.

Ranford, J. (2004). "Pakeha": Its origin and meaning . *Issues in Contemporary Education, 6* (retrieved 28 April 2006 from http: //www.education.auckland.ac.nz/research/cr/papers/ p6.asp).

Read, P. (1983). *The Stolen Generations: The Removal of Aboriginal Children in New South Wales 1883 to 1969.* Sydney: New South Wales Department of Aboriginal Affairs.

Read, P. (1999). *A Rape of the Soul So Profound.* Melbourne/Sydney: Allen & Unwin.

Reconciliation and Social Justice Library (1991). *Royal Commission into Aboriginal Deaths in Custody (October 1987 to November 1990).* Australian Legal Information Institute (available at http://www.austlii.edu.au/au/special/rsjproject/rsjlibrary/rciadic/index.html).

Reynolds, H. (1998). *This Whispering in Our Hearts.* Melbourne: Allen & Unwin.

Reynolds, H. (1999). *Why Weren't We Told?* Ringwood: Viking Press; Sydney: Penguin.

Robinson, R. (1966). *Aboriginal Myths and Legends.* Melbourne: Sun Books.

Rosenfeld, H. (1987). *Impasse and Interpretation.* London: Tavistock.

Rowley, C. D. (1970). *The Destruction of Aboriginal Society.* Canberra: Australian National University Press.

Rushdie, S. (1980). *Midnight's Children.* New York: Knopf.

Sandler, J. (1960). The background of safety. *International Journal of Psychoanalysis, 41*: 352–363.

Schachtel, E. G. (1947). On memory and childhood amnesia. *Psychiatry, 10*: 1–26.

Schilder, P. (1935). The psychoanalysis of space. *International Journal of Psychoanalysis, 16*: 274–295.

Schore, A. N. (1994). *Affect Regulation and the Origin of the Self* (pp. 407–409). Hillsdale, NJ: Lawrence Erlbaum.

Searles, H. F. (1960). *The Nonhuman Environment in Normal Development and Schizophrenia.* New York: International Universities Press.

Segal, H. (1964). *Introduction to the Work of Melanie Klein.* New York: Basic Books.

Sereny, G. (1974). *Into That Darkness: An Examination of Conscience.* London: André Deutsch.

Settlage, C. (1992). Psychoanalytic observations on adult development in life and in the therapeutic relationship. *Psychoanalysis and Contemporary Thought, 15*: 349–374.

Shapiro, E. R. (1997). The boundaries are shifting: Renegotiating the therapeutic frame. In: E. R. Shapiro (Ed.), *The Inner World in the Outer World: Psychoanalytic Perspectives* (pp. 7–25). New Haven, CT: Yale University Press.

Sinason, V. (1994). *Treating Survivors of Satanic Abuse: An Invisible Trauma*. London: Routledge.

Smith, B. (1980). *The Spectre of Truganini*. Sydney: ABC.

Sohn, L. (1983). Nostalgia. *International Journal of Psychoanalysis, 64*: 203–211.

Souter, G. (1963). *New Guinea: The Last Unknown*. Sydney: Angus & Robertson.

Steiner, R. (2000). *It Is a New Kind of Diaspora*. London: Karnac.

Stepansky, P. E. (1988). *The Memoirs of Margaret S. Mahler*. New York: Free Press.

Sterba, E. (1934). Homesickness and the mother's breast. *Psychiatric Quarterly, 14*: 701–707.

Stevens, W. (2005). Anecdote of the jar. In: C. Paglia (Ed.), *Break, Blow, Burn*. New York: Vintage Books.

Stockton, E. (1995). *The Aboriginal Gift*. Sydney: Millenium Books.

Stone, L. (1961). *The Psychoanalytic Situation: An Examination of Its Development and Essential Nature*. New York: International Universities Press.

Strehlow, T. H. (1969). *Journey to Horseshoes Bend*. Sydney: Angus & Robertson.

Strehlow, T. H. (1971). *Songs of Central Australia*. Sydney: Angus & Robertson.

Symington, J., & Symington, N. (1996). *The Clinical Thinking of Wilfred Bion* London: Routledge.

Symington, N. (1994). *Emotion and Spirit*. London: Cassell.

Tacey, D. (1995). *The Edge of the Sacred*. Melbourne: HarperCollins.

Taylor, B. (2004). How far, how near: Distance and proximity in historical imagination. *History Workshop Journal, 57*: 117–122.

Teja, J. S., & Akhtar, S. (1981). The psychosocial problems of FMGs with special reference to those in psychiatry. In: R. S. Chen (Ed.), *Foreign Medical Graduates in Psychiatry: Issues and Problems* (pp. 321–338). New York: Human Sciences Press.

Thomas, H. (1993). *The Conquest of Mexico*. London: Hutchinson.

Tuckett, D. (2006). "Unsettling the Settlers." Paper presented at the Open Day of the Australian Psychoanalytical Society (available on podcast at www.psychoanalysis.asn.au).

Tuckett, D., & Saunders, A. (2006). Freud the philosopher. In: *Philosopher's Zone*. ABC Radio National Transcripts (available at www.abc.net.au/rn/philosopherszone/stories/2006/1733000.htm).

Twemlow, N. (2002). Unspecified threat. *Can We Have Our Ball Back?, 16*. Retrieved 25 April 2003, from http: //web.archive.org/web/20030912233512/canwehaveourballback.com/16twemlow.htm.

Twemlow, N. (2005). *Remote Viewing*. Master's Thesis, Victoria University, Wellington, New Zealand.

Twemlow, N. (2006a). *Black Helicopter*. Poetry manuscript, under consideration.

Twemlow, N. (2006b). From Te Po-tahuri-atu (the night of restless turning). *Landfall, 211*: 124–126.

Twemlow, S. W. (2001a). Maori and Pakeha images and their interrelationships in Jane Campion's *The Piano. Journal of Applied Psychoanalytic Studies, 3*: 85–93.

Twemlow, S. W. (2001b). Modifying violent communities by enhancing altruism: A vision of possibilities. *Journal of Applied Psychoanalytic Studies, 3*: 431–462.

Twemlow, S. W. (2003). A crucible for murder: The social context of violent children and adolescents. *Psychoanalytic Quarterly, 72*: 659–698.

Twemlow, S. W., Fonagy, P., & Sacco, F. (2002). Assessing adolescents who threaten homicide in schools. *American Journal of Psychoanalysis, 62*: 213–235.

Twemlow, S. W., Fonagy, P., & Sacco, F. (2004). The role of the bystander in the social architecture of bullying and violence in schools and communities. *Annals of the New York Academy of Sciences, 1036*: 215–232.

Twemlow, S. W., Fonagy, P., & Sacco, F. (2005). A developmental approach to mentalizing communities II: A model for social change. *Bulletin of the Menninger Clinic, 69*: 265–280.

Twemlow, S. W., & Sacco, F. (2007). The prejudices of everyday life with observations from field trials. In: *The Future of Prejudice: Applications of Psychoanalytic Understanding towards Its Prevention*, ed. H. Parens, A. Mafhouz, S. Twemlow, & D. Scharff. Latham, MD: Rowman & Littlefield.

Twemlow, S. W., & Wilkinson, S. (2004). Topeka's healthy community initiative: A psychoanalytic model for change. In: *Analysts in the Trenches: Streets, Schools and War Zones*, ed. B. Sklarew, S. W. Twemlow, & S. Wilkinson. Hillsdale, NJ: Analytic Press.

Volkan, V. (2004). *Blind Trust: Large Groups and Their Leaders in Times of Crisis and Terror*. Charlottesville, VA: Pitchstone Publishing.

von Franz, M.-L. (1999). *Muhammad ibn Umail's Hall Ar-Rumuz (Clearing of Enigmas)*. Egg, Switzerland: Fotorotar AG.

Ward, I. (1993). Examining Freud's "phantasy" about England. *Psychiatric Times, 10*: 38.

Webb, J., & Enstice, A. (1998). *Aliens and Savages*. Sydney: HarperCollins.

Weiss, S. (1997). The empty space. *Annual of Psychoanalysis, 25*: 189–200.

Werman, D. S. (1977). Normal and pathological nostalgia. *Journal of the American Psychoanalytic Association*, 25: 387–398.

West, J. (1963). *Drovers Road*. London: Dent.

White, H. (1992). Historical emplotment and the problem of truth. In: S. Friedlander (Ed.), *Probing the Limits of Representation: Nazism and the "Final Solution"*. Cambridge, MA: Harvard University Press.

Whitman, W. (1982). *Whitman: Poetry and Prose*, ed. J. Kaplan. New York: Library of America.

Wieviorka, A. (1998). *The Era of the Witness* (trans. J. Stark). Ithaca, NY: Cornell University Press, 2006.

Winnicott, D. W. (1951). Transitional objects and transitional phenomena. In: *Through Paediatrics to Psycho-Analysis*. London: Hogarth Press; New York: International Universities Press, 1975.

Winnicott, D. W. (1953). Transitional objects and transitional phenomena. *International Journal of Psychoanalysis, 34*: 89–97. Also in: *Through Paediatrics to Psycho-Analysis* (pp. 229–242). London: Hogarth Press; New York: International Universities Press, 1975.

Winnicott, D. W. (1954). Metapsychological and clinical aspects of regression within the psycho-analytical set-up. In: *Through Paediatrics to Psychoanalysis*. London: Hogarth Press, 1975.

Winnicott, D. W. (1956). The antisocial tendency. In: *Through Paediatrics to Psychoanalysis* (pp. 306–316). London: Hogarth Press; New York: International Universities Press, 1975.

Winnicott, D. W. (1959). Nothing at the centre. In: *Psychoanalytic Explorations* (pp. 49–52), ed. C. Winnicott, R. Shepherd, & M. Davis. London: Karnac; Cambridge, MA: Harvard University Press.

Winnicott, D. W. (1960a). Ego distortion in terms of true and false self. In: *The Maturational Processes and the Facilitating Environment* (pp. 140–152). London: Hogarth Press; New York: International Universities Press, 1965.

Winnicott, D. W. (1960b). The theory of the parent–infant relationship. In: *The Maturational Processes and the Facilitating Environment* (pp. 37–55). London: Hogarth Press; New York: International Universities Press, 1965.

Winnicott, D. W. (1963a). The development of the capacity for concern. In: *The Maturational Processes and the Facilitating Environment* (pp. 73–82). New York: International Universities Press, 1965.

Winnicott, D. W. (1963b). Fear of breakdown. In: *Psychoanalytic Explorations*, ed. C. Winnicott, R. Shepherd, & M. Davis. Cambridge, MA: Harvard University Press, 1989.

Winnicott, D. W. (1967). Mirror role of mother and family in child development In: *Playing and Reality* (pp. 111–118). London: Routledge; New York: Basic Books, 1971.

Winnicott, D. W. (1971a). *Playing and Reality*. London: Routledge; New York: Basic Books.

Winnicott, D. W. (1971b). *Therapeutic Consultations in Child Psychiatry*. New York: Basic Books.

Winter, J. (2001). The memory boom in contemporary historical studies. *Raritan, 21* (1): 52–66.

Woiwod, M. (1994). *Kangaroo Ground: The Highland Taken*. Yarra Glen: Tarcoola Press.

Woiwod, M. (1997). *The Last Cry*. Yarra Glen: Tarcoola Press.

Woolf, V. (1927). *To The Lighthouse*. New York: Harvest Books.

Zerubavel, E. (1991). *The Fine Line: Making Distinctions in Everyday Life*. New York: Free Press.

INDEX

For Product Safety Concerns and Information please contact our EU
representative GPSR@taylorandfrancis.com
Taylor & Francis Verlag GmbH, Kaufingerstraße 24, 80331 München, Germany